The Performing Pianist's Guide to Fingering

JOSEPH BANOWETZ

With contributions by Philip Fowke and Nancy Lee Harper

The Performing Pianist's Guide to Fingering

INDIANA UNIVERSITY PRESS

This book is a publication of

Indiana University Press
Office of Scholarly Publishing
Herman B Wells Library 350
1320 East 10th Street
Bloomington, Indiana 47405 USA

iupress.org

 The paper used in this publication meets the minimum requirements of the American National Standard for Information Sciences—Permanence of Paper for Printed Library Materials, ANSI Z39.48-1992.

Manufactured in the United States of America

First printing 2021

Library of Congress Cataloging-in-Publication Data

Names: Banowetz, Joseph, author. | Fowke, Philip, author. | Harper, Nancy Lee, author.
Title: The performing pianist's guide to fingering / Joseph Banowetz ; with contributions by Philip Fowke and Nancy Lee Harper.
Description: Bloomington, Indiana : Indiana University Press, 2020. | Includes bibliographical references and index.
Identifiers: LCCN 2020038384 (print) | LCCN 2020038385 (ebook) | ISBN 9780253053138 (hardback) | ISBN 9780253053145 (ebook)
Subjects: LCSH: Piano—Fingering.
Classification: LCC MT232 .B34 2020 (print) | LCC MT232 (ebook) | DDC 786.2/19368—dc23
LC record available at https://lccn.loc.gov/2020038384
LC ebook record available at https://lccn.loc.gov/2020038385

For Alton Chung Ming Chan

Contents

Preface xi
Acknowledgments xv

Part I: Fingering Techniques / Joseph Banowetz 1

1. Fingering Keyboard Works of Selected Composers and Styles 3

Possible Choices of Fingering for the Advanced Pianist 3

Changing a Finger on the Same Note for Legatissimo 3

Crossing Fingers Over or Under 6

Changing Fingers on Repeated Notes in Chords 9

Playing Legato Chords That Span an Octave 9

Retaking Notes Silently 10

Positioning with Fingering for a Jump or Change of Hand Position 11

Using Pattern Fingerings in Passage Work 14

When to Avoid Playing Low Notes of Chords with Fifth Fingers 19

Playing More than One Note with a Finger 20

Using 5–3 to Project Top Melodic Tones 24

Block Fingerings 25

Chromatic Scales in Single Notes 28

Taking Top Notes of Rolls, Runs, and Arpeggios with Strong Fingers 31

Playing Rapid Mordents, Mordent Figurations, and Turns 34

Fingering Turnabout Patterns for Clarity 37

Fingering in Extended Tremolo Passages 41

Playing Legato Octaves 42

Playing Slurred Octaves 48

Playing "Blind" Octaves 49

Skipping a Finger to the Next Note for Clarity and Possible Emphasis 49

Using the Same Finger for Portato Touch 51

Refingering Two-Note Glissandos 52

Composers' Indications for Fingerings 53

The Breaking of Hands and Rolling of Chords by Pianists from the Late Nineteenth and Early Twentieth Centuries 62

2. The Fingering Redistribution of Hands: Pros and Cons 63

Redistributions to Avoid Rolls 67

Redistributing Large Chords and Intervals to Obtain Clarity and Clean Pedal Changes and to Avoid Unwanted Rolls 69

Redistributions for Achieving a Better Hand Position in Preparation for Making Jumps, Moving to Large Chords, and Positioning for Large Intervals 72

Redistributions to Position for Large Skips and Rolls 75

Redistributions for Achieving Controlled Voicing and Technical Clarity 78

Redistributing to Better Shape Slur or Phrase Endings 81

Redistributions for Clarity, to Relieve Stress, for Speed, and for Accuracy 81

Redistributions to Keep Clear Textures and Rhythms 86

Redistributions to Facilitate Finger Pedaling 88

Vladimir de Pachmann's Redistributions in Chopin's Prelude, op. 28, no. 2, as Notated by Leopold Godowsky 90

Videos of Famous Pianists Using Redistributions 92

Appendix: The Fingering of Benno Moiseiwitsch in Manuscript Illustrations / Philip Fowke 95

Part I Bibliography 109

Part II: Baroque Fingering and Interpretation: What Can a Modern Pianist Learn? / Nancy Lee Harper 111

Introduction: The Pianist's Dilemma 113

My Interest in Baroque Fingering and Its Impact on My Playing 115

3. An Overview of General Baroque Fingering Concepts 117

C. P. E. Bach's Approach to Fingering Technique 128

Mention of Baroque Women's Contributions 129

Summary: Axioms for Baroque Fingering 133

4. Articulation (Attack, Decay, Lifting, Slurring, *Affekt*) 136

Attack and Decay 136

Lifting 139

*The Doctrine of Affections (*Affekt*) 140*

Slurring 141

5. Hand Splitting or Redistribution, Stemming, and Cross Hands 144

Hand Splitting or Redistribution 144

Stemming 146

Cross Hands 147

6. Crossing and Turning of the Fingers 149

7. Repeated Notes, Glissandi, and Implied Fingering through Musical Figures 154

Repeated Notes 154

Glissandi 155

Musical Figures Dictating Fingering 156

8. Fingering in Ornamentation 160

Scarlatti's Trills and Tremolo 162

9. Fingering in Chords and in Chordal Realizations 169

10. Bach's Poetic Meter 178

Rhetoric in Speech in Bach's Keyboard Works 178

Rhetoric in Semantics from Bach's Keyboard Works 180

Rhetoric in Structure: Some Dance Examples from Bach's Keyboard Works 181

Notes inégales *182*

The Overdot 184

Fingerings in Metric Shifts 185

11. Singing with the Fingers 189

Finger Substitution 191

Finger Slides 192

Finger Pedaling 192

12. Dancing with the Fingers: A Guide to Understanding Scarlatti's Iberian Sonatas When Choosing a Fingering 195

Brief Case Study of Scarlatti's Sonata-Bolero in D Major, K. 491 203

Conclusion 209

Part II Bibliography 213

Index 219

Preface

General Approaches to Fingering

Choosing the most useful fingering, especially in advanced concert literature, can be a daunting task for even the most accomplished pianist. The choice of fingering can be controversial and challenging based on a wide range of factors, including the period of instruments for which the work was written; differences in each performer's technical approach; physiological differences such as sizes of hands and general physiques; performance approaches used by performers trained in the nineteenth century; and, above all, contrasting awareness and opinions regarding the musical message intended by the composer.

The Performing Pianist's Guide to Fingering is intended to provide much-needed guidance in fingering for the advanced artist/performer. Examples that are used are from original, unedited urtext sources. Hopefully these will stimulate the performer in their playing of each example and will also suggest similar approaches for a wide range of performance literature. This text is not intended for the average student or moderately trained teacher.

Many books contain general reference guides for fingerings, especially in areas where there is broad agreement on traditional approaches used by students and moderately advanced performers. These can be valuable. But too often in more demanding repertory not enough actual performance ability or imagination is reflected in the fingering possibilities. This is especially the case when an edition is made by an accomplished scholar who adds fingerings after constructing a careful edition based on original sources, but unfortunately who is not an accomplished performer. Even when an edition includes added fingerings by a famous performer, the fingering may not be satisfactory for everyone's hands and technical approach. Without doubt all fingerings should be examined. But the performer must always be aware that there is often more than one possibility for choosing a fingering that will function best under the pressure of a performance.

Above all, the advanced performer must explore all aspects of fingering and not simply rely on a given teacher or printed edition. Creativity and originality are characteristics of fingering that are of great importance for any serious performer. Hopefully the present text will help to stimulate these highly meaningful aspects of piano performance!

Redistributions have been a sensitive topic for many pianists, who unfortunately are frequently bound by the layout of the printed score. Too often this limits pianistic capability and artistic possibilities. For this reason, a highly detailed discussion of redistributions has been presented. As well, performers frequently are bound by fingering approaches that do not take into account such factors as utilization of technical patterns, positioning of hands before jumps, use of block fingerings, alternate scale fingerings, octaves, and fingerings for melodic emphasis and special effects, to name but a few.

Each fingering concept is explained in detail so that the principle guiding a particular choice of fingering in a passage can be applied to other pieces. In none of the present discussions are fingerings displayed that have no application in other repertory. But it is critical to remember that at times multiple choices for advanced fingerings will be possible. These must be explored at the piano by the performer, to make absolutely certain that a fingering choice is the right one for use. Some multiple fingering possibilities have often been given in the present text.

Some fingering references are discussed that are from other editors, many of whom were famous pianists. Unfortunately, too many of today's performers ignore editions made by editors such as Bülow, Busoni, Cortot, Godowsky, Mikuli, Moszkowski, Sauer, Schnabel, and many others. Even when you may not completely agree with them, their ideas can be fascinating and stimulating. Fingerings by these editors often give an insight not only into a given composer's style but also furnish glimpses of their own performance approaches. Some of these editors' works are discussed in the present text.

A detailed bibliography is included. Yet to single out various texts becomes a definite problem, because in many cases there is a significant amount of repetition of basic fingering principles. But texts by famous past figures such as Rudolph Ganz, Tobias Matthay, Heinrich Neuhaus, William S. Newman, and Walter Robert, to name but a few, should be mandatory sources for any serious performer.

Of great interest is the appendix by the internationally renowned British pianist and pedagogue Philip Fowke. Through relatives of the legendary pianist Benno Moiseiwitsch (1890–1963), Fowke had access to Moiseiwitsch's personal music library, which includes fascinating fingerings and redistributions made in the score of Rachmaninoff's Piano Concerto No. 2. These are examined in Fowke's section on Moiseiwitsch, and make a strong argument for using redistributions, especially since Moiseiwitsch was a close personal friend of Rachmaninoff's. In addition to Moiseiwitsch's numerous commercial disc recordings, there are videos available on the internet of him performing music by Chopin, Liszt, Medtner, Mendelssohn transcribed by Rachmaninoff, original Rachmaninoff works, Schumann, and Wagner transcribed by Liszt.

Baroque Fingering and Interpretation

The keyboard music of the Baroque era (c. 1600–1750) often took a highly different approach to fingering. Although much keyboard music from that period is now played on the piano, these compositions were written for the harpsichord, clavichord, organ, and early fortepiano. The fortepiano itself was invented near the end of the seventeenth century and beginning of the eighteenth century, but did not until later achieve widespread use. A detailed understanding of Baroque keyboard fingering is comprehensively examined by Dr. Nancy Lee Harper, an internationally renowned pianist, author, and pedagogue.

Choosing a Fingering for Performance

For the mature student and performer, the first basic rule and approach in choosing a fingering is to clearly decide on the composer's musical intent for a given passage. Dynamics, tempi, possible use of rubato, and even aesthetic intent through the choice of fingering must all be examined. Too often, even advanced performers work out a logical and comfortable fingering at a slower tempo only to later discover that when concert speed is reached, the fingering breaks down and becomes unusable.

Knowing the tempo of a passage before actually learning it is imperative. Otherwise it may be necessary to relearn it with a completely different fingering. This not only increases practice time but also creates a subconscious conflict between the two fingering choices. The same guideline applies to dynamics. Too often a fingering is chosen that functions well at a softer dynamic level but that breaks down when concert tempo and a proper high-dynamic level are reached. Especially in editions dating from the nineteenth to early twentieth centuries, fingerings often reflected a more dated technical approach that relied only on finger independence. These did not always take into account a free use of the wrist, single horizontal adjustments of the fingers, arm movements, and other factors. Unfortunately, if knowledge and use of these elements is missing, arriving at a suitable fingering can prove impossible.

A strong warning should be given. If the performer feels pain and physical discomfort, it is a clear indication of a technical problem and possibly of a dangerously bad choice of fingering. The old belief that any pain simply is a sign that "muscles are simply being strengthened" is completely false.

General Rules for Determining Proper Fingering

There are several general "rules" to follow when considering whether to use a fingering recommended by a particular editor or developing your own approach.

1. Under no circumstances simply blindly obey fingerings in a printed score. Even if the editor is a well-known artist, his or her technique may be different in some important aspects. Sizes of hands can make a huge difference as to which fingerings to choose. And a given interpretation can itself often make a great difference regarding what fingering is ultimately chosen. By all means examine different printed editions and compare fingerings. But be aware that too often an edition may be printed that is edited by someone who, although an excellent scholar, may be a mediocre pianist.

Also, especially in many earlier editions, fingerings are at times used that are now considered outdated.

2. Often a given passage may have a number of fingering possibilities. Any given fingering should be tested in concert tempo with correct dynamics and expression. As the old saying goes, "In a slow tempo, anything works." Often an ill-chosen fingering will feel comfortable and reliable until you nearly reach concert tempo; then it will collapse. Assuming there is a better possible choice, the old fingering then has to be unlearned before the new one is mastered. This takes unnecessary time and effort!
3. If possible, try to decide on a given fingering during the earliest stages of learning a piece. Write in the fingering, then experiment to see if it works well. This saves much time in getting a given passage "in the fingers." Too often a work is simply read from the score over and over again, with slight changes in fingering from one time to the next. If a given fingering does not work well, immediately rethink and experiment with modifying it.
4. As a general rule, a fingering should be used that best controls and projects the musical meaning of a particular passage. Possibilities for redistributions are too often ignored, although certainly there are particular passages where a redistribution may be aesthetically inappropriate. But often making redistributions is a way of controlling and projecting the music's artistic message. These pros and cons are all examined in detail in this text.
5. Never forget the old rule "If it works, it's right." This is often the bottom line in learning a passage, especially when there is more than one fingering option.
6. Above all never forget that a fingering is merely a tool in projecting a work's aural and artistic message. It is up to the performer to discover the best fingering tools to achieve this.

Editorial Procedures

All musical examples are based on unedited urtext sources, and include only text indications given by the composer. Occasional examples contain original fingerings by the composer. In these instances, the fingerings are printed as written. All pedaling markings are given exactly as in the original sources, as well as all marks of dynamics, articulation indications, and phrasings. Tempo indications if appearing at a given point in the example are notated without enclosures in parenthesis. But if an example is given that occurs after an earlier tempo indication, then that tempo indication is enclosed in parenthesis. Tempo indications without parenthesis indicate that they appear at that exact place in the original score. Fingerings are not added unless they directly relate to a given problem under discussion. Fingerings for the right hand appear above the top staff, and for the left hand appear below the lower staff. A measure number indication is given at the beginning of each example. The numbers for the examples start and end under each category being discussed.

Acknowledgments

In addition to my deep gratitude and admiration for Nancy Lee Harper and Philip Fowke, both prestigious contributors to this book, I wish to convey my warmest gratitude to Andrew Vagts of the College of Music of the University of North Texas who was extremely helpful in technically organizing the present text and to Jason Patterson and David Falterman for their marvelous construction of the Finale music examples. Generous thanks should be given to Dave Miller, Megan Schindele, Janice Frisch, Allison Blair Chaplin, and Eileen Allen of the Indiana University Press for their valuable editorial suggestions and extremely helpful oversight in preparing the book for final publication. Special credit is be given to the British Library in London for providing and giving permission to use photographs from the Benno Moiseiwitsch Archive, and to Christopher Scobie, Jonathan Summers, and Christopher Rawlings of the British Library staff for their extremely generous help in arranging current access and reproduction permissions for these images. Also special thanks goes to Steven Harlos, Pamela Mia Paul, and Adam Wodnicki of the University of North Texas piano faculty. Their encouragement (and occasional prodding!) has motivated the challenging task of completing this book. Encouragement and advice was given by my late close friend and advisor, Maurice Hinson. Also to be thanked are Donna Arnold, University of North Texas Music Reference Librarian, and Mark McKnight, Head of the Music Library of the University of North Texas. Through their magnificent library, now one of the largest music libraries in the United States, access and help was given in locating important musical references. Further encouragement was given by the eminent British pianist Murray McLachlan, Head of Keyboard at the Chetham's School of Music in Manchester, England. Thanks also must go to many of my pupils who during their lessons presented opportunities to use some of the fingering possibilities discussed in the present book.

Joseph Banowetz
Professor of Piano Performance
College of Music
The University of North Texas

Part I: Fingering Techniques

Joseph Banowetz

1 Fingering Keyboard Works of Selected Composers and Styles

Possible Choices of Fingerings for the Advanced Pianist

Fingering is an endlessly fascinating category of study that too often is carelessly taken for granted by even the advanced pianist. This section addresses some of the potential fingering problems that may occur in many more difficult works. An examination of these problems can aid in addressing similar issues in many other works. This chapter offers numerous examples that should stimulate solutions for many of these performance problems.

It is critical to often test a fingering in concert tempo, using the same dynamics as will be utilized in performance. In many cases, a decision will have to be made not only about which fingering works best under performance pressure but also whether a redistribution (fingering change) is possible and desirable both for performance and aesthetic reasons. Here the performer's musical background, technical approach, and physical build are all important considerations in making a suitable choice.

Changing a Finger on the Same Note for Legatissimo

In an expressive passage, it often will be best to change a finger on a repeated note to achieve a legatissimo and an expressive sound. In example 1.1 from Chopin's Concerto no. 2 in F Minor, first movement, the final two Fs before the rest should be tapered down and not accented. Using a change of fingers, plus a slight raising of the wrist to shape a diminuendo, will help to ensure this effect.

Example 1.1. Chopin, Concerto no. 2 in F Minor, first movement.

A similar melodic shaping is needed at the end of the second phrase of Chopin's Ballade no. 1 in G Minor (ex. 1.2). Either of the two fingerings given will help to reliably achieve this effect.

Example 1.2. Chopin, Ballade no. 1 in G Minor.

In example 1.3, also taken from Chopin's Ballade no. 1 in G Minor, changing fingers on the dotted half notes will help to create a legato. Using this technique, the notes will not sound punched out as the hand position moves downward.

Example 1.3. Chopin, Ballade no. 1 in G Minor.

In several measures from Chopin's Scherzo no. 2 (ex. 1.4), changing fingers on the same note will help maintain an expressive legato with appropriate balance and shaping. To simply use the pedal to give a fake legato would be a great mistake.

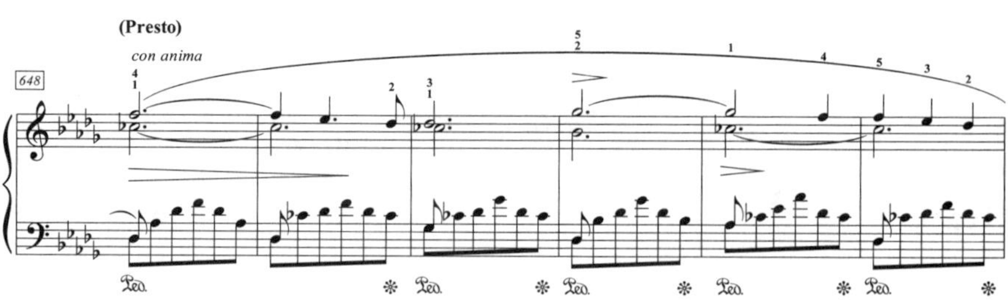

Example 1.4. Chopin, Scherzo no. 2 in B-flat Minor.

In example 1.5 from Chopin's Polonaise-Fantasy, op. 61, changing fingers on the B-flat dotted eighth note will ensure that it can be held through the pedal change that occurs on the second beat. If the hand is simply moved down to the right hand's rolled chord, then an unwanted break will occur between the two B-flats. The same problem occurs in the following measure.

Example 1.5. Chopin, Polonaise-Fantasy, op. 61.

In Chopin's Scherzo no. 2 in B-flat Minor (ex. 1.6), a fingering may be used that will both position the hand for changes of position and help produce a legato between the repeated notes that occur between every other measure. This fingering breaks the common so-called rule that you should not use your thumb to play a black key. However, experience has shown that it works extremely well in concert tempo. Notice also the longer accents in the right hand for the dotted half notes. According to recent research, Chopin made this differentiation in many of his manuscripts, probably to indicate a more expressive tone for a given note.

Example 1.6. Chopin, Scherzo no. 2 in B-flat Minor.

Crossing Fingers Over or Under

There are fingering situations where it may be expedient to cross fingers over or under in order to position the hand better during a given passage. In example 1.7 from Chopin's Scherzo no. 2 in B-flat Minor, playing the right-hand roll can be extremely awkward if the hand is not positioned properly immediately before it. Note that Chopin asks that the rolls in each hand be started simultaneously. Because the pedal must be changed with the low B-flat in the left hand, it also is important that the upper two repeated Fs in the right hand be played legato to avoid an unwanted break in the legato melodic line. Crossing the fifth finger under the third in the right hand will ensure both a smooth legato as well as an accurately played rolled chord. As the fifth finger is played, extend the hand to cover the rest of the notes of the right hand during the rolled chord.

Example 1.7. Chopin, Scherzo no. 2 in B-flat Minor.

Example 1.8 from Liszt's Hungarian Rhapsody no. 8, is an example of how a complex figuration can be made easier to play with brilliance if the best fingering is chosen. To use a typical 2–3–4 fingering for the three grace notes will mean that the octave must be played with the fifth finger, which is on many hands relatively weak. The fingering shown is a better choice. As the octave is played, rapidly push up with the wrist to create a strong accent. Placing the third and fourth fingers together will enhance delivering a strong accent as demanded by Liszt.

Example 1.8. Liszt, Hungarian Rhapsody no. 8.

In example 1.9 from the first movement of Beethoven's Sonata, op. 2, no. 2, it is important that a smooth legato be maintained in the right hand. This fingering ensures that there are no unwelcome breaks in the textures of either part. Note that you must slide your thumb from the G-sharp to the A and B.

Example 1.9. Beethoven, Sonata, op. 2, no. 2, first movement.

The fingering given for Beethoven's Sonata, op. 109, third movement (ex. 1.10), may at first seem a bit strange. But it is important to maintain the sempre ***pp*** demanded by Beethoven. Starting the single-note figuration with the fifth finger cuts down on the distance the hand must move upward. Care must be taken that the hand does not tighten slightly as it is moved higher, thus creating an unwanted accent immediately before it.

Example 1.10. Beethoven, Sonata, op. 109, third movement.

Chopin's Ballade no. 1 in G Minor in example 1.11 also shows how crossing the fingers over can aid in keeping a smooth legato.

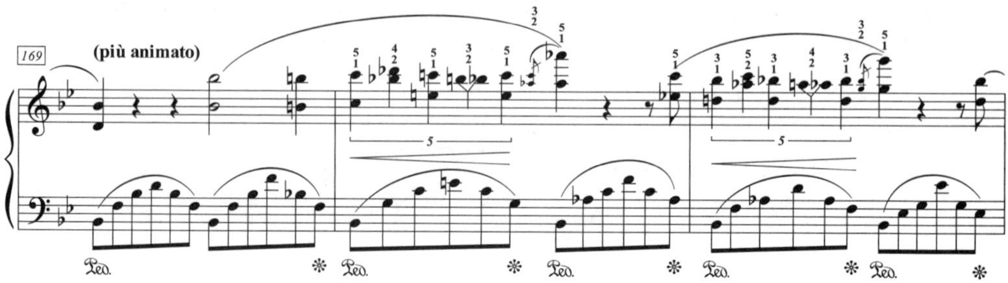

Example 1.11. Chopin, Ballade no. 1.

In example 1.12 from the first movement of Beethoven's Sonata, op. 2, no. 3, using the recommended fingering will help to ensure that the turn is played both rapidly and clearly. Taking the top B-flat with the fourth finger allows the upward-moving melody to be played smoothly.

Example 1.12. Beethoven, Sonata, op. 2, no. 3, first movement.

Example 1.13, from the fourth movement of Prokofiev's Sonata no. 2 in D Minor, has an awkward passage because of the placement of the black notes in the right hand. At concert speed, the placing of the second finger over the thumb will facilitate the high-speed jumps that must be made. This is yet another example of how a passage must be tested at speed and with the correct dynamics to see which fingering will work the best.

Example 1.13. Prokofiev, Sonata no. 2 in D Minor, fourth movement.

Changing Fingers on Repeated Notes in Chords

Rapid repeated notes in chords can create problems. Normally the achievement of a clear playing of repeated notes at high speeds will benefit from changing fingers on each repeated note. But at times this may be more difficult if the repeated notes are within chords. In Beethoven's Sonata, op. 106, second movement (ex. 1.14), this difficulty is compounded by the slur endings coming on each sixteenth note. A slight upward movement of the wrist at the end of each slur followed by a small downward movement of the wrist on each downbeat will facilitate the rapid changing of fingers between the chords, as will the changing of fingers on each repeated note. Note that the metronome indication in this example is from Beethoven.

Example 1.14. Beethoven, Sonata, op. 106, second movement.

Playing Legato Chords That Span an Octave

Example 1.15 from Chopin's Ballade no. 3 shows two short groups of chords spanning an octave. The slurs indicate that these should be played as legato as possible. Several fingerings can perhaps be used, depending in part on the size of the performer's hand.

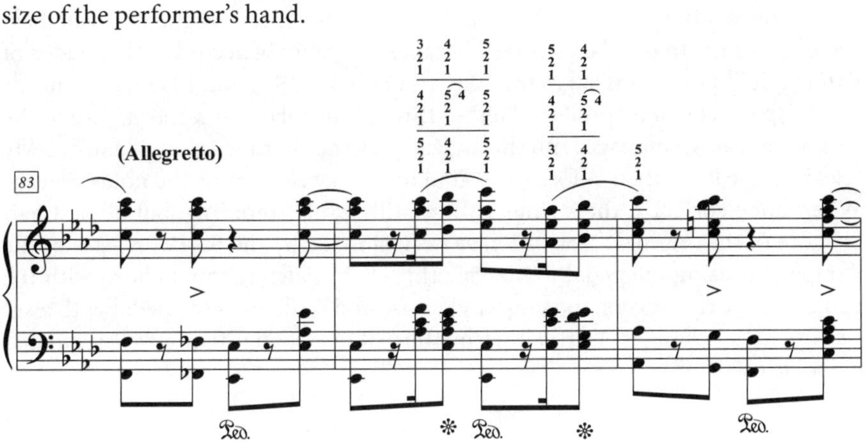

Example 1.15. Chopin, Ballade no. 3.

Retaking Notes Silently

In rare situations, it may be desirable to retake a note silently with the other hand. In example 1.16 from Prokofiev's Sonata no. 3, the rolled chord not only needs to be played forcefully, but the top E-natural extremely well projected, so that it continues to sound alone before dissolving into the *pianississimo* triplets. A reliable way to accomplish this voicing is to take the left-hand D with the right hand, then cross over the left hand to play forcefully the top E. Next, the right hand can silently hold down the depressed E as the damper pedal is released following the fermata.

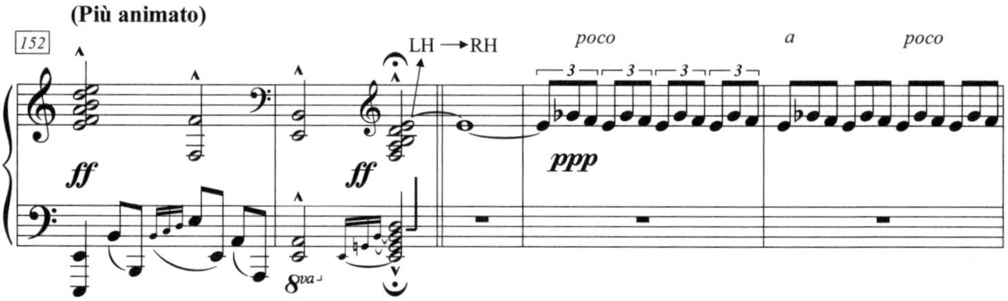

Example 1.16. Prokofiev, Sonata no. 3 in A Minor.

An unusual possible use of this technique appears in the opening of the first movement of Beethoven's Sonata, op. 13 (*Pathétique*; ex. 1.17). In Beethoven's urtext copy he clearly indicates that in the first three measures, a ***fp*** should come on each downbeat chord. After that he simply writes ***sf*** indications. Some performers have felt that each of the ***fp*** chords should immediately drop in dynamics as if played by an orchestra. The great pianist Edwin Fischer (1886–1960) wrote in his book *Beethoven's Pianoforte Sonatas*: "The ***fp*** of the very first chord offers a further difficulty: should this be played ***f*** to begin with and then the whole chord ***p*** until the demisemiquaver? Difficult though it is to reproduce today, the orchestral effect of the ***fp*** is to be preferred because it is more in accord with the idea of *Pathétique*."[1] Fischer manages this effect on both his 1938 and 1952 recordings.[2]

The ***fp*** effect can be produced either through fingering or a special use of the damper pedal. To manage with the fingers, play the chord without pedal, quickly releasing the keys, then before the sound dies away re-depress the notes silently. When done correctly, the strings will be still lightly sounding, but a good half or more of the original *forte* will have been stopped by the partial release of the dampers. If using the pedal to manage this effect, catch the first chord with the pedal, release the fingers, then rapidly release and re-depress the pedal with a series of partial changes. With either method, it is essential that a well-regulated piano be used.

Example 1.17. Beethoven, Sonata, op. 13.

Positioning with Fingering for a Jump or Change of Hand Position

Often a wise choice of fingering can aid in either preparing for a jump or a change of hand position. This may at times necessitate breaking the old-fashioned rule of not putting the thumb on a black note. In example 1.18, if you follow this rule while playing the left hand's five sixteenth notes, the rolled tenth, especially for a smaller hand, is awkward to play in time. Either of the other two fingerings that are given will make the rolled-tenth interval considerably easier to play.

Example 1.18. Liszt, Hungarian Rhapsody no. 8.

Positioning the hand for a jump can at times be facilitated through a wise choice of fingering. In example 1.19, taking the final sixteenth and eighth notes immediately before the two right-hand octaves with the fifth and fourth fingers will be awkward at high speed, because the hand must quickly find the new octave interval position. Moving instead to the second finger and thumb allows the hand to be slightly extended, in preparation for the jump to the octaves.

Example 1.19. Schumann, "Coquette," from *Carnaval*, op. 9.

In Ravel's *Miroirs* no. IV, "Alborada del grazioso" (ex. 1.20), placing the thumb on the fifth sixteenth note allows for the hand to be in position for the downbeat chord in the next measure. At the high speed demanded, the slight break in legato will not be noticed, especially because most players will keep the damper pedal depressed throughout this measure.

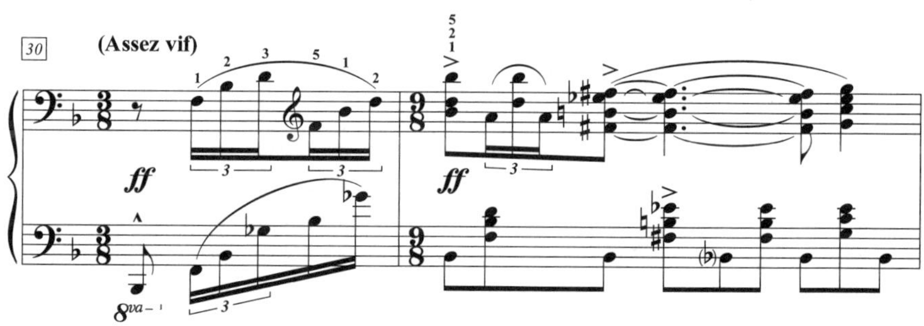

Example 1.20. Ravel, *Miroirs* no. IV, "Alborada del grazioso."

Example 1.21 is a notoriously difficult passage even for performers whose hands can easily span a tenth! On an instrument of Beethoven's own day, with its slightly narrower keys and shallower action, this still would have proved to be a technically demanding passage. The fingering given in example 1.21 solves the problem of the skips by positioning the hand.

In example 1.22, placing the thumb on the D immediately before the hand must change position on the second beat will enable the sixteenth notes to be played legato. This is especially important because the pedal cannot be used for achieving a legato due to the notes in the right hand.

Example 1.23 presents a problem with its large left-hand rolled chord. The sixteenth notes must be played smoothly, and the roll must not disturb the rhythmic flow with an "emergency rubato." Rachmaninoff had extremely large hands, but the average performer's hands will be challenged by this passage. This alternative approach will help. On the third beat in the left hand, omit the C because it is also played in the right hand. This will enable the thumb to be easily placed on

Example 1.21. Beethoven, Sonata, op. 2, no. 2, first movement.

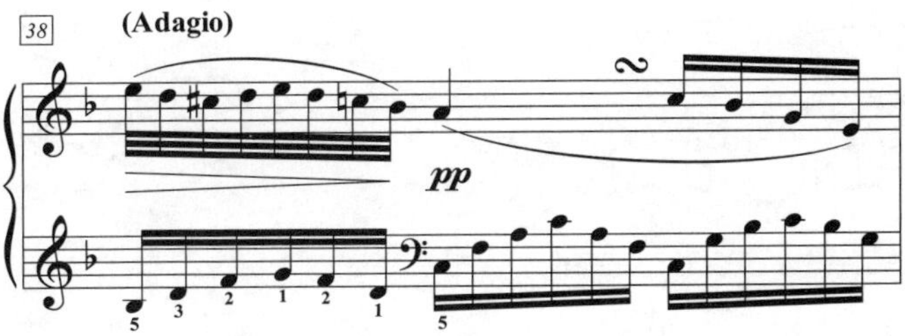

Example 1.22. Beethoven, Sonata, op. 2, no. 1, second movement.

Example 1.23. Rachmaninoff, Prelude, op. 23, no. 6.

the E-flat immediately before the rolled chord. With this fingering, the hand can be positioned to move smoothly to the low B-flat on the fourth beat.

Example 1.24, as in several previous examples, calls for the placing of the thumb on a black note in order to position the hand for moving to a jump before a larger interval. Some editors, using the tired "avoid putting your thumb on a black note" rule, finger the sixteenths on the third beat with the thumb on the Cs, and the second finger on the final B-flat, thus twisting the hand away from positioning for the jump to the high C on the fourth beat.

Example 1.24. Beethoven, Sonata, op. 111, first movement.

In example 1.25, the fingering given aids in positioning the hand for the extensions of intervals that immediately follow.

Example 1.25. Schumann, *Fantasiestücke*, op. 111, no. 1.

Using Pattern Fingerings in Passage Work

In some instances, definite recurring patterns may be found in rapid passage work. Using a pattern fingering can greatly facilitate muscle memory. In example 1.26 from Beethoven's Sonata, op. 109, third movement, the sixteenth-note passage work in the left hand can be fitted into a repeated four-note pattern. Placing the thumb on black notes should not be a problem, even though some editions suggest following this old-fashioned rule. Later in example 1.26, when the sixteenth-note figuration is played by the right hand, a recurring fingering can be used for each four eighth notes.

Example 1.26. Beethoven, Sonata, op. 109, third movement.

Often a figuration that repeats may not be the same as the rhythm of a given passage. In examples 1.27 and 1.28, both from Chopin's Scherzo, no. 4, op. 54, four-note patterns may be used. Placing the thumbs on black notes is not a problem if you avoid a rigid hand position.

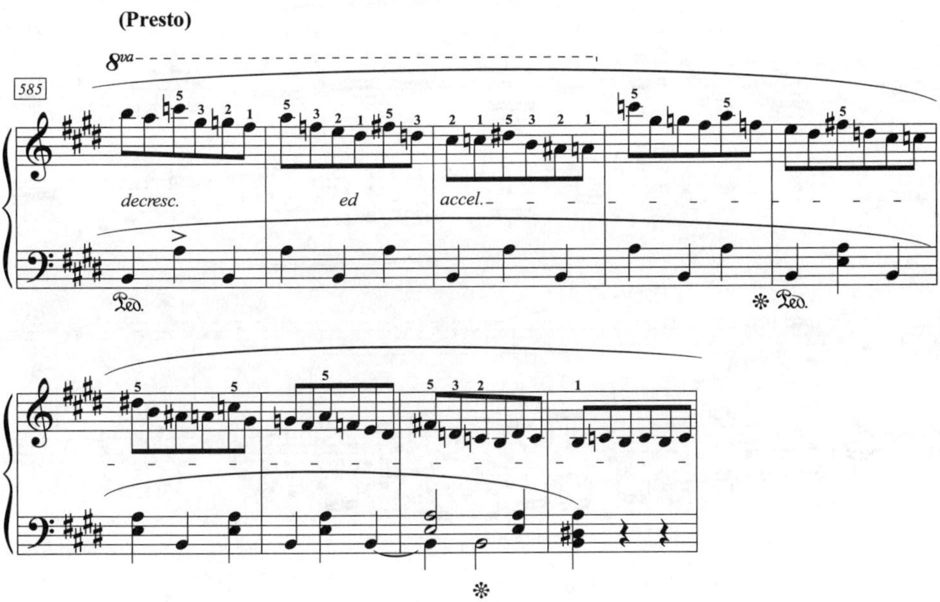

Example 1.27. Chopin, Scherzo, no. 4, op. 54.

Example 1.28. Chopin, Scherzo, no. 4, op. 54.

Similar pattern fingerings may function well in examples 1.29 and 1.30. In example 1.30, placing the thumb on a black note following a white note may seem strange at first. But at high speed, and with a flexible hand position, it proves practical and comfortable.

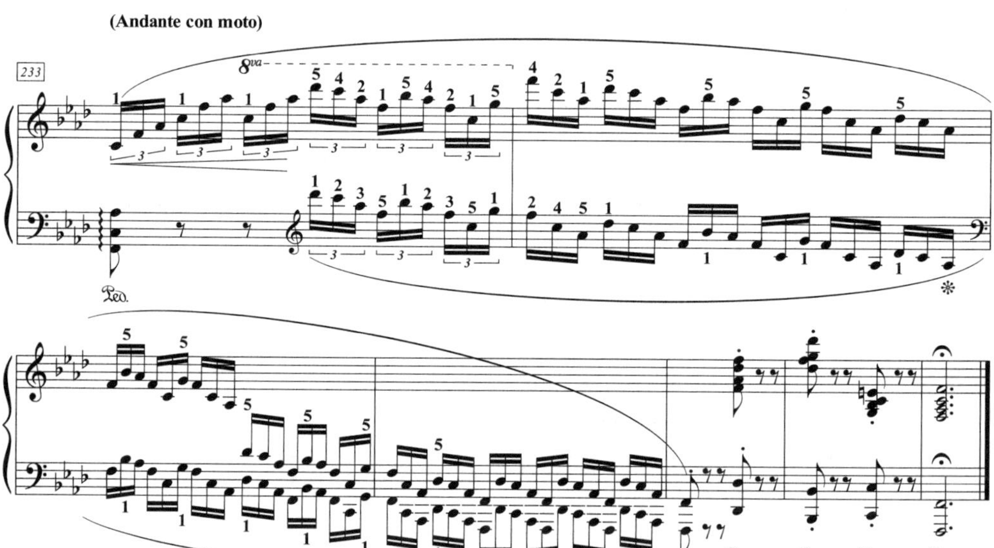

Example 1.29. Chopin. Ballade, no. 4, op. 52.

Example 1.30. Chopin, Ballade, no. 1, op. 23.

In example 1.31, maintaining the same fingering for the left hand in the two measures containing sixteenth-note scales makes memorization easier. Moving the hand slightly forward will facilitate using the thumb to play the F-sharps.

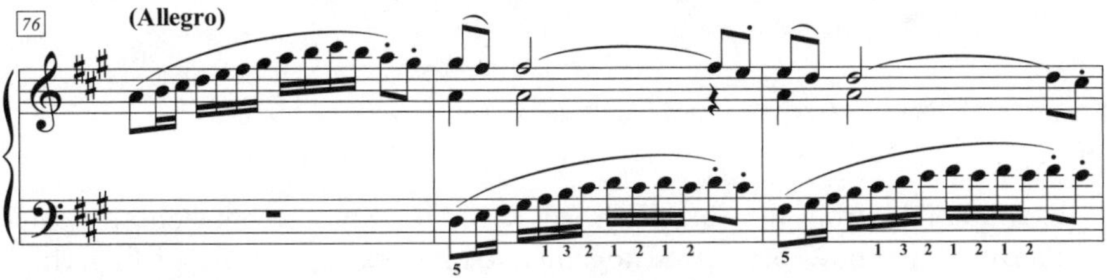

Example 1.31. Mozart, Concerto in A Major, K. 414, first movement.

Each hand plays upward-moving chromatic scales in parallel motion in a passage from Liszt's Variations on a Basso Continuo from the Cantata "*Weinen, Klagen, Sorgen, Zagen*" (ex. 1.32). Here, instead of using traditional fingerings, the same fingerings can be used by the hands together, with the thumbs played together simultaneously.

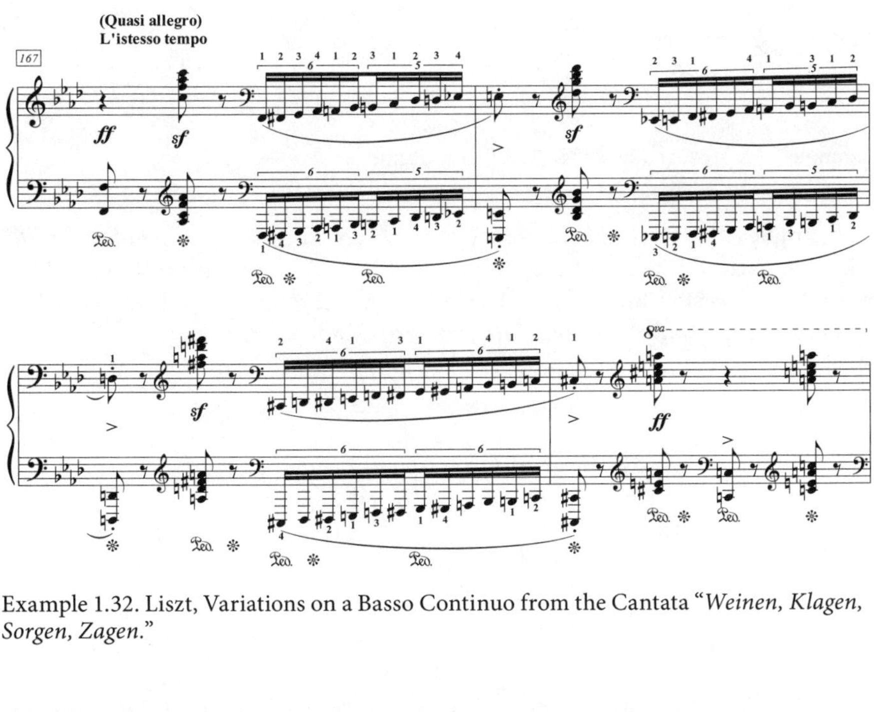

Example 1.32. Liszt, Variations on a Basso Continuo from the Cantata "*Weinen, Klagen, Sorgen, Zagen.*"

In example 1.33 from Saint-Saëns's Concerto no. 2, second movement, the upward moving arpeggios can be fingered so that the shifts of position occur at the same time in each hand. For clarity, take the final A and F both with the right hand.

Example 1.33. Saint-Saëns, Concerto no. 2, second movement.

Example 1.34, from the Mozart Sonata K. 333, first movement, contains pairs of chords that should be slurred together. Using the same pairs of fingerings solves this problem of playing with an unbroken legato during each slur. In those editions that avoid placing the thumb on a black note, this obvious fingering pattern is upset while also preventing the creation of a perfect legato.

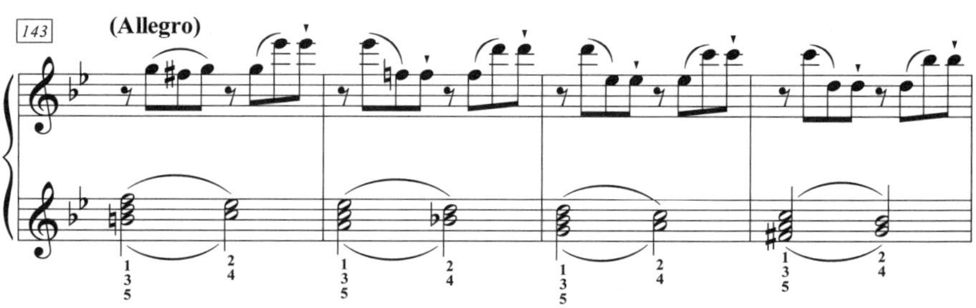

Example 1.34. Mozart, Sonata, K. 333, first movement.

Example 1.35, from the Chopin Concerto no. 2, third movement, contains a hidden pattern that is not easy to detect at first. But as with earlier examples, using the suggested fingering will help facilitate the rapid speed demanded in this passage, partially by using more strong and independent fingers.

Example 1.35. Chopin, Concerto no. 2, third movement.

When to Avoid Playing Low Notes of Chords with Fifth Fingers

When chords in the left hand follow a bass note an octave or more below, especially when performed in a rapid tempo, avoid playing the chords with the fifth finger. In example 1.36 from the fourth movement of Beethoven's Sonata, op. 101, using the fifth finger to play the chords will create possible accuracy problems. To see this clearly, simply play the first two eighth notes of each measure in tempo with the fifth finger alone. Pieces influenced by the waltz have many examples of similar patterns.

Example 1.36. Beethoven, Sonata, op. 101, fourth movement.

The following fingering (ex. 1.37), which uses the fifth finger for lower chords, should not to be used.

Example 1.37. Beethoven, Sonata, op. 101, fourth movement.

Playing More than One Note with a Finger

At times it may be desirable to play more than one note with a finger. This will be especially true in a larger chord when two notes can be played with the thumb (see ex. 1.38 from Liszt's Variations on a Basso Continuo from the Cantata "*Weinen, Klagen, Sorgen, Zagen*"). Similar fingering possibilities are shown in example 1.39, from Liszt's *Paganini* Étude no. 6 and example 1.40 from Chopin's Scherzo no. 2.

Example 1.38. Liszt, Variations on a Basso Continuo from the Cantata "*Weinen, Klagen, Sorgen, Zagen*."

Example 1.39. Liszt, *Paganini* Étude no. 6.

Example 1.40. Chopin, Scherzo no. 2.

In example 1.41 from the Chopin Ballade no. 1, playing the A and B with the thumb permits the more independent third and fifth fingers to be used to achieve clarity when playing the rapid grace notes above. This is preferable to using the less independent fourth and fifth fingers to play these grace notes, if the first and second fingers are used when playing the A and B. In the following measure, using the thumb to play the D and E permits the hand to be moved more easily from the higher chord immediately before, as well as to keep more of a legato when moving to the chord on the third beat.

Example 1.41. Chopin, Ballade no. 1.

In example 1.42 from Mozart's Sonata in A Minor, K. 310, first movement, playing the chords with the thumb on the top two notes permits a perfect legato to be maintained when moving to the following chords. Relying on the pedal to achieve a legato would be at best unreliable.

Example 1.42. Mozart, Sonata in A Minor, K. 310, first movement.

In example 1.43 from the Chopin Polonaise-Fantasy, op. 61, taking the D-sharps in the left hand with the right-hand thumb can avoid having to roll the chords. Many hands can stretch from a B-natural to a D-natural but not from a B-natural to a D-sharp.

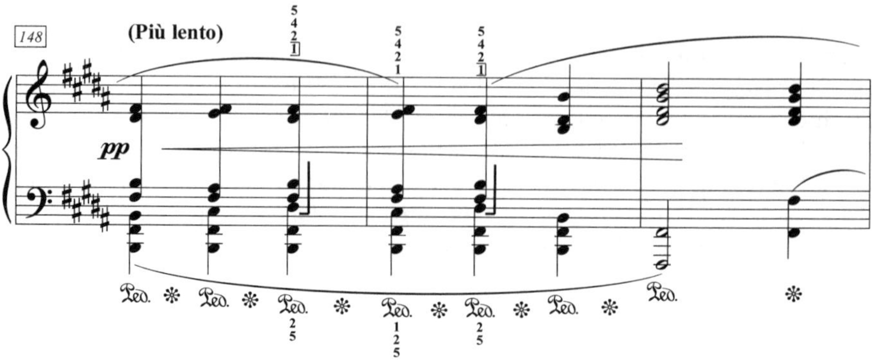

Example 1.43. Chopin, Polonaise-Fantasy, op. 61.

In example 1.44 the right-hand chord in the second measure of Rachmaninoff's Concerto no. 2, first movement, creates a problem for even a fairly good-sized hand. Here the C and D-flat can be played with the thumb. Position the thumb pointing downward, pressing the side of the D-flat key as it is pushed simultaneously with the C. Also in the following measure, play the Cs and D-naturals with the thumb pressed flat on both keys.

Example 1.44. Rachmaninoff, Piano Concerto no. 2, op. 18, first movement.

A similar redistribution will avoid rolling a larger interval in Brahms's *Variations on a Theme by Schumann*, op. 9 (ex. 1.45). Here the left-hand D can be taken

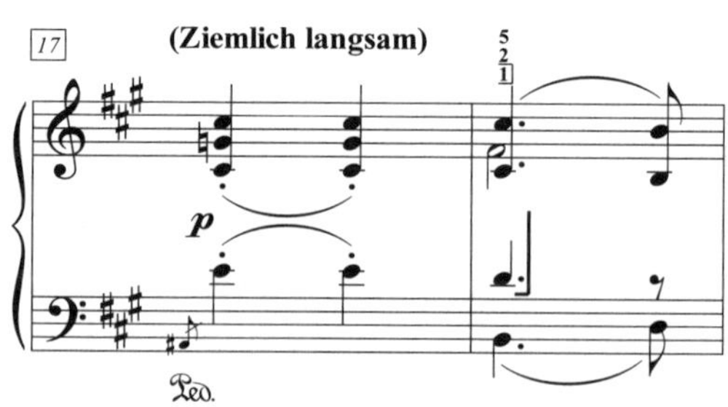

Example 1.45. Brahms, *Variations on a Theme by Schumann*, op. 9.

with the right hand, and as in example 1.44, the C-sharp and D played with the thumb pointing downward. Or the fingering in the right hand could be 2–1–3–5. Another solution, assuming the player can span an interval of a ninth, would be to take the bottom right-hand C-sharp with the left hand and the left-hand D with the right hand.

There are times the fingers may be bunched together for strength. In example 1.46 from Beethoven's Sonata, op. 57, first movement, playing the repeated-note D-flats with either 3–2 or 3–2–1 with the fingers pushed together ensures both great strength and that the fingers will not slip off the keys.

Example 1.46. Beethoven, Sonata, op. 57, first movement.

The skip in Chopin's Scherzo no. 2 (ex. 1.47) is dangerous for any performer. It must be not only loud but also accurate. Too often one hears an expressive "emergency rubato!" Bracing the fingers helps in this difficult jump.

Example 1.47. Chopin, Scherzo no. 2.

In Prokofiev's Sonata no. 5, second movement (ex. 1.48), no pedal should be used because of the staccato chords. Holding the E can be a problem even for a larger hand. It is helpful to play the E, then silently push the above F down with the palm of the hand. This allows the hand to expand slightly and play the piano chords above, while still holding the E.

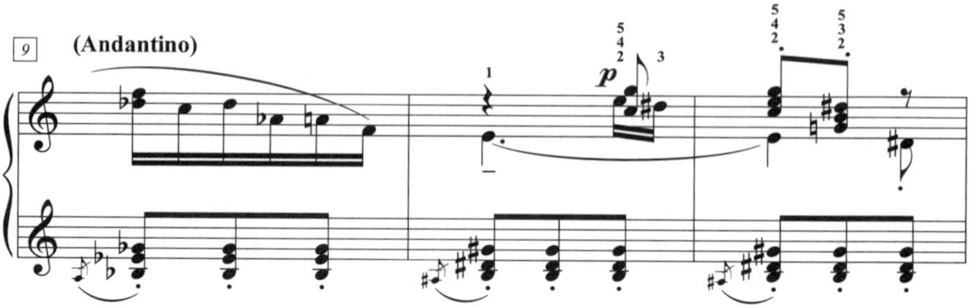

Example 1.48. Prokofiev, Sonata no. 5, second movement.

Using 5–3 to Project Top Melodic Tones

In Chopin's Étude, op. 25, no. 7 (ex. 1.49), the four-note chords would normally be played with 5–4. But because of the high dynamic level this may make it difficult to bring out the top melodic tones of each chord. A better solution is to play each chord with 5–3. This allows you to shift some weight more easily to the top tones.

Example 1.49. Chopin, Étude, op. 25, no. 7.

A similar example occurs in the first movement of Beethoven's Sonata, op. 111 (ex. 1.50). Above all, the performer must listen to the sonority between the hands, particularly the balance between the right-hand melody tones and the left-hand octaves and chords. Using 5–3 on the four-note chords will help in achieving a suitable balance of melody versus left hand.

Example 1.50. Beethoven, Sonata, op. 111, first movement.

Block Fingerings

Although for the less advanced performer putting the thumb over or under the fifth finger can seem awkward and clumsy, it can often solve problems of gaining speed and smoothness in runs and arpeggios. Major composers have themselves at times indicated such fingerings, as in these examples by Liszt (ex. 1.51), Busoni (ex. 1.52), and Prokofiev (ex. 1.53).

Example 1.51. Liszt, Spanish Rhapsody.

Example 1.52. Busoni, *Elegy* no. 4, "Turandots Frauengemach" (intermezzo).

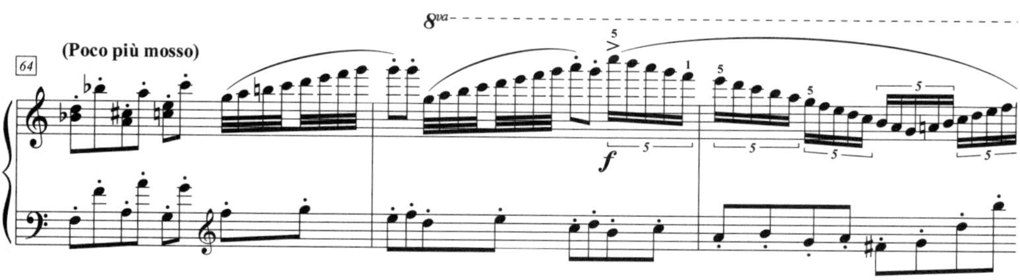

Example 1.53. Prokofiev, Concerto no. 1 in D-flat Major.

Other possible passages where block fingerings could be used are shown in examples 1.54, 1.55, and 1.56.

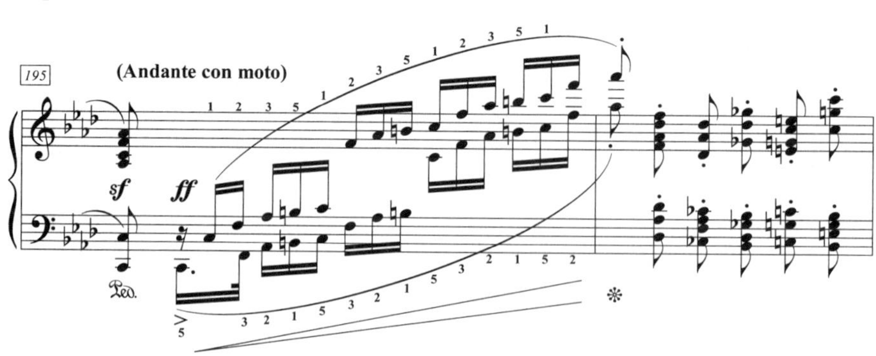

Example 1.54. Chopin, Ballade no. 4 in F Minor, op. 52.

Example 1.55. Liszt, *Transcendental* Étude no. 8, "Wilde Jagd."

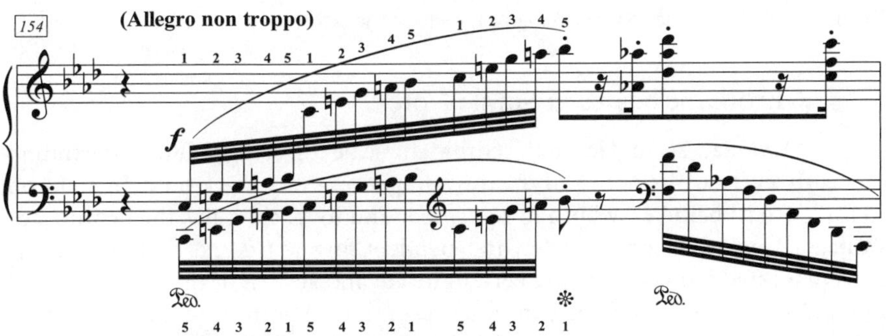

Example 1.56. Brahms, Concerto no. 2, first movement.

In Liszt's Piano Concerto no. 1 (ex. 1.57), the final downward run near the conclusion of the coda is difficult to maintain at the rapid tempo demanded. Using a block fingering in both hands for about half of the run greatly facilitates maintaining the necessary speed, without having to resort to the too-often heard "emergency rubato," which is clearly not called for in the score.

In practicing the block-finger technique, avoid using an adjustment of the wrist or hand. Instead, think of each five notes as a rapid rolled chord, then move extremely rapidly to the next position of the hand over the next five notes. At a high speed, maintaining a legato between the fifth fingers and thumbs is not necessary, assuming an unwanted accent does not occur during the rapid change of hand position.

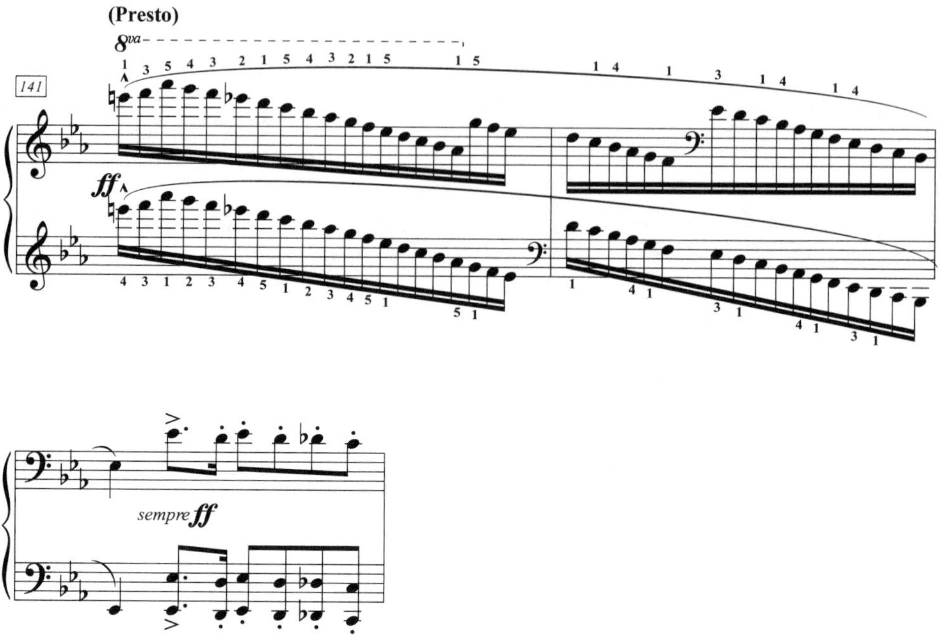

Example 1.57. Liszt, Piano Concerto no. 1, coda of the last movement.

Chromatic Scales in Single Notes

Most pianists first learn the chromatic scale fingering that uses the thumb on nearly every white note and the third finger on every black note. In addition to this pattern being easy both to remember and to teach, it has the definite advantage of using strong, relatively independent fingers (see ex. 1.58). But if it is used in a rapid tempo, there are certain disadvantages. First, the thumb is used in rapid succession, which may in some cases tighten both the hand and joint of the thumb. This is especially true if the performer is relying excessively on mere finger independence. Also, at high speed the sound may degenerate into a rough non-legato that may not be appropriate for a given passage. In this case, alternate chromatic scale fingerings can prove extremely beneficial. Three basic possible alternate chromatic scale fingerings are shown in examples 1.59–1.61.

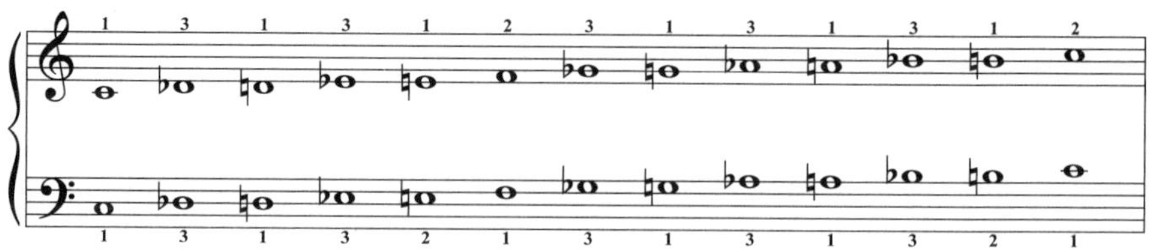

Example 1.58. Standard chromatic scale fingering.

Example 1.59 is a two-octave pattern: the thumb in each hand plays every other white note, followed by the next fingers in order. No finger should be skipped. After playing for two octaves, the pattern starts all over again.

Example 1.59. First alternate chromatic scale fingering.

Example 1.60 is a slight modification of the thumb on every other white-note pattern, with the use of the first and third fingers at the conclusion of an octave. This modifies the two-octave pattern in example 1.59 to a one-octave pattern.

Example 1.60. Second alternate chromatic scale fingering.

The fingering in example 1.61 will seem at first strange to many performers, but once mastered is of incalculable help in rapid passages requiring both high speeds and smoothness. It can be effectively used in chromatic scales going in either direction.

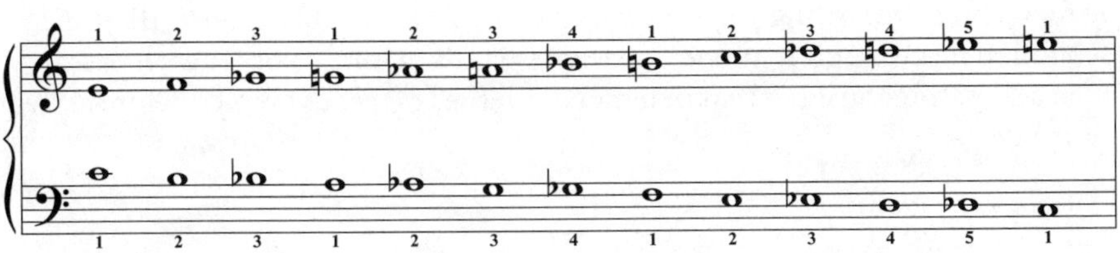

Example 1.61. Third alternate chromatic scale fingering.

The given performer's technical approach should not be tight and rigid. There must be some flexibility in the hand and wrist, this being too often missing even with relatively advanced performers. Assuming this flexibility, then it is possible to utilize to great advantage the fingering given in example 1.61.

Examples 1.62–1.65 demonstrate possible uses of these chromatic scales patterns. In Chopin's Ballade no. 1, mm. 242–245 (ex. 1.62), playing the chromatic scale demands a high speed and a feeling of upward motion and legato. But this often creates technical problems. There are three fingering possibilities, each based on one of the three basic patterns given in examples 1.59, 1.60, and 1.61.

Example 1.62. Chopin, Ballade no. 1.

Further example of alternate fingering possibilities can be found in examples 1.63, 1.64, and 1.65. It cannot be stressed enough that the performer must make the final choice regarding what fingering is the most reliable. Above all, it must accommodate best a given mood and the demands of tone color for each passage. Often a fingering must be tried in tempo with the correct dynamics before arriving at a decision.

Example 1.63. Beethoven, Sonata, op. 7, first movement.

Example 1.64. Liszt, Hungarian Rhapsody no. 8.

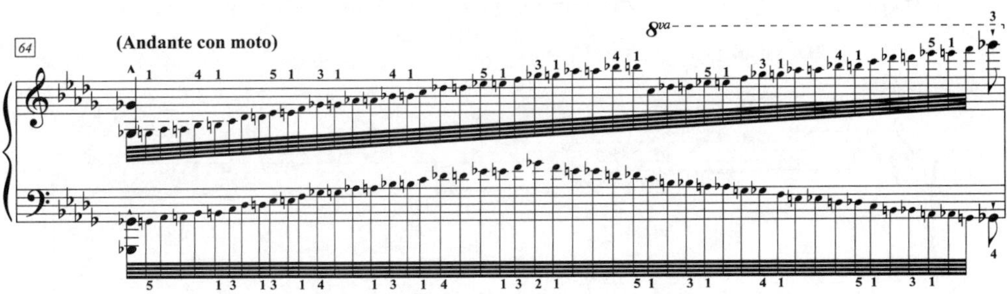

Example 1.65. Liszt, *Transcendental* Étude no. 12, "Chasse neige."

Taking Top Notes of Rolls, Runs, and Arpeggios with Strong Fingers

A rolled chord can often benefit from crossing to the top note with a strong finger. This is especially true if the roll of the chord is to be played both rapidly and at a high dynamic level. In Liszt's *Don Juan Fantasy* (ex. 1.66), playing the rolled chords in the right hand with the fourth and fifth fingers, and the left hand with the second finger and thumb, will probably place a strain on even a large hand. In the right hand, the fifth finger can also easily slip off the top notes. The fingering shown can help to alleviate this problem.

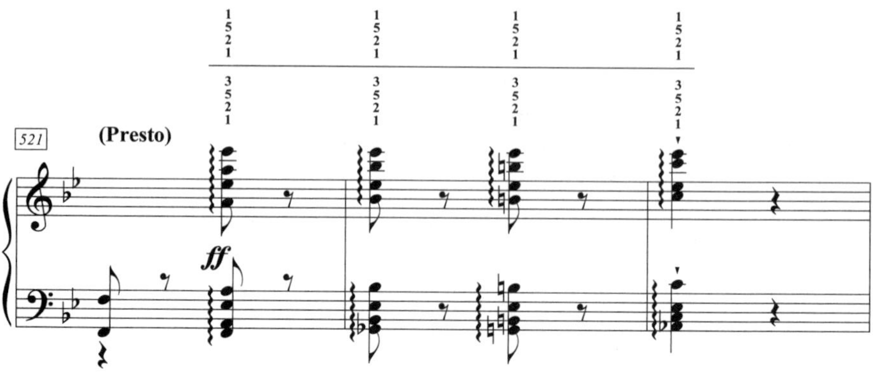

Example 1.66. Liszt, *Don Juan Fantasy.*

Liszt's Variations on a Basso Continuo from the Cantata "*Weinen, Klagen, Sorgen, Zagen*" (ex. 1.67) has a similar example of a rapid rolled chord. Only a player with a large hand can manage to use the fifth, third, second fingers, and thumb. One of these two possible fingerings shown in example 1.67 is more secure. If the thumb, second, and third fingers are used together to play the top A-flat, quickly bunch the fingers together when moving from the F immediately below.

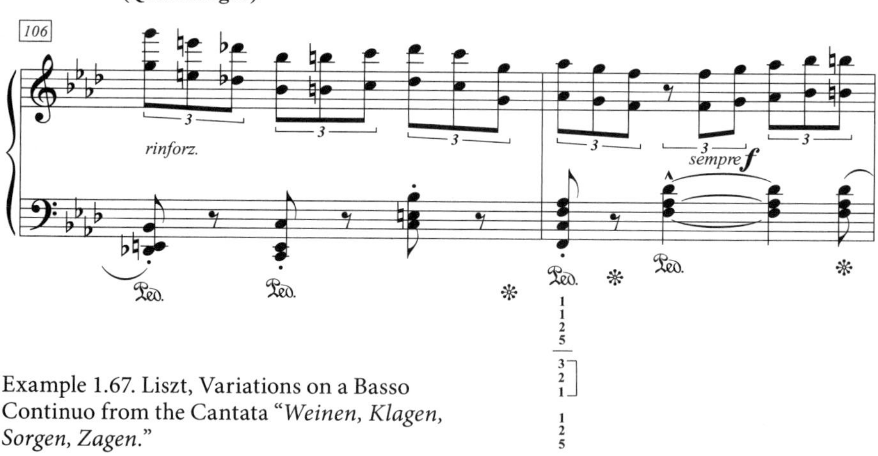

Example 1.67. Liszt, Variations on a Basso Continuo from the Cantata "*Weinen, Klagen, Sorgen, Zagen.*"

In Beethoven's Sonata, op. 57, third movement (ex. 1.68), the *fortissimo* eighth notes in the right hand can best be played with the thumb, especially when they fall on black notes. This ensures that a strong finger will be used and that it will not slip off the black key at high speed.

In Liszt's *Paganini* Étude no. 6 (ex. 1.69), using the right-hand thumb immediately after each triplet ensures that a strong finger will be used for each accent within the *sempre più di forza* dynamics. It also ensures that the hand will be positioned to move immediately upward to the following octave.

Example 1.68. Beethoven, Sonata, op. 57, third movement.

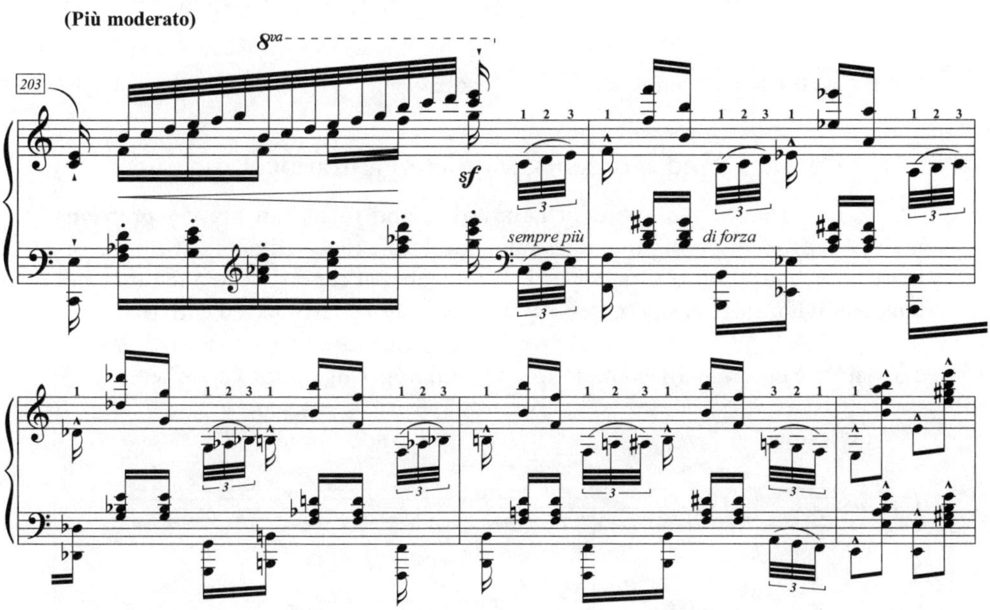

Example 1.69. Liszt, *Paganini* Étude *no. 6.*

This passage from Chopin's Concerto no. 1, third movement (ex. 1.70), will benefit from taking the top notes of each run with strong fingers. Using a block fingering in the arpeggios so that shifts take place at the same time in each hand will also help to maintain the rapid tempo and brilliancy that is required. Several fingering choices are given, all of which should be explored to see which one functions the most consistently at the necessary tempo and dynamic level.

Example 1.70. Chopin, Concerto no. 1, third movement.

Playing Rapid Mordents, Mordent Figurations, and Turns

Rapid mordents, mordent figurations, and turns can present problems if played with a fingering that does not address the repeated note within the ornament or figuration. At high speed, the finger that repeats very often may not have enough time to easily re-depress the key after it is first played with that same finger. Choosing a fingering that avoids using the same finger twice will help to alleviate the problem. In example 1.71, several fingering options are offered.

Example 1.71. Beethoven, Sonata, op. 31, no. 2, third movement.

Care should be taken that the wrist is elevated slightly at the end of each slur in order to properly shape it with a small diminuendo. In example 1.72 from the same work,[2] either of two similar fingerings may be used. Putting the thumb on a black key will not prove the least bit awkward.

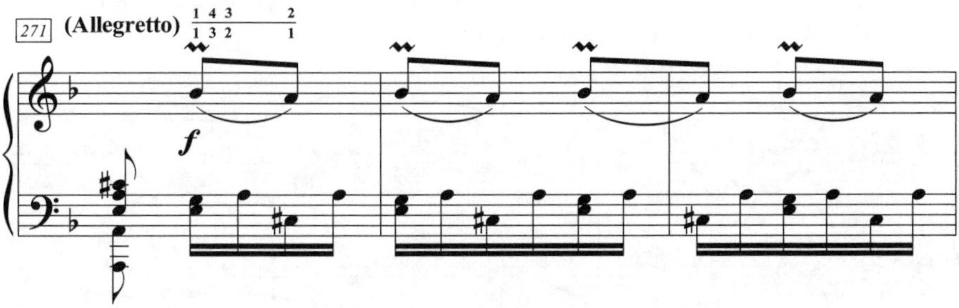

Example 1.72. Beethoven, Sonata, op. 31, no. 3, third movement.

In Chopin's Nocturne, op. 27, no. 2 (ex. 1.73), the mordent must be played with the upper fingers of the right hand. Nonetheless, the same principle of changing fingers on the rapid repeated note can be maintained. Regardless of which fingering is used, keep the right-hand thumb close to the C-sharp to avoid an unnecessary in-and-out movement that could tighten the hand, thus interfering with playing the mordent clearly.

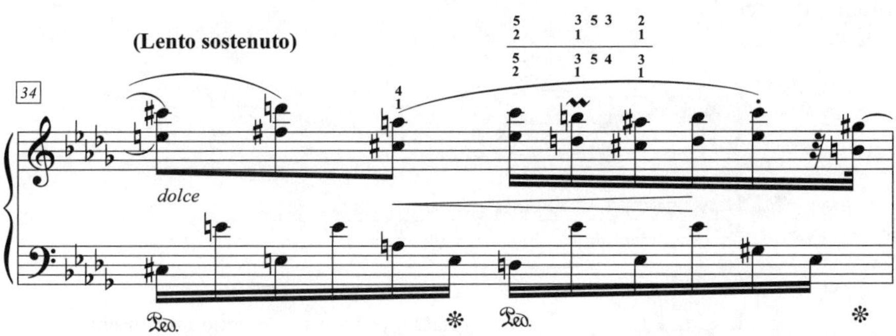

Example 1.73. Chopin, Nocturne, op. 27, no. 2

A similar fingering may be found three measures later (ex. 1.74).

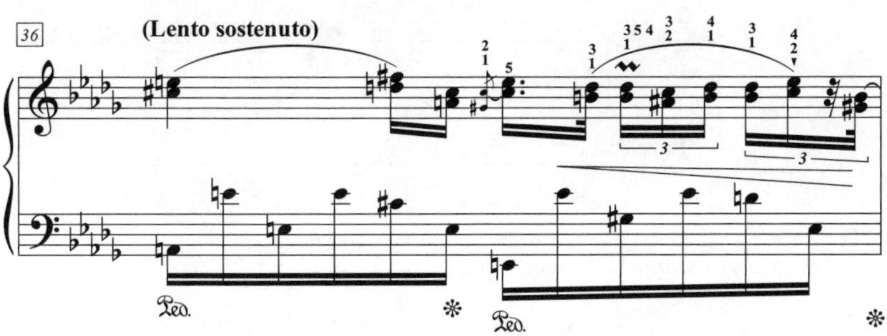

Example 1.74. Chopin, Nocturne, op. 27, no. 2.

In some cases, a mordent figure cannot be played with a change of finger on the repeated note. In these situations, try to use fingers that have a natural independence. In example 1.75, using 4–5–4 or 3–4–3 will prove to be much less reliable than 3–5–3 at a relatively high speed.

Example 1.75. Chopin, Concerto no. 1, third movement.

Turns or turn figurations can present the same problems as rapid mordents. Do not use the fingering that is given in some piano editions using the fourth finger (see ex. 1.76). On most hands, the fourth finger does not have the rapid independence of the others. The fingering choices shown in example 1.77 will be much more reliable.

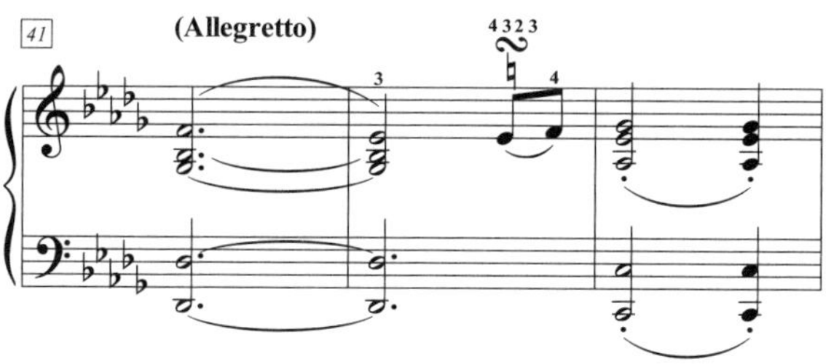

Example 1.76. Beethoven, Sonata, op. 10, no. 2, second movement.

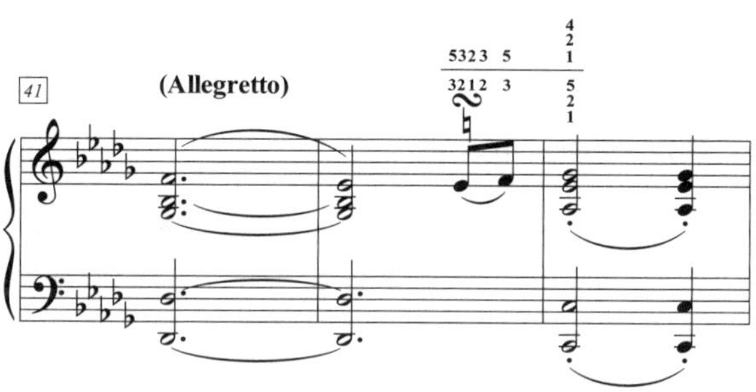

Example 1.77. Beethoven, Sonata, op. 10, no. 2, second movement.

In the turn-like figurations shown in example 1.78, either of the two suggested fingerings that utilize a change of fingers on the repeated notes will be much more reliable than the commonly used 4–3–2–1–2.

Example 1.78. Beethoven, Sonata, op. 2, no. 1, first movement.

In measures 7 and 8 of this same work, several alternate fingerings are possible (ex. 1.79). The performer should slightly elevate the wrist in order to shape with a small but clear diminuendo the last note of the slur.

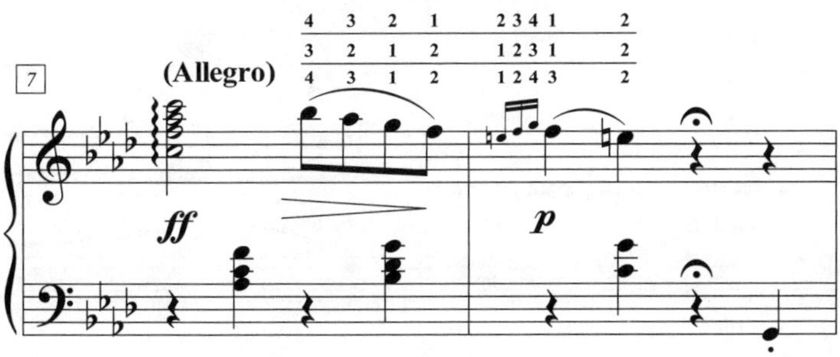

Example 1.79. Beethoven, Sonata, op. 2, no. 1, first movement.

A similar figuration is found in Beethoven's Sonata, op. 10, no. 2, first movement (ex. 1.80). Either of the two fingering choices that are given will be better than the 3–2–4–3 fingering given in some editions.

Example 1.80. Beethoven, Sonata, op. 10, no. 2, first movement.

Fingering Turnabout Patterns for Clarity

In rapid passage work, obtaining clarity when playing a turnabout pattern of notes may present a problem, especially if the third and fourth or fourth and fifth fingers are overused in sequence. In Liszt's Hungarian Rhapsody no. 9, clarity will be easier to obtain if instead of using 3–5–4, the fingering given in example 1.81 is used. Similar situations occur in example 1.82. Using 3–5–3 avoids using 3–4–3 or 4–5–4. If 3–5–3 is used at the turnabout, then the traditional A-major scale fingering must be altered (see ex. 1.82). If the performer prefers the traditional A-major scale fingering, then the fingering shown in example 1.83 might be used.

Example 1.81. Liszt, Hungarian Rhapsody no. 9.

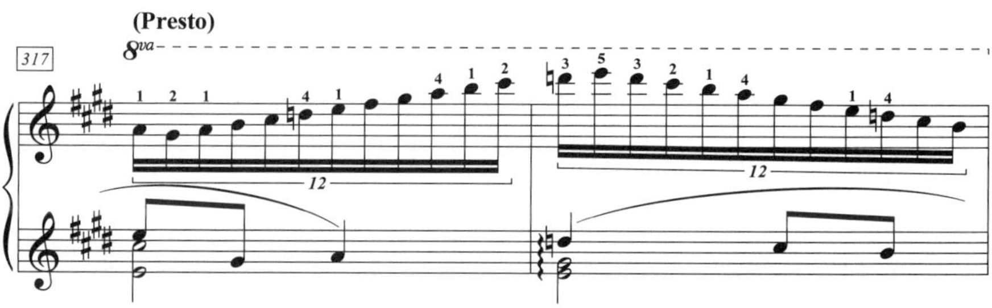

Example 1.82. Liszt, Hungarian Rhapsody no. 9.

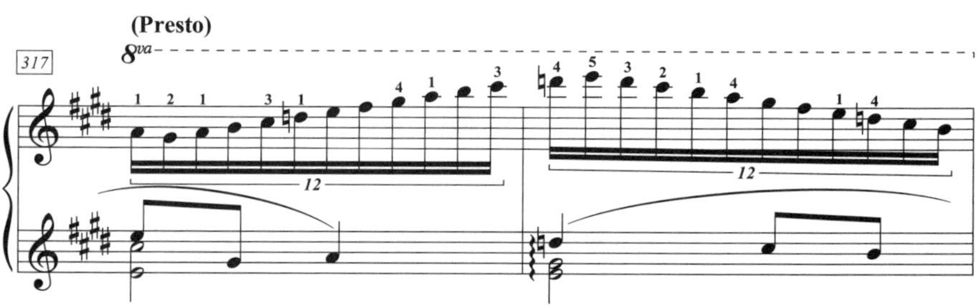

Example 1.83. Liszt, Hungarian Rhapsody no. 9.

Similar situations with turnabout patterns occur in examples 1.84, 1.85, 1.86, and 1.87.

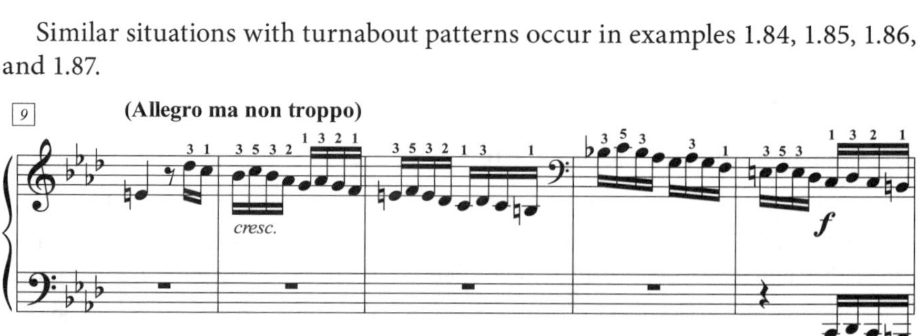

Example 1.84. Beethoven, Sonata, op. 57, third movement.

Example 1.85. Beethoven, Sonata, op. 53, first movement. Note the alternate choice of fingerings.

Example 1.86. Beethoven, Sonata, op. 2, no. 3, fourth movement.

Beethoven's Sonata, op. 57, third movement, contains an extended series of turnabout passages that many pianists find awkward. Example 1.87 features an interesting footnote and fingering by Liszt's pupil, Hans von Bülow (1830–1894). Bülow's fingerings will work well especially for a smaller hand.

Performers with larger hands will probably prefer the fingering shown in example 1.88. It works extremely well, assuming the player does not keep the hand

Example 1.87. Beethoven, Sonata, op. 57, third movement.

in a five-note rigid position but adjusts toward the fourth and fifth fingers with a horizontal movement of the wrist. My honored friend the music teacher Franz Kroll of Berlin developed this fingering; Kroll's editions of the classics have done so much for the instruction of artists and the public alike. It has a singular look at first, but the practical test of years has proven it to be of unrivalled excellence. It fits the musical phrasing so perfectly that by consistently carrying it out the entire movement might be transposed all'improvvista into any other desired key. Without exactly repudiating the use of the thumb on C on the second beat, the passing over of the third finger (as if with a spring) renders the needful accent less sharp, and—as only practicing players, not readers, can convince themselves—dismembers the whole phrase very little (Bülow's remarks).[3]

Example 1.88. Beethoven, Sonata, op. 57, third movement.

A third choice of placing the fourth finger over the fifth finger when going from a white to a black note is given in example 1.89 by Artur Schnabel (1881–1951).

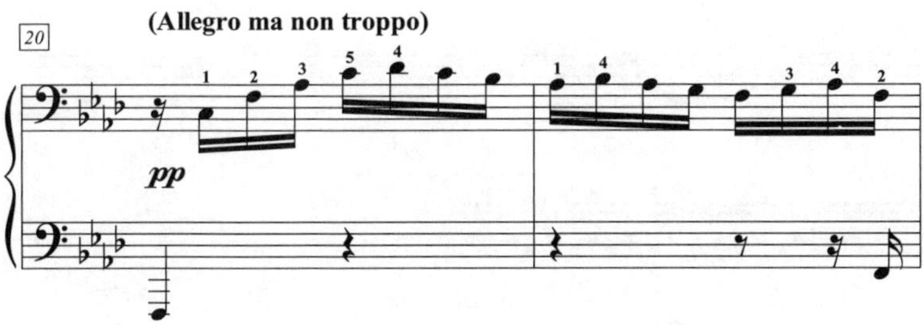

Example 1.89. Beethoven, Sonata, op. 57, third movement.

In Ravel's *Miroirs* no. IV, "Alborada del grazioso" (ex. 1.90), playing the F-double-sharp and A-natural with the side of the thumb solves the problem of placing the fingers for the turnaround at the top of the run. As the run ends, slightly elevate the wrist to aid with the diminuendo.

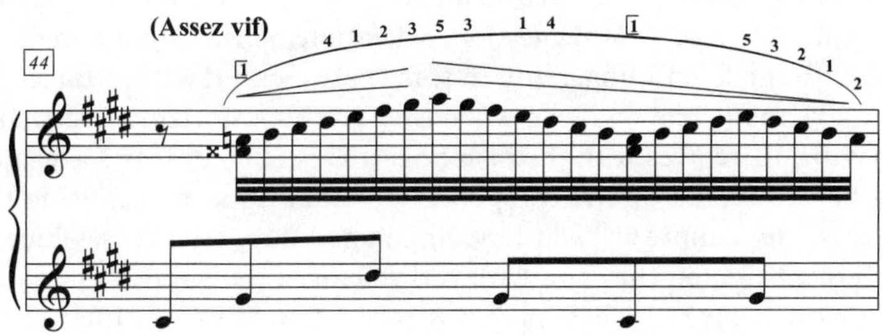

Example 1.90. Ravel, *Miroirs* no. IV, "Alborada del grazioso."

Fingering in Extended Tremolo Passages

Rapid and extended tremolos can possibly cause tension problems, even if the performer uses a satisfactory technical approach such as forearm rotation. Many players use a 1–3–2–3–1–3–2–3 alternation of fingers in rapid trills; the same approach can be used in tremolo passages. Care must be taken that the arm and hand remain loose and not in a fixed rigid position. The first movement of Beethoven's Sonata, op. 57 (ex. 1.91) shows how this type of fingering may be used. In this example, it is best to begin the four-note pattern with 4–2, so that at the end of the tremolo figuration the thumb will be played, and therefore can be slightly pulled away from the left hand as it comes in on the downbeat of measure 81.

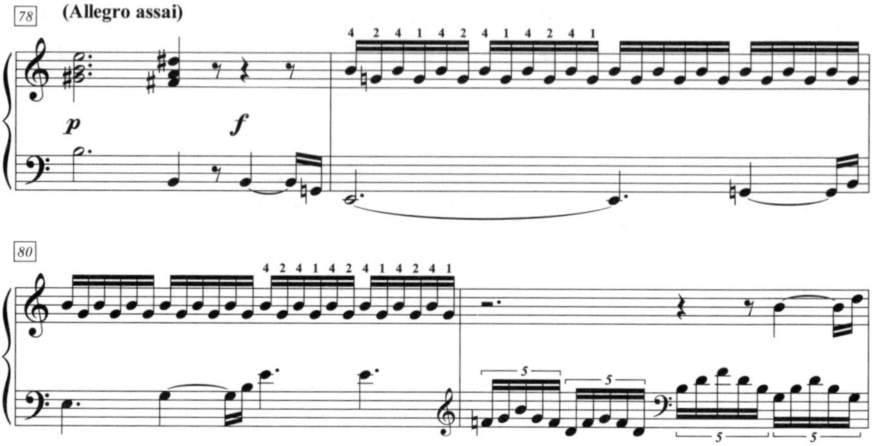

Example 1.91. Beethoven, Sonata, op. 57, first movement.

Playing Legato Octaves

There are many pieces that demand octaves that are to be played as legato as possible. As a general suggestion, black-note octaves should in most cases be played with the fourth finger and in some cases with the third finger. It is astonishing how many players, even when they have comfortably large hands, insist on playing all octaves with the fifth finger. This often destroys a legato touch that may be demanded by the composer. Of equal importance, using the fifth finger necessitates a more awkward moving in and out of the keys, which at high speed will often tighten the arm. Unless the span of the hand is extremely limited, black-note octaves are best played with the fourth finger. The exception to this is when so-called blind octaves occur. This will be shown in a later discussion.

One of the most famous works containing legato octaves is Chopin's Étude, op. 25, no. 10 (ex. 1.92). To primarily rely on the fifth finger when playing the black notes, even when the proper speed can be achieved, will usually create a touch and sound that is percussive and inexpressive. Playing many of the octaves with the fourth finger, as well as occasionally using the third finger, will help to project Chopin's expressive shaping of the melodic line. A technical help is to keep the thumb relatively close to the next black key instead of jerking the arm in and out, as will be done if the fifth finger is used throughout.

The examples 1.93 and 1.94, from Beethoven's Sonata, op. 7, first movement, and Sonata, op. 14, no. 1, first movement, respectively, show how a legato can be maintained using not only the fourth and fifth fingers but the third as well. Relying on the damper pedal to obtain an artificial legato will create audible unwanted blurs of sound.

Example 1.92. Chopin, Étude, op. 25, no. 10.

Example 1.93. Beethoven, Sonata, op. 7, first movement.

Example 1.94. Beethoven, Sonata, op. 14, no. 1, first movement.

A passage from the first movement of Saint-Saëns Concerto no. 2 (ex. 1.95) demands a similar fingering to the Chopin Étude, op. 25, no. 10 (ex. 1.92). The sempre legato marking is by the composer; although the pedal certainly can be used, it should not be simply a cheap substitute for a legato.

Chopin's Ballade no. 4 (ex. 1.96) is a famous passage demanding a difficult legato touch. Using the third, fourth, and fifth fingers will help to achieve this. A light, rapid changing of pedal will act as an aid, but should not be trusted to produce a *pianissimo* legato sound.

Facing top Example 1.95. Saint-Saëns, Concerto no. 2, first movement.

Facing bottom Example 1.96. Chopin, Ballade no. 4.

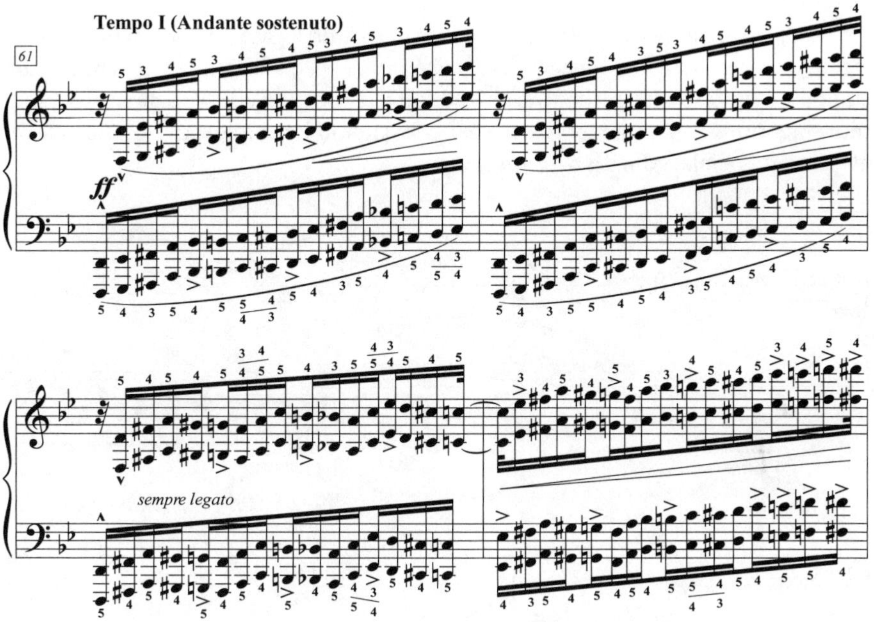
61
Tempo I (Andante sostenuto)
ff
sempre legato

38
(Andante con moto)
pp
legato
mezza voce

There are instances when an expressive, slower legato melody will be written in octaves. But even if the pedal is used to ensure a legato, a fingering legato should be used to aid in shaping the melody. In Beethoven's Sonata, op. 57, first movement (ex. 1.97), a generous use of pedal should be employed. But the octaves also should be played with a legato touch.

Example 1.97. Beethoven, Sonata, op. 57, first movement.

In some passages, slurs may be interspersed with staccatos. In Liszt's *Paganini Étude* no. 2 (ex. 1.98), using the fourth finger after the fifth will help to control such short articulations, especially because they often will require an emphasis on the first note of each slur. This will be the case even if two notes in the slur are on white keys.

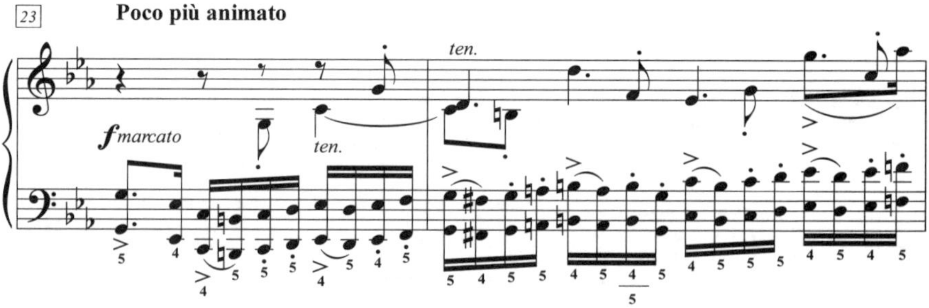

Example 1.98. Liszt, *Paganini* Étude no. 2.

Beethoven's Sonata, op. 57, third movement (ex. 1.99) has three fingering possibilities that will ensure a legato for the top notes of all the octaves. Using the pedal alone to keep the octaves legato will blur the sixteenth-note figuration beneath. It is also important to show a diminuendo to *piano* touch, which can be aided by using a legato octave fingering.

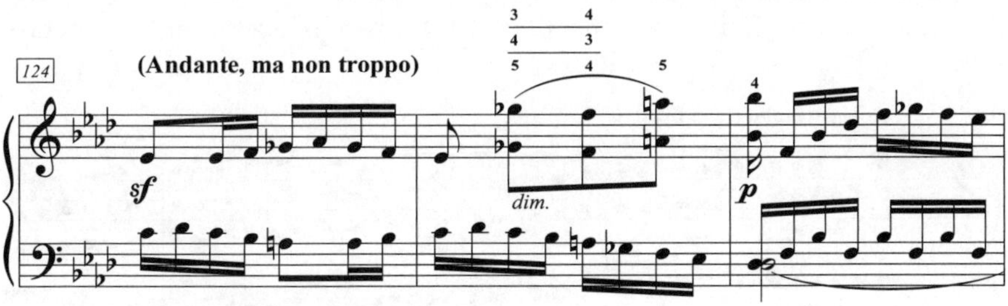

Example 1.99. Beethoven, Sonata, op. 57, third movement.

Beethoven's Sonata, op. 53, first movement (ex. 1.100) shows the importance of being aware of different touches taking place simultaneously. The left hand's touch must be a *pianissimo* staccato, in imitation of the opening measures in the movement. The right hand must, however, be legato. Using the pedal is impossible, as to do so would immediately create slurs in the left hand. Here a continual changing of fingers from four to five is essential, while keeping the thumb close to the key surface in order to minimize the slight non-legato that is unavoidable.

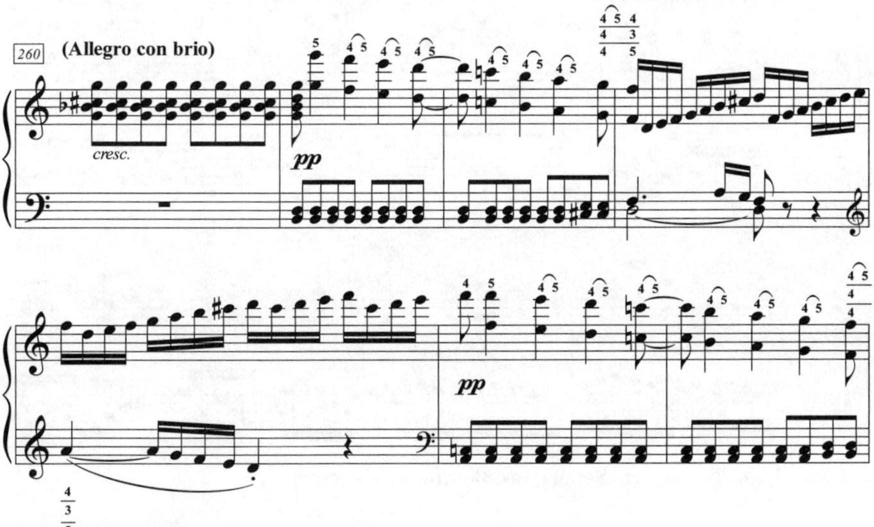

Example 1.100. Beethoven, Sonata, op. 53, first movement.

Playing Slurred Octaves

There are passages that demand that pairs of octaves be slurred. It is important in these situations that the slur connects the two top notes of each pair of octaves. In most cases, the first of each pair will receive an accent followed by a diminuendo. This effect is facilitated by connecting with the fingers. In Beethoven Sonata, op. 7, first movement (ex. 1.101), there is a series of these octave slurs.

Example 1.101. Beethoven, Sonata, op. 7, first movement.

In Beethoven's Sonata, op. 81a, third movement (ex. 1.102), the thumb is always placed on a black note before the following octave. This is helpful so that the top notes of each pair of octaves can be played legato and the thumb can be slid easily from one note to the next with a smoothly connected legato.

Example 1.102. Beethoven, Sonata, op. 81a, third movement.

Playing "Blind" Octaves

So-called blind octaves occur when during a chromatic scale pattern the hands play an octave apart, with the thumbs of each hand interlocking. In these passages. it is much better to use only the thumb and fifth finger in each hand (see Liszt's *Paganini* Étude no. 2, example 1.103).

Example 1.103. Liszt, *Paganini* Étude no. 2.

Skipping a Finger to the Next Note for Clarity and Possible Emphasis

There are instances where a finger may in a rapid tempo be skipped to the next note in order to achieve clarity and emphasis. In the first movement of Beethoven's Sonata, op. 111 (ex. 1.104), playing the left-hand thumb twice in succession will help to ensure clarity. In the right-hand part immediately above, using the first, second, and third fingers will add strength to this important theme. Note that the same sets of fingers will be used in each hand.

Example 1.104. Beethoven, Sonata, op. 111, first movement.

In from Liszt's *Paganini* Étude no. 6 (ex. 1.105), skipping the left hand's thumb to the following octave will help gain agility and brilliance through the use of stronger and more independent fingers in each triplet. A skipping of the thumb to the next note helps similarly in the right-hand part. As in example 1.104, the same sets of fingers are used simultaneously in each hand. This is the kind of fingering that will not always be seen to work well until a piece is played up to tempo with correct dynamics. In a slow tempo, often a questionable fingering will work well but will then break down when a concert tempo is reached.

Example 1.105. Liszt, *Paganini* Étude no. 6.

Beethoven's Sonata, op. 2, no. 3, first movement (ex. 1.106), contains a passage that frequently gives pianists problems. These measures open the entire piece, before the performer may be properly warmed up. It is common for performers to begin too loudly, then to freeze in the middle of the right-hand thirds. The fingerings given may appear a bit strange at first, but when practiced and played in tempo at the correct dynamic level, they prove to have great value. If possible, choose similar fingerings for both passages. For instance, if the top fingering is used in the first two measures, see if it will work in the next two measures. This will depend on whether the hand position is flexible and whether the performer's fingers are not too thick to fit between the black keys.

Example 1.106. Beethoven, Sonata, op. 2, no. 3, first movement.

A fascinating example of using the same finger in succession appears in Chopin's Nocturne, op. 37, no. 1 (ex. 1.107). Here the composer indicates that in the right hand, a row of four notes in the expressive melody should be played with the third finger. This is possibly an indication for a slight expressive rubato and to ensure that each note receives a deep sound. This fingering was notated by Chopin in a teaching copy for one of his pupils.

Example 1.107. Chopin, Nocturne, op. 37, no. 1.

Using the Same Finger for Portato Touch

The same finger can be used for a succession of notes requiring a portato touch, as in Liszt's Ballade no. 2 in B Minor (ex. 1.108). In this expressive passage, Liszt demands a small, expressive rubato, which can be better obtained through using the same finger for the lightly disconnected portato notes. Although Liszt gives no pedaling either in the manuscript or in the first edition, most performers assume that pedal changes are made with each low downbeat bass note. The pedaling given in example 1.108 is by Emil von Sauer (1863–1942), one of Liszt's most famous pupils. When performing an expressive portato touch, keep the wrist supple and loose.

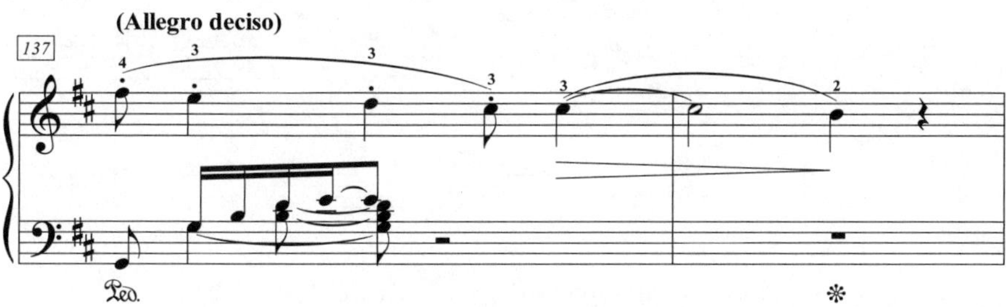

Example 1.108. Liszt, Ballade no. 2 in B Minor.

A similar portato touch may be found in Chopin's Nocturne, op. 37, no. 1 (ex. 1.109). But in this case, the fingering is by Chopin himself. As in example 1.108, the pedal indication (also by Chopin) will create a legato. But here Chopin obviously desires a strong touch, with emphasis on each note. As in example 1.108, the fingering used offers fascinating examples of expressive possibilities.

Example 1.109. Chopin, Nocturne, op. 37, no. 1.

Refingering Two-Note Glissandos

Passages with two-note glissandos that were intended by the composer to be played with one hand present problems for most of today's pianists. Composers such as Mozart and Beethoven occasionally indicated such glissandos. The fortepianos of the mid- to late eighteenth century and early nineteenth century, of course, had both slightly narrower keys and a shallower and less heavy touch. But today's pianos have a far greater depth and heaviness of touch, as well as a wider key width. Therefore, it is often necessary to work out an alternate fingering solution for double-note glissandos that are written to be played with one hand.

An example may be found in Mozart's Variations on "Lison dormait," KV 315d (264), which was first composed in 1778, then revised in 1786 (ex. 1.110). Here the glissando can easily be divided between the hands. In this section, which is named earlier as "cadenza," Mozart probably intended for the left hand to hold the octave Gs. The problem is that when the glissando is divided, the pedal alone cannot hold the Gs. One possible solution would be to first play the left-hand G octave, quickly catch it with the sostenuto pedal, then continue with the glissando divided between the hands. Mozart's free timing notation is given as in the original score.

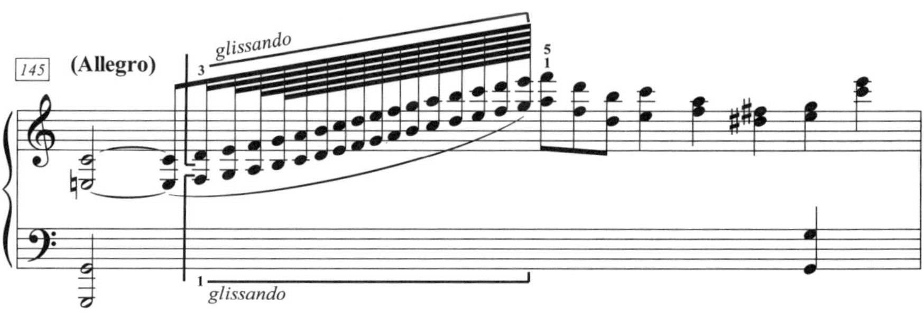

Example 1.110. Mozart, Nine variations on "Lison dormait," K. 315d (264).

A famous example of a two-note octave cadenza occurs in the last movement of Beethoven's "Waldstein" Sonata, op. 53. Beethoven relatively rarely indicated fingerings in his piano works, but here he clearly indicates his desire for glissandos in both hands (ex. 1.111).

Most pianists try to work out a fingering that permits the prestissimo tempo, legato indications, and *pianissimo* dynamics. For instance, the editions by Hans von Bülow (1830–1894) and Moritz Moszkowski (1854–1925) give alternate fingering solutions that divide the glissandos between the hands. Unfortunately, they omit a significant number of notes. (Artur Schnabel [1882–1951] in his edition gives a version that does not omit notes.) My version (ex. 1.112) maintains all the notes. Any performer should carefully examine any redistributed versions of the octave glissandos and then make a carefully informed artistic choice.

Example 1.111. Beethoven, "Waldstein" Sonata, Op. 53: Original fingering.

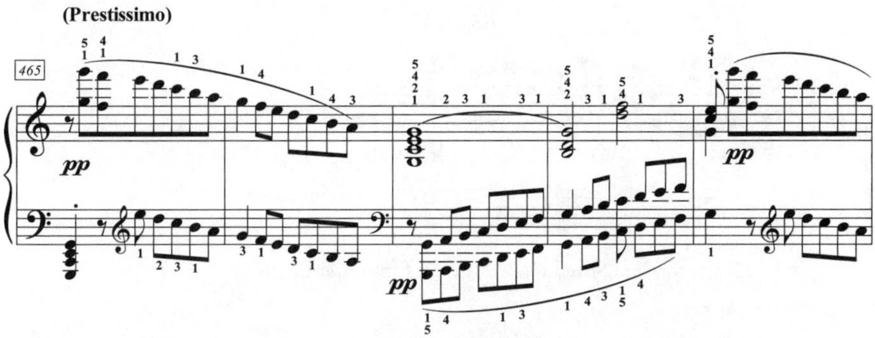

Example 1.112. Beethoven, "Waldstein" Sonata, Op. 53: Banowetz's fingering.

Composers' Indications for Fingerings

In addition to implying a certain fingering through notating the notes in either the top or bottom clefs, there are instances when a composer actually writes in fingering indications. These should always be carefully considered, for in some instances a composer's given fingering may convey a strong musical implication for the intended performance. At other times, however, a composer's suggested fingering may seem strange or even unusable. Regardless, these fingerings should be considered before the performer makes a final personal decision regarding whether they are relevant. Fortunately, there are excellent editions available that carefully include any fingering indications made by the composer. A number of these have been listed in the bibliography.

The following are a few selected examples of composers' own indications for fingerings. All these fingerings are given in italics. Beethoven occasionally writes in fingerings. However, it must be remembered that the action on the pianos in Beethoven's day was much shallower and the keys slightly narrower. For example, Beethoven's fingerings in this passage from his Sonata, op. 2, no. 2 (ex. 1.113), are not practical for today's pianists. Most pianists will play the first note of each three-note triplet with the left hand (ex. 1.114). But Beethoven's fingering clearly indicates that the triplets should be played legato and without a percussive accent on the opening note of each triplet. Other possible redistributions, although at first more difficult to learn, can help to control the placing of exaggerated accents on the first notes of each triplet figuration (ex. 1.115).

Example 1.113. Beethoven, Sonata, op. 2, no. 2, first movement.

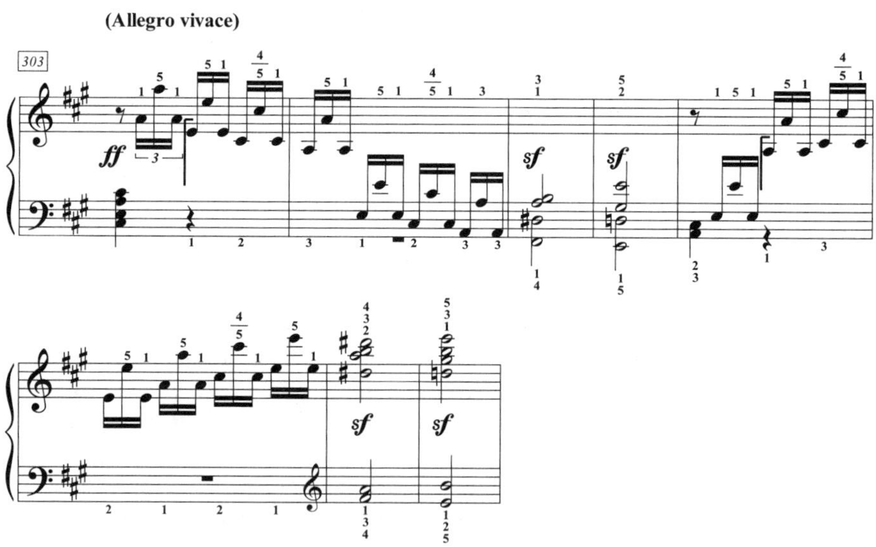

Example 1.114. Beethoven, Sonata, op. 2, no. 2, first movement: Frequently used redistributions.

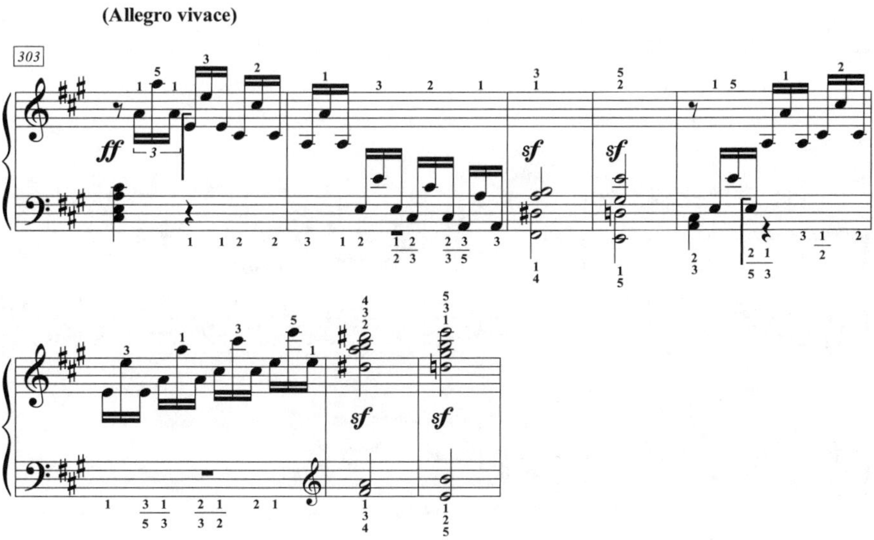

Example 1.115. Beethoven, Sonata, op. 2, no. 2, first movement: Other possible redistributions.

In example 1.116 from the third movement of Beethoven's Sonata, op. 2, no. 1, the composer's fingering clearly indicates his desire for a legato touch. Beethoven's fingering works reasonably well, although there are some possible slight modifications that could perhaps make this easier to obtain (ex. 1.117). This modified fingering redistributes some notes between the hands while also avoiding the playing of adjoining notes with the same finger. With this approach, a near perfect legato can be maintained without relying on the damper pedal.

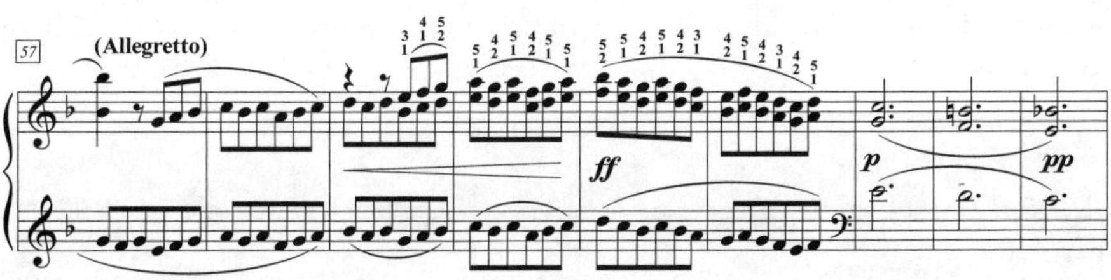

Example 1.116. Beethoven, Sonata, op. 2, no. 1, third movement.

Example 1.117.

Beethoven's fingering for the fourth movement of his Sonata, op. 2, no. 3 (ex. 1.118), is reliable and practical. His fingering easily creates the desired staccato touch.

Example 1.118. Beethoven, Sonata, op. 2, no. 3, fourth movement.

A famous example of Beethoven's fingering occurs in his Sonata, op. 106, third movement (ex. 1.119). His slurs indicate the shaping of each pair of notes, combvined with a one-note legato. It is of interest that he indicates a 4–3 pattern in the first printed edition; then, in a slightly later edition printed in England, he indicates a 3–2 pattern. Regardless of the fingering used, the player should maintain a one-note legato between each pair of notes. A slight raising of the wrist as the second note of the pair is played will help to maintain the correct shaping of dynamics.

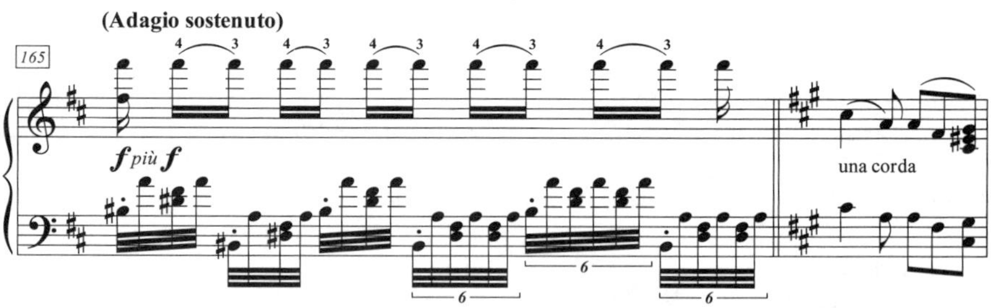

Example 1.119. Beethoven, Sonata, op. 106, third movement.

Chopin's compositions have many indications for fingerings, many of which were added in copies of music used by his pupils during lessons. They give a rich insight into his attitude toward phrasing, implied rubato, and melodic shaping.

In Chopin's Nocturne, op. 9, no. 2 (ex. 1.120), the moving of the right hand's fifth finger from D to C clearly shows the ending of the slur and implies perhaps a slight rubato hesitation. There naturally is no actual break in the sound because of the notated pedaling by Chopin.

Example 1.120. Chopin, Nocturne, op. 9, no. 2.

Chopin's fingerings in examples 1.121 and 1.122 give fascinating glimpses of his apparent using the same finger in succession and of crossing one finger under another. According to later written accounts of his teaching and playing, this was an approach to fingering that he commonly used in both his performances and teaching.

Example 1.121. Chopin, Nocturne, op. 9, no. 2.

Example 1.122. Chopin, Nocturne, op. 48, no. 1.

In Chopin's Nocturne, op. 37, no. 1 (ex. 1.123), the third finger of the right hand is used three times in succession during an emphasized legato part of the melody. Chopin indicates that the entire first two beats should be held in the pedal. The sixteenth-note rest perhaps implies a slight rubato hesitation.

Example 1.123. Chopin, Nocturne, op. 37, no. 1.

In Chopin's Nocturne, op. 62, no. 1 (ex. 1.124), his use of the first and third fingers of the right hand in succession perhaps indicates that he feels better control and evenness can be obtained with this unusual fingering. Although in the original there is no decrescendo starting at the top of the group of sixteenth notes in m. 84, the performer may wish to add one.

Example 1.124. Chopin, Nocturne, op. 62, no. 1.

A clear use of block fingering may be seen in Chopin's Nocturne, op. 15, no. 2 (ex. 1.125). Here it is completely logical because the four black notes precede the thumb playing on B, then are repeated as the hand changes position when it places the fifth finger on A-sharp.

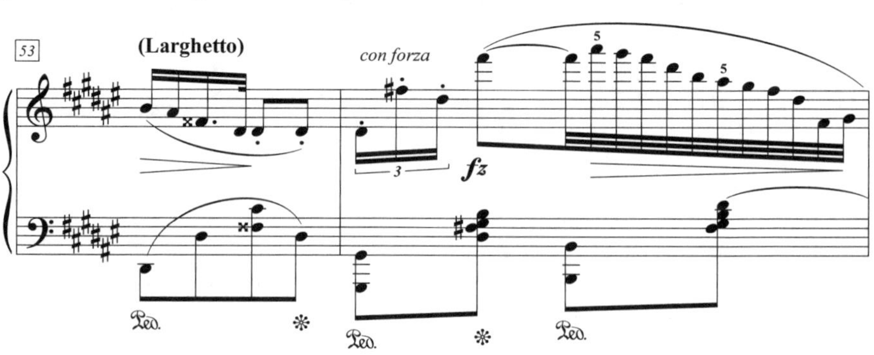

Example 1.125. Chopin, Nocturne, op. 15, no. 2.

In Chopin's Nocturne, op. 48, no. 1 (ex. 1.26), there is a significant example of his use of a redistribution technique, as notated in a pupil's teaching copy. Here he clearly indicates possible hand groupings that are clearly different from his original score.

Example 1.126. Chopin, Nocturne, op. 48, no. 1.

Chopin's original fingering for his Nocturne, op. 27, no. 1, is shown in example 1.127a. Two examples of Chopin's indications for the redistribution of hands in this same passage are found in copies of this piece used by his pupils (exx. 1.127b and 1.127c).

Example 1.127a. Chopin, Nocturne, op. 27, no. 1: Chopin's original score.

Example 1.127b. Chopin, Nocturne, op. 27, no. 1: a suggested redistribution by Chopin.

Example 1.127c. Chopin, Nocturne, op. 27, no. 1: another suggested redistribution by Chopin.

Liszt's *Vallée d'Obermann* (ex. 1.128) clearly shows the composer's use of legato fingering for octaves. This type of fingering was also utilized often by Chopin, as for instance in his Étude, op. 25, no. 10.

Example 1.128. Liszt, *Vallée d'Obermann*.

In Liszt's *Transcendental Étude no. 4,* "Mazeppa" (ex. 1.129), the fingering clearly demands a loud and percussive touch. Difficult as this fingering may prove to be in performance, it should be explored, if for no other reason than to understand the kind of sound Liszt probably wished for this passage.

Example 1.129. Liszt, *Transcendental* Étude no. 4, "Mazeppa."

A passage from the Brahms Intermezzo, op. 118, no. 1 (ex. 1.130) clearly shows a block fingering that is used to help project and shape four-note groups of the overall phrase.

Example 1.130. Brahms, Intermezzo, op. 118, no. 1.

In Brahms's Rhapsody, op. 119, no. 4 (ex. 1.131), the composer clearly shows a use of finger crossings to maintain a smooth line and shaping of the melody. It is the same kind of fingering found in some Chopin works.

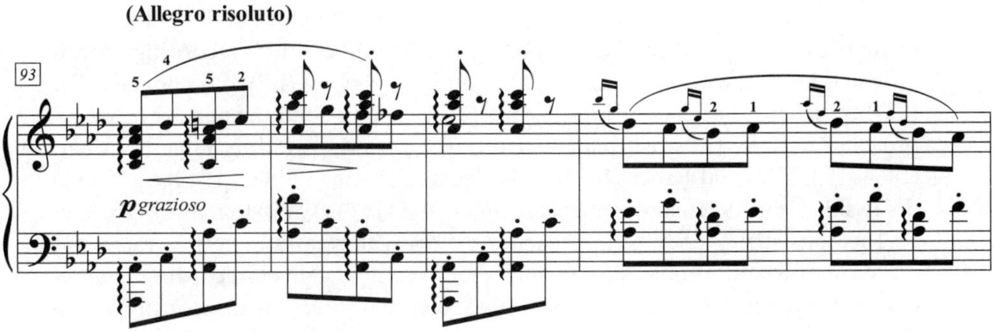

Example 1.131. Brahms, Rhapsody, op. 119, no. 4.

Brahms's Rhapsody, op. 119, no. 4 (ex. 1.132), shows an interesting use of block fingerings.

Example 1.132. Brahms, Rhapsody, op. 119, no. 4.

The Breaking of Hands and Rolling of Chords by Pianists from the Late Nineteenth and Early Twentieth Centuries

A significant number of pianists from the late nineteenth and early twentieth centuries employed a breaking of hands and rolling of chords in their performances. This is evident from early sound disc and cylinder recordings, many of which have now been made available on long-playing (LP) and compact disc (CD) transfers. These recordings give priceless insights into the performance approaches used by the great pianists from this period, including Eugen d'Albert (1864–1932), Harold Bauer (1873–1951), Ignaz Friedman (1882–1948), Ignaz Paderewski (1860–1941), and Sergei Rachmaninoff (1873–1943), to name but a few.

The consistency of their approaches differs widely, and of course raises the question of whether today's performer should imitate a given recording. To give one instance, in the opening measures of Rachmaninoff's own recording of his Piano Concerto no. 2 (ex. 1.133), he breaks the chords by playing the bottom Fs slightly before the notes above. This can be heard in two recordings, one made in 1924 and the second in 1929, both with the Philadelphia Orchestra conducted by Leopold Stokowski. Yet Rachmaninoff had extremely large hands that could easily play these chords without breaking!

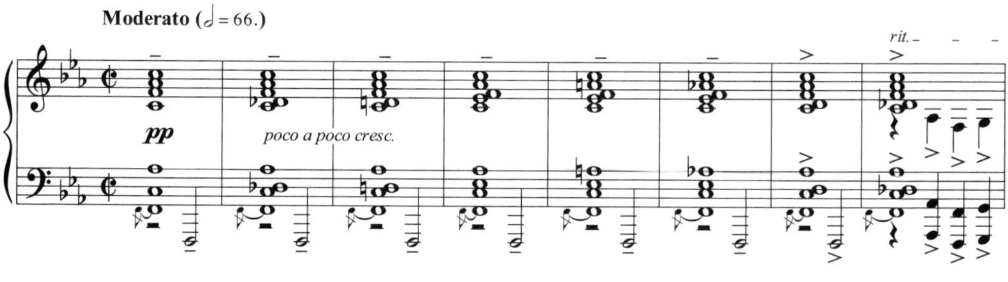

Example 1.133. Rachmaninoff, Piano Concerto no. 2, as performed by Rachmaninoff.

The question is raised as to where and when a large chord should possibly be redistributed to enable playing without a roll or break, and if the hands should be played exactly together in other passage work. This is something that each performer needs to personally consider and decide when working out a fingering.

Notes

1. Edwin Fischer, *Beethoven's Pianoforte Sonatas*, trans. Stanley Godman with the collaboration of Paul Hamburger (London: Faber and Faber, 1959), 47.

2. Recorded in November 1938, for His Master's Voice, HMV DB 3666–7, 78-rpm discs; recorded in October 1952, for His Master's Voice, HMV ALP 1094, 331/3-rpm LP disc.

3. Ludwig van Beethoven, *Sonatas for the Piano*, ed. Hans von Bülow and Sigmund Lebert (New York: G. Schirmer, 1923).

2 The Fingering Redistribution of Hands: Pros and Cons

The question of redistributions of fingerings remains controversial. A significant number of performers and pedagogues are apparently wedded to the idea that each hand should, without exception, play whatever notes are assigned to it by a given composer, regardless of whether the composer was a virtuoso pianist or not. Some even feel that using a redistribution is a form of cheating. Kendall Taylor, in his book *Principles of Piano Technique and Interpretation*, writes: "Such rearrangements abound and in general should be strongly discouraged. . . . Those addicted to altering and rearranging hands may be accused of practicing 'Swindle-technique'!"[1] It is even felt by some that using a redistribution is a form of "cheating," as if piano playing is some kind of sport!

But there are valid concerns when deciding for the sake of convenience, reliability, or ease of performance whether a redistribution is desirable and, most importantly, artistically valid for a performance of a given work. What are the criteria for deciding when to utilize a redistribution? First and foremost, this decision should depend on the sound image that the performer wishes to project. For instance, in a passage that has a large interval that cannot be negotiated by the performer and that would demand an awkward roll, there is no artistic virtue in not taking a note or notes with the other hand. This holds especially true if the composer himself, as in the case of Rachmaninoff and Busoni, possessed large hands. Under no circumstances, however, should notes be omitted or played for convenience in a different register or at a different time than what is written.

One of the primary things a performer must do is to decide on the exact sound that is needed for a given passage. A composer's style is, of course, a strongly determining factor. Obviously, much of Bartók's or Prokofiev's piano music demands a different tone quality than do Debussy's works. These considerations will at times influence the choice of a possible redistribution. When, for instance, a possible redistribution will alter the sound obtained by playing the composer's original distribution, then careful soul searching has to be done by the performer. Beethoven at times has passages that, through redistributions, can immediately be performed more easily from a sheer physical standpoint but often at the cost of a subtle change in the physical sound and feeling of musical tension.

The factors that should be considered when making a decision whether or not to use a given distribution include the following:

1. Is the basic sound given by adhering to the original distribution changed in too drastic a manner?
2. What are the technical risks in adhering to the original distribution? Will these risks be worth taking under the pressure of an actual public performance or recording?
3. Does keeping the original distribution create obstacles in achieving the musical meaning of a given passage?
4. Is there an unacceptably extreme change in the actual physical appearance of the passage in a public performance?

Controversial examples of redistributions can be found in several examples from Beethoven. These demand careful consideration on the part of the performer.

In the first movement of Beethoven's Sonata, op. 106 (ex. 2.1a), the opening left-hand jumps are notably dangerous, especially if Beethoven's original metronome indication of a half note equaling 138 is followed. Three well-known historically important editions by Hans von Bülow and Sigmund Lebert (ex. 2.1b), Donald Francis Tovey and Harold Craxon (ex. 2.1c), and Moritz Moszkowski (ex. 2.1d) suggest different redistributions.

Example 2.1a. Beethoven, Sonata, op. 106: original score.

Example 2.1b. Beethoven, Sonata, op. 106: Hans von Bülow and Sigmund Lebert edition.

Example 2.1c. Beethoven, Sonata, op. 106: Donald Francis Tovey and Harold Craxon edition.

Example 2.1d. Beethoven, Sonata, op. 106: Moritz Moszkowski edition.

Yet another example of a passage that often receives a redistribution occurs in the first movement of Beethoven's Sonata, op. 57 (ex. 2.2a). There are a good number of redistributions possible, some of which, like that found in the alternation of every other note with the other hand, will unfortunately possibly make the sound too percussive (ex. 2.2b). Another example that has a more discrete taking of one note in every group of six with the left hand, however, can be effectively used (ex. 2.2c). A video of the great English pianist Dame Myra Hess (1920–1995) shows her utilizing this last redistribution.

Example 2.2a. Beethoven, Sonata, op. 57: Original version.

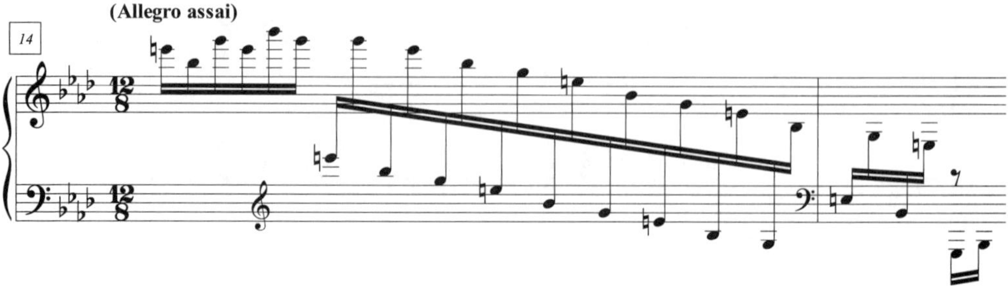

Example 2.2b. Beethoven, Sonata, op. 57: First possible redistribution.

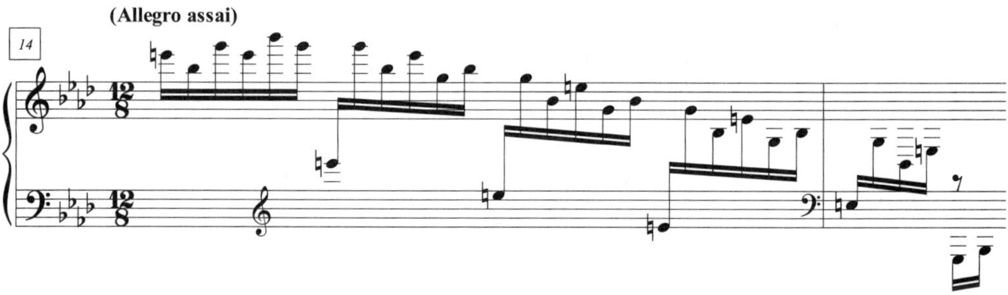

Example 2.2c. Beethoven, Sonata, op. 57: Second possible redistribution.

A final example of a borderline possible redistribution in Beethoven can be found in the opening cadenza of the first movement of his Concerto no. 5. The slightly uncomfortable hand shifts here can be immediately made more comfortable and reliably smooth, especially for performers with small hands, by the redistributions shown in example 2.3. Incidentally, I saw Arturo Benedetti Michelangeli (1920–1995) use these redistributions in a public concert in London.

Example 2.3. Beethoven, Concerto no. 5, opening cadenza.

There are many other similar examples where redistributions may be either entirely suspect or demand stylistically careful modification choices. This is particularly true when changes in sound are created from the original, especially when the composer was himself a virtuoso performer.

Redistributions to Avoid Rolls

The pedantic and outdated "rule" that the player should never take a note written for the other hand with a redistribution simply does not have merit, especially when dealing with larger intervals or chords that must be broken if not redistributed. This is not, as some would say, "cheating." Chopin's Concerto no. 2 in F Minor (ex. 2.4) offers a clear example of this necessity. If the opening tenth interval, and even possibly the following ninth, cannot be stretched by the left hand, a redistribution is necessary. This will not only avoid an unwritten roll on the downbeat but, even more importantly, allow the holding of the F dotted half note in the left hand its full time, as needed support for the changing harmony above. Chopin's "il basso sempre legato" indication is not editorial.

Example 2.4. Chopin, Concerto no. 2 in F Minor, first movement.

A similar example occurs in the second movement of Chopin's Concerto no. 2 in F Minor (ex. 2.5). Chopin asks for a roll on the downbeat in the right hand but then gives no indication for a roll on the second beat, where there is a large interval that cannot be managed by smaller hands. The obvious solution is to play the right hand's B-flat with the left hand.

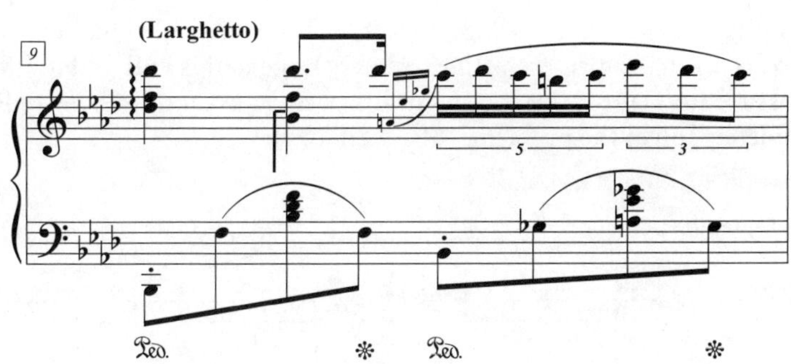

Example 2.5. Chopin, Concerto no. 2 in F Minor, second movement.

In Liszt's Sonetto no. 123 (ex. 2.6), most pianists will not be able to play the major tenths on the fourth beats in the left hand. Taking the Gs with the right hand will solve this problem. If the B-flat in the melody cannot be held legato to the next downbeat, catch it with the pedal. There should, of course, be a change of pedal on each beat throughout each measure.

Example 2.6. Liszt, *Sonetto* no. 123.

Liszt's *Paganini* Étude no. 6 (ex. 2.7) demands a rapid tempo. Even if a tenth can be stretched, the high speed makes getting both to and away from this large interval difficult. Taking the top notes of the tenths with the other hand helps to solve the problem of obtaining both accuracy and brilliance.

Example 2.7. Liszt, *Paganini* Étude no. 6.

In Chopin's Ballade no. 3 (ex. 2.8), the large chords in the left hand are marked without rolls. Even performers with extremely large hands will find it difficult, if not impossible, to play all the chords in this passage without rolls. A redistribution completely solves the problem.

Example 2.8. Chopin, Ballade no. 3.

In Liszt's *Transcendental* Étude no. 10 in F Minor (ex. 2.9), even a performer with the span of a tenth will find this passage extremely difficulty to play at its rapid tempo. Taking the top note of each tenth in the left hand with the thumb of the right hand enables both speed and accuracy.

Example 2.9. Liszt, *Transcendental* Étude no. 10 in F Minor.

Redistributing Large Chords and Intervals to Obtain Clarity and Clean Pedal Changes and to Avoid Unwanted Rolls

Although from the mid-nineteenth to early twentieth centuries the breaking of hands and rolling of chords were very common, there are numerous situations that demand redistributions in order to avoid unwanted rolls, obtain clarity of texture, and ensure clean pedal changes. In Liszt's *Transcendental* Étude no. 9, "Ricordanza" (ex. 2.10), many hands will not be able to play the left-hand chords without rolling them. Taking the top notes of each chord with the right hand solves the problem.

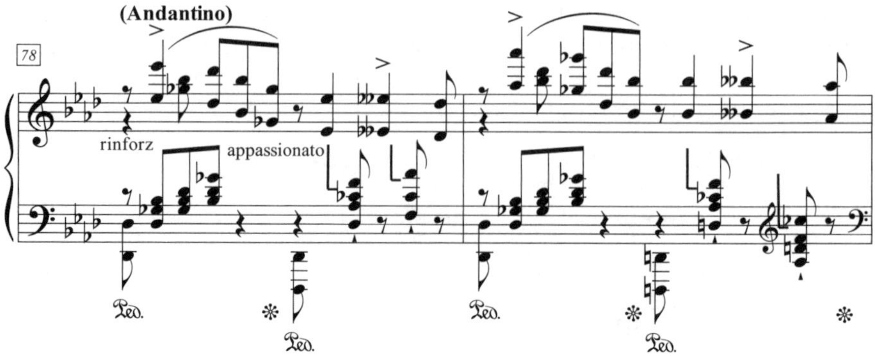

Example 2.10. Liszt, *Transcendental* Étude no. 9, "Ricordanza."

In Beethoven's Sonata, op. 109, third movement (ex. 2.11), the repeated chords in the left hand during the first two beats will for many hands be difficult or impossible to play without rolls. On the third beat, taking the F-sharp with the left hand facilitates playing a smooth and even trill with independent fingers.

Example 2.11. Beethoven, Sonata, op. 109, third movement.

More reliably smooth pedal changes will occur in Liszt's Ballade no. 2 in B Minor (ex. 2.12) if the top notes of the rolls are taken with the right hand. In pedaling the first roll, the pedal must be changed with the top note, not the bottom, of the roll, to keep a full legato between the quarter note before and the dotted half note. When the pedal is changed, this bottom note of the roll must be held with the finger to make certain the bass line does not get lost. A redistribution will ensure the necessary legato.

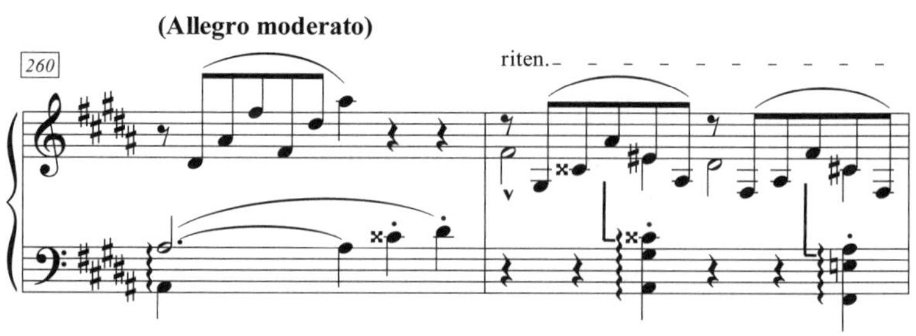

Example 2.12. Liszt, Ballade no. 2 in B Minor.

In Liszt's *Paganini* Étude no. 6 in A Minor (ex. 2.13), the tenths in the left hand will present problems for many performers. At the rapid speed of this passage, rolls become awkward. Redistributing the top note of each tenth interval solves this problem easily.

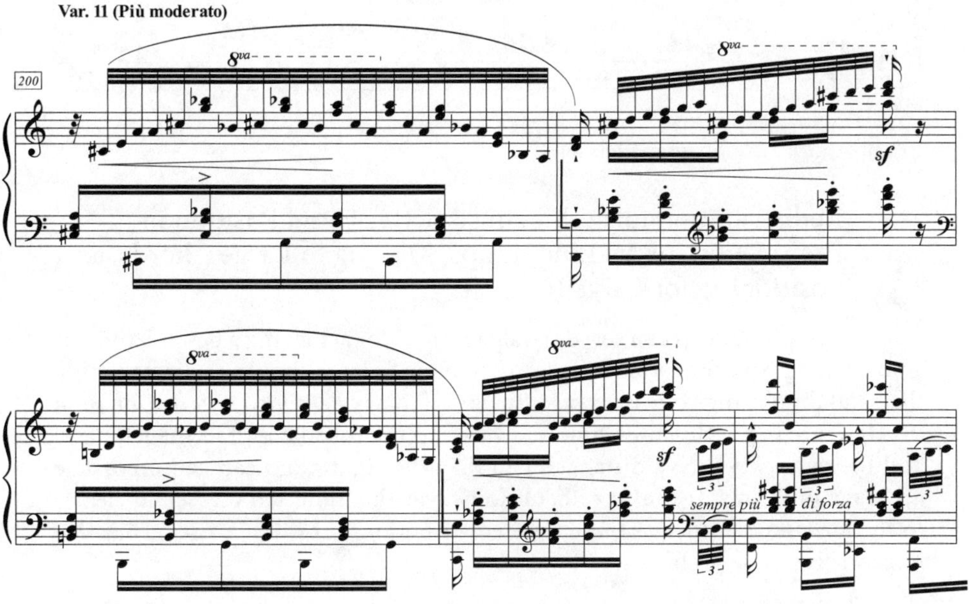

Example 2.13. Liszt, *Paganini* Étude no. 6 in A Minor.

The excerpts from Liszt's *La Leggierezza* Étude (ex. 2.14) and his Spanish Rhapsody (ex. 2.15) show clearly how a redistribution can eliminate an unwanted roll for a large interval or chord. Note that Liszt does not indicate a roll for the chord spanning an eleventh but does write rolls for previous chords covering smaller intervals.

Example 2.14. Liszt, *La Leggierezza* Étude.

Example 2.15. Liszt, Spanish Rhapsody.

Redistribution for Achieving a Better Hand Position in Preparation for Making Jumps, Moving to Large Chords, and Positioning for Large Intervals

Redistributions can serve as valuable aids for achieving a better hand position when preparing for making leaps, moving to large chords, and positioning the hand for playing large intervals. In Liszt's fantasy *Réminiscences de Don Juan* (S. 418), moving both hands simultaneously to the rolled chord in the left hand and the over two-octave distanced chord in the right hand can cause possible accuracy problems. It is also difficult to deliver the indicated crescendo clearly to the *fortissimo*. Either of these two redistributions (exx. 2.16a and 2.16b) will largely solve these problems.

Example 2.16a. Liszt, *Réminiscences de Don Juan* (S. 418). First redistribution.

Example 2.16b. Liszt, *Réminiscences de Don Juan* (S. 418). Second possible redistribution.

A similar difficulty can be found in Liszt's *Mephisto* Waltz no. 1. If this passage is played with an alternation of hands starting with the right hand, the left hand cannot be well positioned for the rapid rolled chord. Liszt's pupil Emil von Sauer suggests the redistribution shown in example 2.17. Be sure to use the 2–1 fingering in the left hand on the D–E-flat, and the 1–2 fingering in the right hand on the A-flat–C. This will place the hands in a better position for the jumps to the chords. As with so many other examples, this fingering must be played at tempo to sense its full usefulness.

Example 2.17. Liszt, *Mephisto Waltz no. 1.*

Liszt's technically demanding *Transcendental* Étude no. 8, "Wilde Jagd" ("Wild Hunt"), has many places that demand large, rapid jumps. Two possible redistributions allow for more technical security without resorting to the "emergency rubatos" that are so often heard. Either of these redistributions (shown in exx. 2.18a and 2.18b) will greatly facilitate playing these dangerous passages.

Example 2.18a. Liszt, *Transcendental* Étude no. 8, "Wilde Jagd" ("Wild Hunt"): First possible redistribution.

Example 2.18b. Liszt, *Transcendental* Étude no. 8, "Wilde Jagd" ("Wild Hunt"): Second possible redistribution.

Purists will undoubtedly react adversely to the suggested redistributions in the second movement of Beethoven's Sonata, op. 111 (ex. 2.19). However, keeping a sharply defined dotted rhythm, together with concerns for accuracy in negotiating the rapid and awkward skips, may make these suggested redistributions extremely useful.

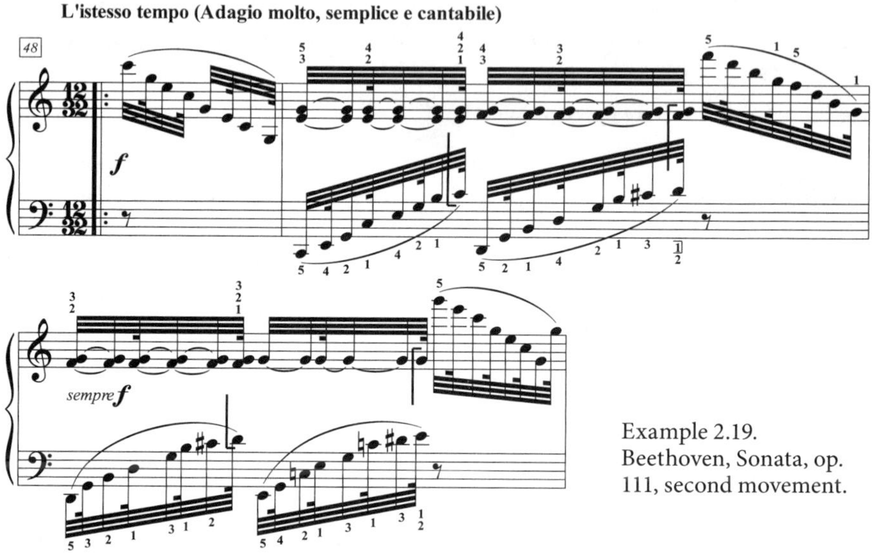

Example 2.19. Beethoven, Sonata, op. 111, second movement.

In the first movement of Beethoven's Sonata, op. 14, no. 2, the ends of several phrases stop on the downbeats, which are then followed by awkward skips. There should be no accent on each of the downbeat phrase endings, and each downbeat F should not be played with a jagged staccato touch, as this will give the impression of an accent. Even allowing for a slight hesitation between the downbeat Fs and the Ds a tenth lower, the skip is difficult to manage with proper melodic shaping. Utilizing the fingering shown in example 2.20 will make this awkward passage much more manageable.

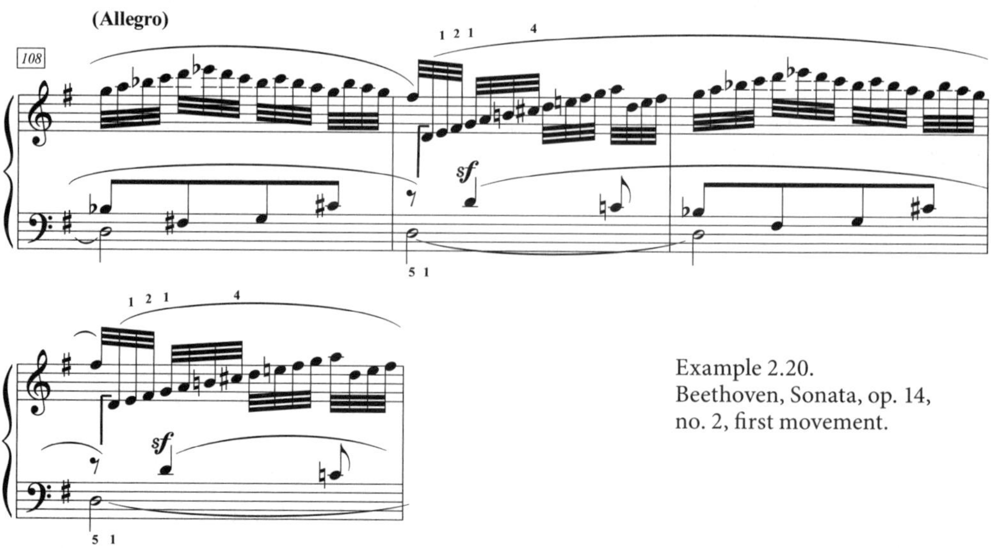

Example 2.20. Beethoven, Sonata, op. 14, no. 2, first movement.

There are situations when the hands may have to suddenly move simultaneously to a new position. In some cases, a facilitation can be made to allow one hand to move a split second earlier, thereby perhaps avoiding an unwanted accent and helping to ensure technical accuracy, as in the first movement of Chopin's Piano Concerto no. 1, op. 11 (ex. 2.21). Note that accents on the downbeats are not desirable because they are the last notes in slurs that Chopin marks with accents on the first notes. Moving suddenly away with both hands at the same time can create slight tension, resulting in unwanted downbeat accents.

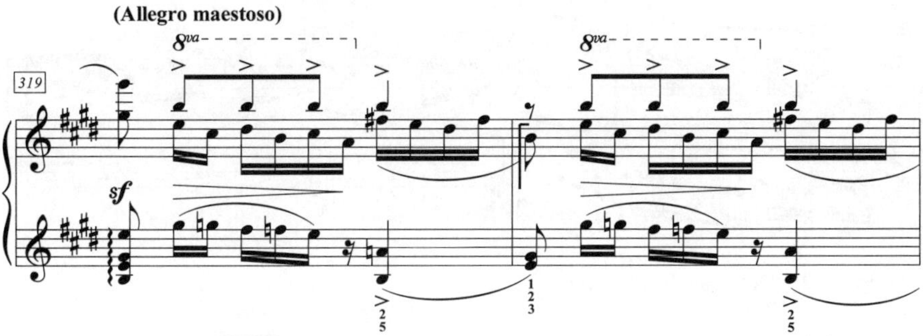

Example 2.21.
Chopin, Piano Concerto no. 1, op. 11, first movement.

Redistributions to Position for Large Skips and Rolls

A redistribution can be a tremendous aid in gaining a necessary musical effect as well as a consistent technical command of a given passage. In example 2.22 from Debussy's *Cloches à travers les feuilles* (*Images*, Book 2), the redistributions facilitate the awkward shifts of hand position. If the performer feels that

Example 2.22. Debussy, *Cloches à travers les feuilles* (*Images*, Book 2).

Debussy intended hesitations in making the shifts (which the present writer does not feel were intended), then these can be played while the redistributions are still used for technical security.

In Debussy's Étude 1 *pour les "cinq doigts" d'après Monsieur Czerny* (ex. 2.23), taking the top note of each of the large rolls will increase technical security, especially for a smaller hand. The tempo is rapid, and the rolls should be played before the beats, with the As in each hand coming together.

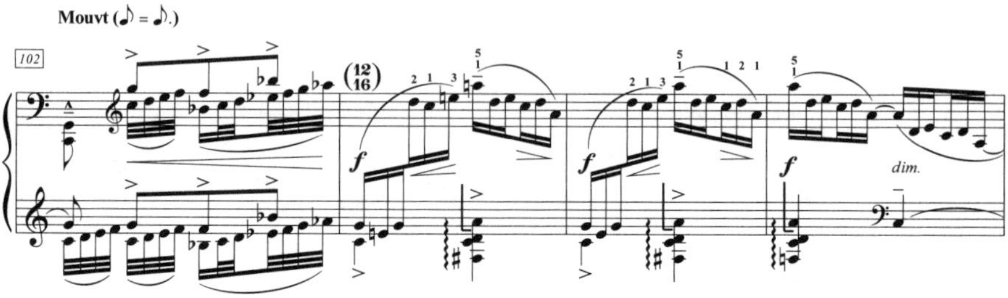

Example 2.23. Debussy, Étude 1 *pour les "cinq doigts" d'après Monsieur Czerny.*

Chopin's Scherzo no. 2 (ex. 2.24) contains an extremely awkward passage if a traditional fingering is used for the trill that is played just before the rapid leap of over five octaves. Taking the two finishing notes of the trill with the left hand not only reduces the upward travel time to the high F but also allows there to be more accuracy because the hand can move to the F a bit earlier. Chopin himself indicates this redistribution in a copy of music used during a lesson with his student Camille O'Meara.

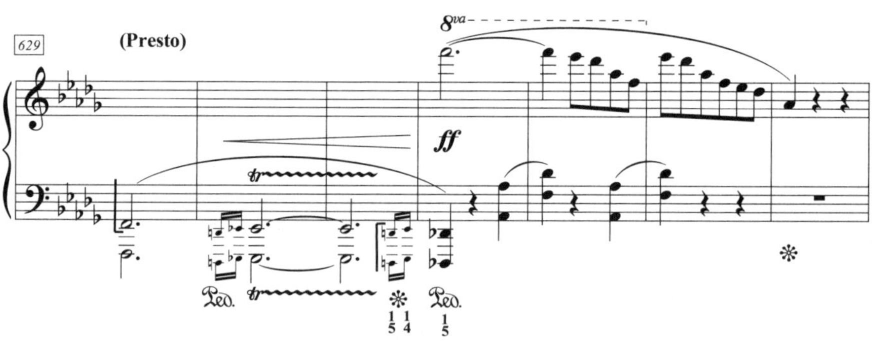

Example 2.24. Chopin, Scherzo no. 2.

Schumann's "Arlequin" from his *Carnaval*, op. 9 (ex. 2.25) contains large jumps in the right hand that, even for a performer with a moderately sized hand, can prove to be uncomfortable. Taking the bottom tied notes of the right hand—plus making certain that the thumb, even if playing a black note, is used before each skip of a tenth—helps to ensure both rhythmic and note accuracy. This passage, because of the skips, is frequently heard with a total distortion of the actual notated rhythm!

Example 2.25. Schumann, "Arlequin," from *Carnaval*, op. 9.

Beethoven's Concerto no. 5, first movement (ex. 2.26), contains a passage with difficult skips. Not only must the sixteenth notes be played at a fairly rapid tempo, but they must also remain leggiero and *piano.* If the hand tightens slightly as it changes position, an unintentional crescendo may occur. The suggested redistributions will aid in keeping control of both the dynamics and touch that are demanded.

Example 2.26. Beethoven, Concerto no. 5 "Emperor," op. 73, first movement.

When playing Beethoven's Sonata, op. 111, first movement, it is difficult to maintain a strong crescendo and non-legato touch while avoiding an "emergency rubato" hesitation right before the fortissimo downbeat. Any of the three possible redistributions shown in example 2.27 will help to solve the problem. They should all be tried out in concert tempo with the correct dynamics, then a decision made as to which one is most comfortable and reliable.

Example 2.27. Beethoven, Sonata, op. 111, first movement. Three possible redistributions.

Redistributions for Achieving Controlled Voicing and Technical Clarity

Redistributions can be remarkably helpful in achieving control when balancing voicing and in gaining technical clarity in a passage. As with redistributions in general, care should always be taken that the composer's initial musical idea is not altered. As emphasized before, each performer must decide whether a given redistribution in some way interferes with the composer's artistic intentions or, to the contrary, whether it clarifies the music's message and makes it easier for the performer to deliver successfully in a public performance. But to apply a hard and fast rule to never "cheat" by using a redistribution seems at best shortsighted and at worst pedantic!

In the first movement of Beethoven's Sonata, op. 2, no. 3 (ex. 2.28), the dotted half-note Gs may be taken with the right hand, to allow the stronger, more independent fingers to play the left-hand sixteenths and eighths. This facilitation is suggested for instance in editions made by Hans von Bülow (1830–1894), Moritz Moszkowski (1854–1925), and Artur Schnabel (1881–1951).

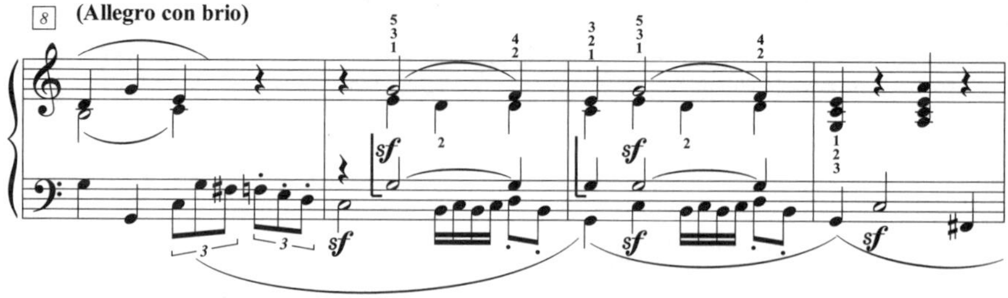

Example 2.28. Beethoven, Sonata, op. 2, no. 3, first movement.

In Chopin's Scherzo no. 4 (ex. 2.29), taking the tied B in the bass with the right hand allows for a better control of legato and diminuendo throughout the left hand's melodic material.

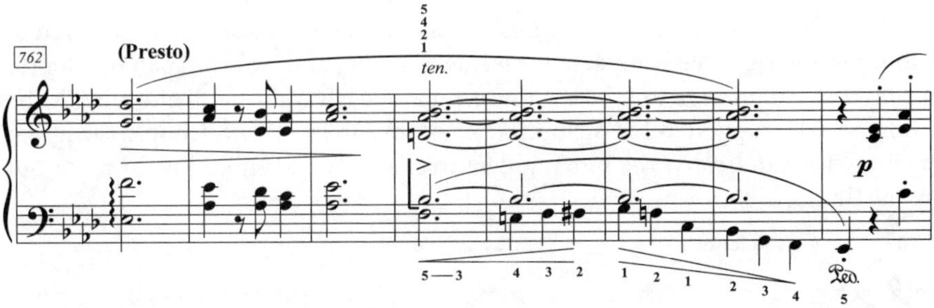

Example 2.29. Chopin, Scherzo no. 4.

At times, composers write passages that may create a great deal of awkwardness for the average pianist's span. For instance, in Schumann's *Kinderszenen*, op. 15, no. 8, "Am Kamin" ("At the Fireside"), much of the piece is written with the thumbs of each hand interlocking. Bass notes are at times indicated to be held when this would demand a handspan of an easy tenth. Holding many of these long bass notes with the pedal would create a significant blurring of harmonies. In example 2.30a, Schumann's original text is given and then a suggested redis-

Example 2.30a. Schumann, *Kinderszenen*, op. 15, no. 8, "Am Kamin" ("At the Fireside"). Original version.

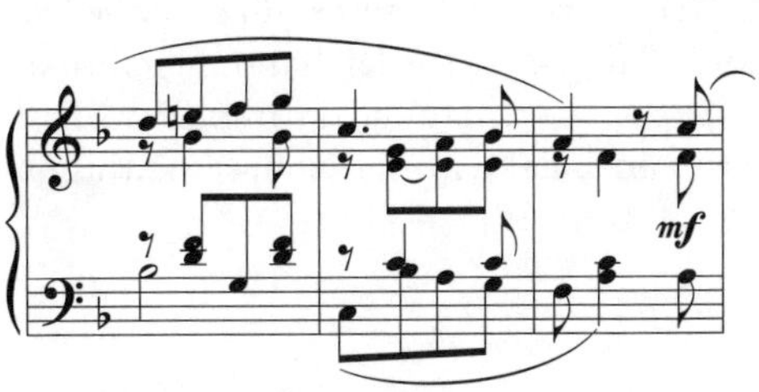

Example 2.30b. Schumann, *Kinderszenen*, op.15, no. 8, "Am Kamin" ("At the Fireside"). Suggested redistribution.

tribution (ex. 2.30b). The metronome indication is by Schumann. Harold Bauer (1873–1951) in his edition of the *Kinderszenen* gives a similar redistribution throughout "Am Kamin," but he changes Schumann's metronome indication.

A similar keyboard layout occurs in the trio section of the second movement of Chopin's Sonata no. 2 (ex. 2.31). If there is a slavish insistence on not redistributing, the right hand must play chords covering at times the span of a tenth. An obvious solution is to take the lower note of each right-hand chord with the left hand. The suggested redistribution does not interfere with Chopin's original layout, which indicated the moving part in the left hand should be brought out by the thumb.

Example 2.31. Chopin, Sonata no. 2, second movement.

A small redistribution can be very helpful at times when the hands are rapidly switching position, especially when an unwanted accent or crescendo needs to be avoided that may result from muscular tension when making a change of hand position. In Debussy's Étude 1 *pour les "cinq doigts" d'après Monsieur Czerny* (ex. 2.32), the hands must rapidly alter position, all within a *pianissimo* dynamic level. Taking the first D-flat with the right hand allows enough extra time for the left hand to then change position without excessive difficulty.

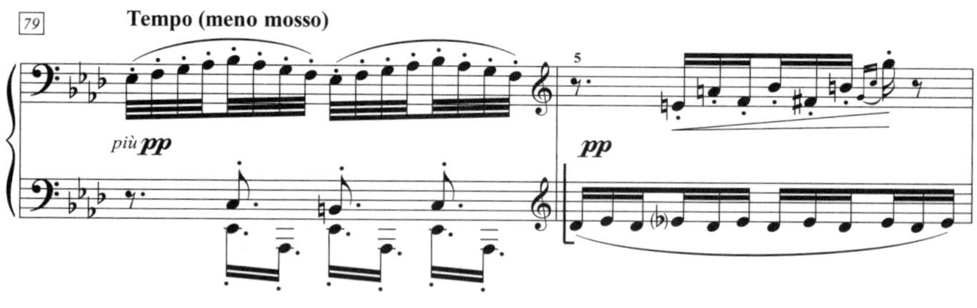

Example 2.32. Debussy, Étude 1 *pour les "cinq doigts" d'après Monsieur Czerny.*

A similar instance of a rapid position change is shown in the first movement of Rachmaninoff's Concerto no. 2 (ex. 2.33). There is a decrescendo over the last two beats, with the right hand playing an E-flat octave. The left hand then immediately plays the lower E-flat, which is supposed to remain held through the first beat of the next measure. Taking the left-hand E-flat with the right-hand thumb solves the problem of voicing and holding the E-flat the full time after it is played twice earlier.

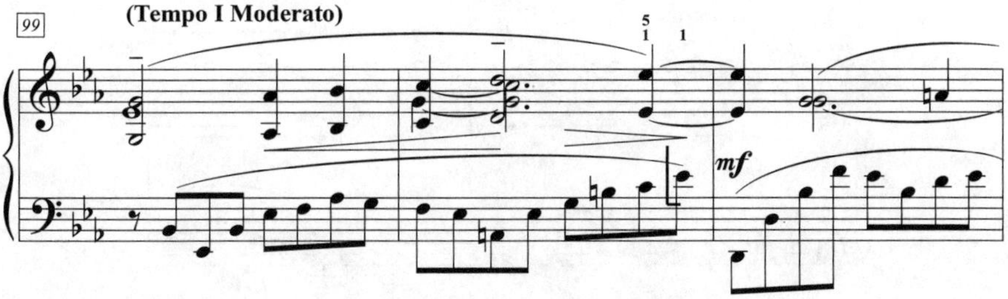

Example 2.33. Rachmaninoff, Concerto no. 2, first movement.

Redistributing to Better Shape Slur or Phrase Endings

In some instances, a redistribution may be used to give better control over shaping the end of a slur or phrase. Such an ending generally will demand a drop in dynamics. This will particularly become a problem if the tempo is not slow and one or both of the hands must move away quickly to another part of the keyboard. In Beethoven's Sonata, op. 109, third movement (ex. 2.34), the right hand must leave the low B to move upward for over two and a half octaves, all within tempo and without accenting the B as a result of the hand tightening slightly in anticipation of the jump upward. Taking the B with the left hand solves this problem. It also allows the B to be held its full time and will ensure that the phrase ending does not receive an unwanted accent.

Example 2.34. Beethoven, Sonata, op. 109, third movement.

Redistributions for Clarity, to Relieve Stress, for Speed, and for Accuracy

Redistributions can often be effectively used to achieve clarity and technical control, to achieve high velocity, for accuracy, and to relieve stress. In the third movement of Beethoven's Sonata, op. 10, no. 3 (ex. 2.35), taking the F-sharp and E with the left hand will ensure that the trill can be played in a uniformly smooth manner. If the player's hand cannot hold down the dotted half notes in the left hand, simply depress the pedal until the downbeat of the following measure. At the speed of the passage, this will not result in an objectionable blur.

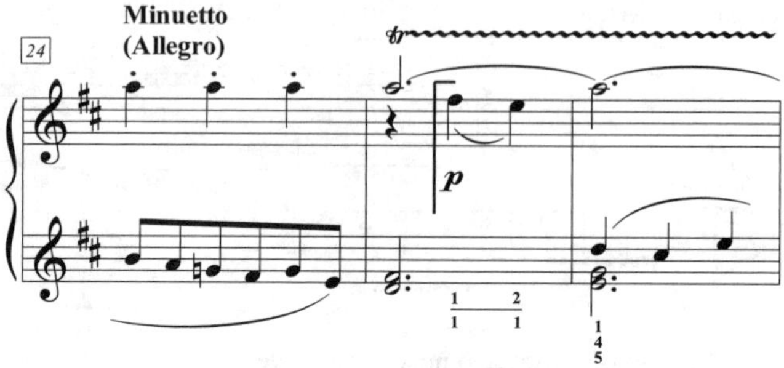

Example 2.35 Beethoven, Sonata, op. 10, no. 3, third movement.

The opening of the Chopin Sonata no. 3, first movement, features a difficult passage to perform. The usual fingering given is to place the thumb on the B, then cross over to the third finger on the downbeat F-sharp half note. However, starting the piece cold, being a bit tense, or having a slight amount of dampness on the tip of the third finger can easily result in slipping off the F-sharp. There is the story of a famous pianist who had such a mishap. She immediately stopped playing, took out her handkerchief, dusted off the F-sharp, then with a great deal of bravura took the F-sharp with the left hand! This problem can be much more easily solved with the fingering and redistribution shown in example 2.36.

Example 2.36. Chopin, Sonata no. 3, first movement.

In Chopin's Ballade no. 3 (ex. 2.37), many pianists redistribute the octaves between the hands. This helps to give a smooth legato, without having to play under tempo. If the performer chooses to play all the octaves with the right hand alone, the fingering shown in example 2.37 should be used. Otherwise, the redistributions shown in examples 2.38a and 2.38b can be made. Fingerings can be paired so that the same sets of fingers play together.

Chopin's Ballade no. 4 has a notoriously difficult passage in the coda. Many performers try to keep the dotted-sixteenth-note–thirty-second-note rhythm in the left hand, not realizing that Chopin was still using an older form of nota-

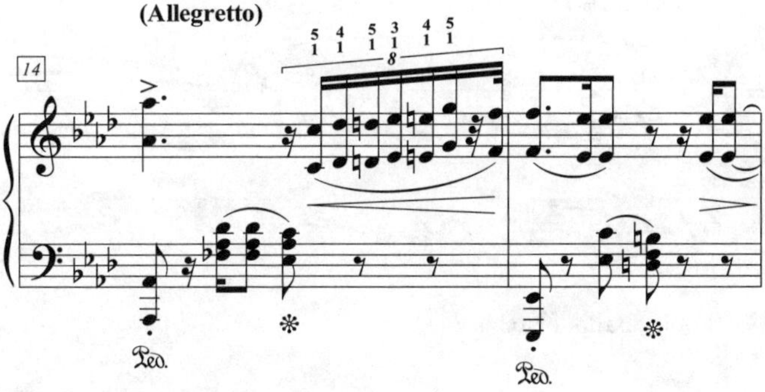

Example 2.37. Chopin, Ballade no. 3.

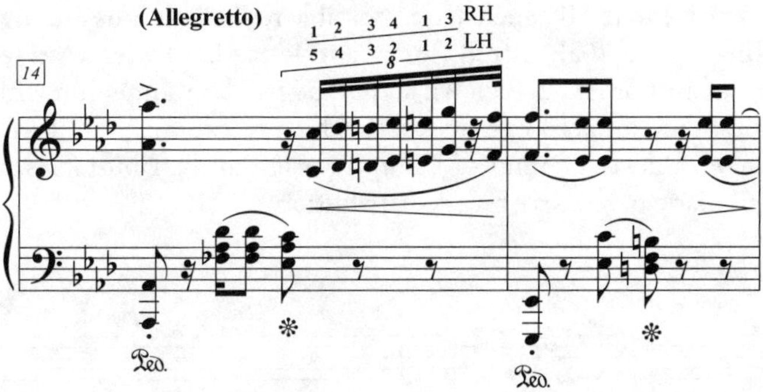

Example 2.38a. Chopin, Ballade no. 3. Redistribution.

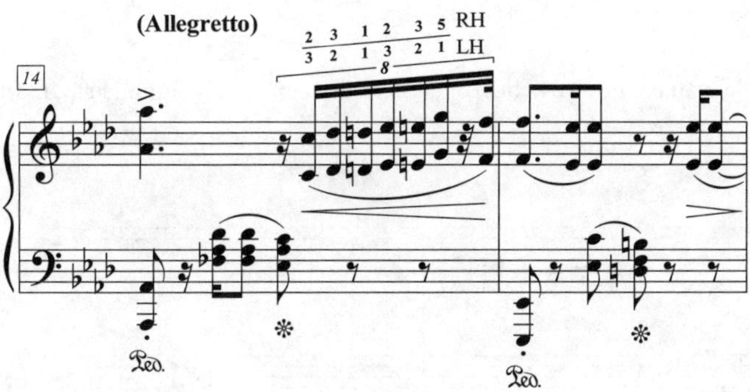

Example 2.38b. Chopin, Ballade no. 3. Redistribution.

tion that was common during Bach's day. Here the thirty-second notes should be played against the third of each triplet in the right hand. The redistribution that solves the difficult technical layout of Chopin's original scoring is shown in example 2.39.

Example 2.39. Chopin, Ballade no. 4.

This passage from the Chopin Scherzo no. 2 is difficult from an accuracy standpoint even for a player who can easily stretch the interval of a tenth. A long unbroken stretch of pedal is necessary, so even a very minor finger slip will be obvious and offensive to the listener. Three possible redistributions are suggested by Ignaz Friedman (ex. 2.40a), Alfred Cortot and Ignaz Jan Paderewski (ex. 2.40b), and the present author (ex. 2.40c). All should be tried out in tempo with the correct dynamics, then a decision made as to which one, if any, will be used. Care should be taken that the sound of Chopin's original distribution is not overly modified and made percussive by a redistribution.

Example 2.40a. Chopin, Scherzo no. 2. Redistribution by Ignaz Friedman.

Example 2.40b. Chopin, Scherzo no. 2. Redistribution by Alfred Cortot and Ignaz Jan Paderewski.

In Liszt's *Mephisto* Waltz no. 1 (ex. 2.41), the extended broken-octave passage is demanding, especially for players with smaller hands. No diminuendo is

Example 2.40c. Chopin, Scherzo no. 2. Redistribution by Joseph Banowetz.

marked, although often one is added in the last measure, along with a ritard. Taking with the left hand the bottom last three notes of the right-hand's broken octaves largely solves the problem of maintaining a bravura sound and speed.

Example 2.41. Liszt, *Mephisto* Waltz no. 1.

Liszt's *Transcendental* Étude no. 10 (ex. 2.42) presents a similar endurance test. Redistributing the hands as in example 2.41 can make it easier to play while

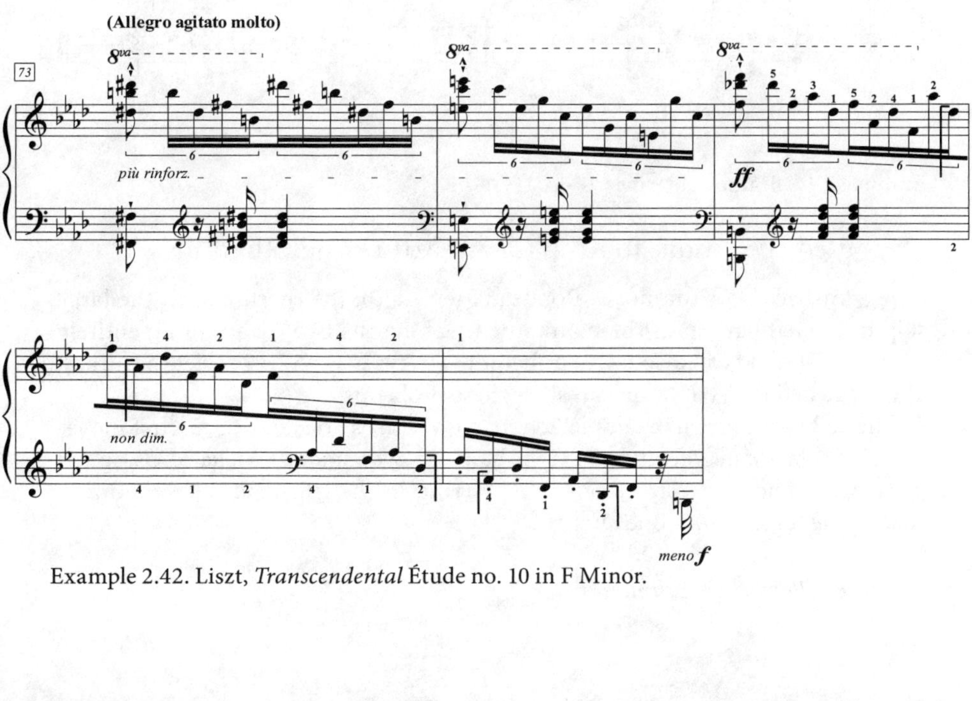

Example 2.42. Liszt, *Transcendental* Étude no. 10 in F Minor.

allowing the player to maintain the più rinforzando and *fortissimo* demanded by Liszt.

In Schubert's Impromptu, op. 142, no. 4 (ex. 2.43), some performers add an "emergency rubato" to the twenty-three-note rapid run. Using a fingering related to block fingering can help. When playing this passage at the correct concert speed, holding the pedal through the entire measure will not create a problem. Or the chord can be held with the sostenuto pedal, and the damper pedal changed if necessary.

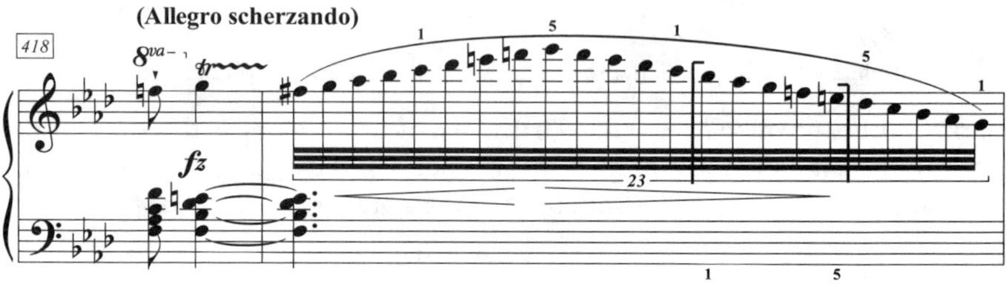

Example 2.43. Schubert, Impromptu, op. 142, no. 4.

The charming Brahms Intermezzo, op. 119, no. 3 (ex. 2.44) can easily be marred if a finger slip occurs in the final measures. Using the suggested redistribution will not change the basic sound but will virtually ensure accuracy.

Example 2.44. Brahms, Intermezzo, op. 119, no. 3.

Redistributions to Keep Clear Textures and Rhythms

In Bach's Partita no. 2, Rondeaux (ex. 2.45), the rhythm with the large skip in the left hand must be maintained. Taking the two-octave jump entirely with the left hand can also prove difficult to always play with complete accuracy. The suggested redistribution can solve these problems.

The redistribution in example 2.46 from Mozart's Sonata, K. 333, first movement, will facilitate keeping the right-hand octaves smoothly legato. Using the pedal would not only create possible blurring in the left hand but would also change the texture and tone quality.

Example 2.45. Bach, Partita no. 2, Rondeaux.

Example 2.46. Mozart, Sonata, K. 333, first movement.

In Brahms's Trio for Clarinet, Violin, and Piano, op. 114, first movement (ex. 2.47), the awkward skip in the left hand of the piano part must not disturb rhythmically the other two instruments. Accuracy is also a possible problem. The redistribution of a single note easily solves these difficulties.

Example 2.47. Brahms, Trio for Clarinet, Violin, and Piano, op. 114, first movement.

In Liszt's Hungarian Rhapsody no. 8 (ex. 2.48), the rhythms in the grace notes and the dotted-sixteenth–thirty-second note rhythms must be kept sharp and clear. Taking the grace notes with the thumb of the left hand—especially the A in the large roll—will help to facilitate the keeping of a firm rhythmic outline.

In Debussy's *Estampes* (Prints), no. III, *Jardins sous la pluie* (ex. 2.49), a long, tied-A pedal point is indicated for two measures. Although some pedal can be used, to simply hold the A with the pedal will create an extremely muddy texture. Taking all the sixteenth notes in the last two measures of the crescendo with the

Example 2.48. Liszt, Hungarian Rhapsody no. 8.

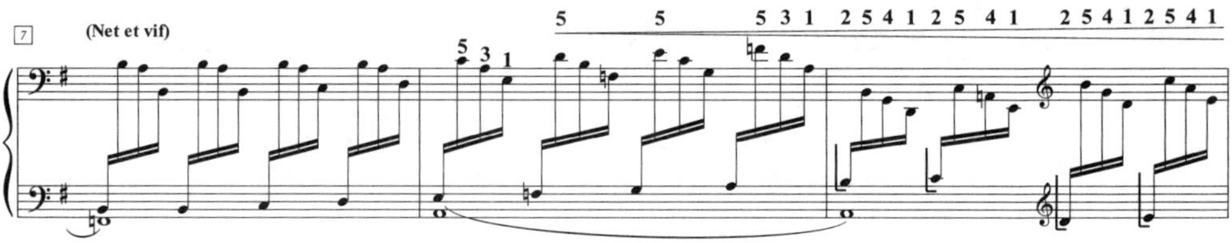

Example 2.49. Debussy, *Estampes* (Prints), no. III, *Jardins sous la pluie.*

right hand solves the problem of holding the A without creating a large unwanted smear of pedal.

Redistributions to Facilitate Finger Pedaling

There are many examples of passages that demand a use of finger pedaling to hold over harmonies while changes of pedal are made to accommodate other parts. In Franck's Prélude, Chorale, and Fugue, FWV 21 (ex. 2.50), a low pedal point G needs to be maintained. With the distribution given in the original, as well as the constant changes of harmony, it is not possible to hold the G. Even using the middle *sostenuto* pedal will create a problem for many performers. A simple redistribution will solve the problem easily.

Example 2.50. Franck, Prélude, Chorale, and Fugue, FWV 21.

In Liszt's *Transcendental* Étude no. 11, "Ricordanza" (ex. 2.51), the G on the downbeat will probably blur the basic A-flat tonic harmony too much. A redistribution helps to keep the harmony more transparent. The downbeat A-flat in the left hand should be held as the pedal is changed a note later.

Example 2.51. Liszt, *Transcendental* Étude no. 11, "Ricordanza."

Chopin's Sonata no. 2, third movement (ex. 2.52) has places in the melody that demand a change of pedal. Yet to do so will momentarily lose the bass support given by the low left-hand octaves. The player must find a way to give the illusion that pedal changes occur only each half measure. The suggested redistributions solve the problem.

Example 2.52. Chopin, Sonata no. 2, third movement.

Chopin's Piano Concerto no. 1 in E Minor, first movement (ex. 2.53), contains a similar problem, namely the maintaining of the supporting bass line in spite of necessary changes of pedal that are necessary to keep the shifting harmony clear.

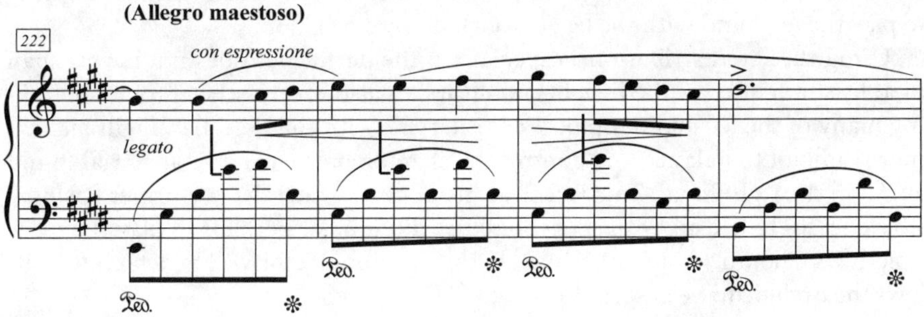

Example 2.53. Chopin, Piano Concerto no. 1 in E Minor, first movement.

When a slow melody moves stepwise, it may be necessary to change the pedal to avoid an ugly blur. If a basic harmony needs to be maintained, a redistribution may be helpful. This problem occurs in Brahms's Intermezzo, op. 118, no. 2 (ex. 2.54). The suggested redistribution is particularly helpful because of the slowing of the tempo and the diminuendos.

Example 2.54. Brahms, Intermezzo, op. 118, no. 2.

Vladimir de Pachmann's Fingering Redistributions in Chopin's Prelude in A minor, op. 28, no. 2, as Notated by Leopold Godowsky

Vladimir de Pachmann (1848–1933) was one of the nineteenth and early twentieth century's most famous pianists. He was respected for his masterful performances, especially of Chopin's works, and was equally famous for his often notoriously amusing behavior on stage. His suggested redistributions for Chopin's Prelude in A minor, op. 28, no. 2, were first printed in the February 1925 edition of *Good Housekeeping* magazine.[2] It was notated by Leopold Godowsky (1870–1938), who was of course one of the greatest pianists of the era, and a close personal friend of Pachmann.

The fingerings in the Pachmann/Godowsky edition (ex. 2.55) raise questions relating to redistributions. Pachmann was not of large physical stature, and he did not have a huge handspan. Therefore, many of the intervals found in the left hand of Chopin's score would present problems in performance. Pachmann indicated in an interview with Alice Booth in the same issue of *Good Housekeeping* that it is important to avoid tension when performing. His indications for redistributions are obviously intended to avoid stiffness in the hand when attempting to play the left hand with the legato touch desired by Chopin.

Using these redistributions, especially if the performer does not have a span of at least a tenth, can be beneficial, but it can also create other problems. Taking many of the left-hand top notes of intervals with the right hand will make it more difficult to balance and control the shaping of the melodic material found above in the right hand. This is a clear instance in which the performer has possible choices to use all or part of the redistributions or perhaps to play the piece exactly as Chopin wrote it. Ultimately the deciding factor will be which way allows the prelude to be best performed!

Example 2.55. Chopin, Prelude, op. 28, no. 2. Pachmann's fingering as notated by Leopold Godowsky.

Videos of Famous Pianists Using Redistributions

Two examples of videos that show famous pianists using redistributions justify this approach to fingering. Vladimir Horowitz (1903–1989) played Chopin's Ballade no. 1 in 1968, live in New York City's Carnegie Hall.[3] He takes the Coda starting in m. 208 at a breathtaking speed, then divides the last part of the rapid sixteenth-note scale starting in m. 248 so as to keep in rhythm. (Horowitz's redistribution is approximately as shown in ex. 2.56.) Many pianists at this point use an "emergency rubato" and add at least an additional half measure of time to the downward run.

Example 2.56. Chopin, Ballade no. 1. Horowitz's redistribution.

Example 2.57 is from a video of the Chopin Polonaise, op. 53, as performed in 1978 during a concert given by Emil Gilels at the Moscow Conservatory.[4] Here Gilels crosses his left hand over the right hand to ensure accuracy and to clearly accent the right-hand B-flat.

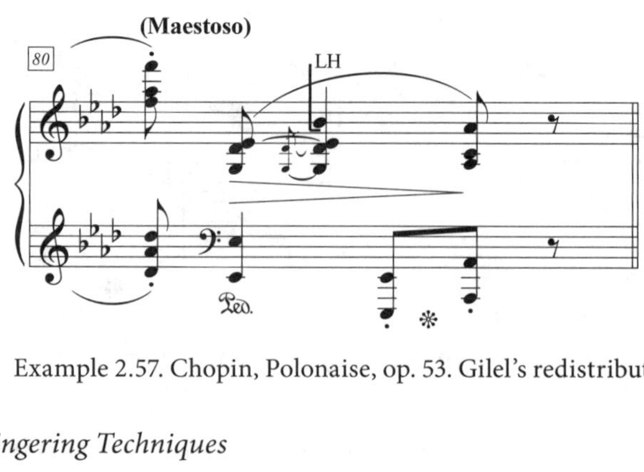

Example 2.57. Chopin, Polonaise, op. 53. Gilel's redistribution.

Notes

1. Kendall Taylor, *Principles of Piano Technique and Interpretation* (Borough Green, Kent, England: Sevenoaks, 1981), 47.

2. Alice Booth, "Vladimir de Pachmann," *Good Housekeeping*, February 1925, 52–53, 193.

3. *Vladimir Horowitz at Carnegie Hall*, performed by Vladimir Horowitz (1968; New York: Sony Classical, 2013), DVD.

4. *Emil Gilels Live in Moscow, Vol. 4*, performed by Emil Gilels (1978; Pleasantville, NY: Video Artists International, 2008), DVD.

Part I Appendix: The Fingering of Benno Moiseiwitsch in Manuscript Illustrations

Philip Fowke

Over the years, I have encountered widely divergent views over the question of keyboard redistribution, rearrangements, and discreet omissions, or in some pianists' parlance, "cheating." There are teachers and performers who consider these practices as anathema, and there are those who take a more relaxed and practical view. I belong to the latter group.

In forty years of performing in public, often under considerable learning pressure for high-profile events, I have had to find ways of solving technical and musical problems quickly, effectively, and, above all, reliably. Technique, so often misappropriated to mean "facility," is a word that should encompass a range of strategies from posture, use of arm, wrists, fingers, and feet . . . not to mention visual and cerebral resources. The aim should be economy of movement, and this can only be achieved through exploration of a wide range of physical choices. To play with ease, comfort, and security requires a mind open to many possibilities, the sound and musical context always being the priority.

In a talk I gave at the Chetham's International Summer School and Festival of Pianists in Manchester entitled "To Cheat or not to Cheat," I drew the distinction between "justifiable enablement" and "inappropriate facilitation." A good example of the latter would be the opening bars of Beethoven's Sonata, op. 111. To divide the octave leaps between the hands reduces the musical and dramatic impact; there is also the visual component of the left hand's commanding gesture that generates a sense of risk and musical tension. To use both hands destroys these essential elements. Still drawing from Beethoven's works, an example of "justifiable enablement" would be the octave glissandi in the finale of the "Waldstein" Sonata, op. 53, which, although possible on the modern piano for agile pianists with strong fingernails, is more safely performed as regular scales between the hands.

More contentious would be the reversal of hands in the Presto con Fuoco of op. 31, no. 3 from the second beat of bar 278 to bar 300. This requires sharing the two final eighth notes, D-flat and G, in the right hand of bar 299 in order to get back to the normal distribution of hands. However, most performers will find this a practical solution, and it will reduce anxiety over the usual right-hand figuration. As a kind of justification for such ingenuities, I recall a story told by my late teacher Gordon Green (1905–1981), about a recital he attended given by Richter in which Beethoven's Sonata, op. 2, no. 1 was performed. The left hand's statement of the opening theme from bars 8 to 11 is a familiar stumbling block for less able pianists. The great Richter took no risks and played these bars in the right hand much to Gordon's amusement!

Knowing the extent of my own solutions to a galaxy of pianistic challenges, I was reassured to see a similar approach shown by the legendary pianist Benno Moiseiwitsch (1890–1963). Like many great pianists, he was born in Odessa and studied with Theodor Leschetizky (1830–1915). Leschetizky studied with Carl Czerny (1791–1857), who in turn studied with Beethoven (1770–1827). This distinguished genealogy in itself gives authenticity to the performing continuity and tradition as inherited by Moiseiwitsch. Gordon Green links into this distinguished musical pedigree via Frank Merrick (1886–1981), a student of Leschetizsky. As custodian to Benno Moiseiwitsch's music score library for some years before donating it to the British Library in 2003, I had ample opportunity to study the scores while they were in my possession. As my own career developed, his scores were an inspiring and often affirming resource of practical performing insights.

For this appendix, I have taken four concertos closely associated with and recorded by Moiseiwitsch: Beethoven's Piano Concerto no. 5 in E-flat, op. 73; Tchaikovsky's Piano Concerto no. 2 in G Major, op. 44; and Rachmaninoff's Piano Concerto no. 1 in F-sharp Minor, op. 1, and Piano Concerto no. 2 in C Minor, op. 18. It would be impossible to enumerate all the fingerings and annotations of these works, so I have taken the ones that are of particular interest and reflect Moiseiwitsch's brand of keyboard ingenuity and practical performing strategies. I found that Rachmaninoff Piano Concerto no. 1 had the most detailed annotations and have outlined most of them here. In his manuscripts, Moiseiwitsch marks the places where a wax disc had to be changed in the 78-rpm recording format. He simply writes, "1st side," or whichever number was relevant to the side being recorded.

Rachmaninoff's Piano Concerto no. 2 has fewer annotations, but they are of considerable interest. Furthermore, they reflect a broadness and freedom of execution that would be frowned on today. Moiseiwitsch is fearless when it comes to some compositional "improvements." For this reason, I decided not to list the annotations and omissions in Tchaikovsky's Piano Concerto no. 2 because, for one thing, they are too numerous, and for another it is simpler to reproduce a few pages to give an idea of the extensive cuts, redistributions, and recompositions that Moiseiwitsch employed. It should be noted that he used the original, longer version of this concerto.

I have used bar numbers in all cases except Rachmaninoff Piano Concerto no. 2. It was simpler to number the annotated bars in relation to the nearest rehearsal cue. In the case of Rachmaninoff's Piano Concerto no. 1, I decided to number the bars because there was some discrepancy between editions regarding rehearsal cue numbering.

Beethoven Piano Concerto No. 5.

Two-piano score. Peters edition.

London Philharmonic Orchestra, conducted by George Szell, recorded at the Kingsway Hall, London, October 21, 1938. (A recording of a live concert given in 1963 at the Royal Festival Hall, London, also exists by the BBC Symphony Orchestra conducted by Sir Malcolm Sargent.)

Note 2.1. First movement, Allegro

Bar 208. The first four sixteenth notes and following eighth-note triplets are reversed to match the arrangement in bar 466. It makes more rhythmical sense following the triplets in bars 207 and 465. It is also more logical to remember and to perform. Furthermore, it is undetectable in performance! Moiseiwitsch performs the two groups of five sixteenth notes as a four and a six.

Bar 221. The lower F on the first beat is "corrected" to a G-flat. This is, arguably, rather questionable in view of Beethoven's clear intention of a dissonance of a ninth between the piano and strings.

Bar 333. Moiseiwitsch cannot resist continuing to top G. (Who can?)

Bar 363. Moiseiwitsch reconfigures each two groups of four thirty-second notes as a three and a five. This enables greater force and clarity at the start of each E-flat arpeggio.

Bars 578 and 580. Moiseiwitsch adds an octave E-flat in the left-hand E-flat chords.

Note 2.2. Third movement, Rondo

Bars 172–173. Moiseiwitsch takes the right-hand C-flats and B-flats in the left hand. For some pianists, including myself, this falls dangerously within the frontiers of "inappropriate facilitation."

Bar 423. Moiseiwitsch adds an octave A-flat to the left hand. Irresistible!

Rachmaninoff Piano Concerto No. 1

Two-piano score. Gutheil Nouvelle edition (copyright 1919).

Benno Moiseiwitsch with the Philharmonia, conducted by Malcolm Sargent, HMV Studio 1 Abbey Road, London, December 23, 1948.

Note 2.3. First movement, Vivace

Bar 13. Moiseiwitsch suggests that the third beat of the right hand also plays the first F-sharp of the following right-hand group of six sixteenth notes. (The author thinks there is an even easier solution.)

Bar 25. Moiseiwitsch takes the final two sixteenth notes of the penultimate group of five sixteenth notes in the left hand and the first three sixteenth notes of the last group of five in the right hand and final two in the left hand. A neat solution.

Bar 46. Moiseiwitsch takes the last C-sharp of the second beat group of five sixteenth notes in the left hand! (This is an effective extra flourish that allows for a smart landing on the D and F-sharp).

Bar 149. Moiseiwitsch takes the third sixteenth note of each group in the right hand.

Bar 178. Moiseiwitsch takes the first four notes of the group of six sixteenth notes in the right hand. The B-natural is also played in the right hand but tied to the same following B-natural of the arpeggiated chord in the right hand. Very neat.

Bar 204. Moiseiwitsch takes the C-sharp of the third beat alto triplet eighth notes with the E-natural of the left hand.

Bar 238. Moiseiwitsch adds the lower octave beneath the first two eighth notes of the fourth beat left hand eighth notes (F-sharp and E). Irresistible.

Bar 251. Moiseiwitsch takes the last two eighth notes of the fourth beat eighth-note triplet in the right hand and the last two eighth notes of the second and fourth beats in the left hand in bar 252. This makes the general flow more comfortable.

Bar 262. The first beat B-flat in the right hand is taken in the left hand (which is effective pianistically, tonally, and visually)!

Bar 264. The right hand second beat alto G-flat and F are taken in the left hand.

Bar 269. In his 1948 recording, Moiseiwitsch omits the second half of this bar and resumes with the second half of the following bar.

Bars 272–274. Moiseiwitsch omits these in the 1948 recording.

Bar 283. Moiseiwitsch adds octave A-sharps to match the register of the fourth left-hand sixteenth-note chord.

Bar 284. Moiseiwitsch adds a left-hand first inversion, octave chord of F-sharp above the bass C-sharp.

Note 2.4. Second movement, Andante

Bar 10. Moiseiwitsch takes the alto F-sharp eighth note of the right-hand triplet immediately prior to the first mf in the left hand. (The author takes the next eighth note as well.)

Bar 10. Moiseiwitsch indicates that he treats the final four sixteenth notes and triplet eighth notes as a group of seven sixteenth notes (presumably with appropriate rhythmical/rubato adjustment).

Bar 12. Moiseiwitsch takes the left-hand C-sharp, and quarter-note F-sharp in the right hand.

Bar 13. Moiseiwitsch takes the right-hand, half-note middle-C in the left hand (thus repeating it twice?).

Bar 21. Moiseiwitsch indicates that he plays the second and third left-hand eighth notes, D and B-sharp, together (presumably with appropriate rhythmical adjustment).

Bar 36. Moiseiwitsch suggests the right-hand, alto, sixteenth-note A of the first beat be played in the left hand. This would in turn suggest that he may tie it to the following A, thus making a pattern of syncopated ties for the rest of the bar in the left hand.

Bar 53. Moiseiwitsch plays the last two eighth-note beats all in the right hand. This makes the jump to the first beat of the next bar in the left hand more leisurely.

Bars 70–71. Moiseiwitsch rewrites these bars. By adding a full quarter-note beat following the second beat of bar 70, a bar line is inserted following the first group of sixteenth notes. Bar 71 now begins on what was originally the last beat of bar 70. Bar 72 is treated as a bar of three-quarters. This would possibly make the ensemble a little more straightforward and secure. (Could this have been Malcolm Sargent's idea? He was an able pianist himself.)

Bar 72. Moiseiwitsch takes the penultimate right-hand sixteenth notes, C-sharp and A, in the left hand together with the E. Conversely, the last three sixteenth notes are all taken in the right hand. Very neat!

Note 2.5. Third movement, Allegro vivace

Bar 78. Moiseiwitsch takes the last four eighth notes in the left hand

Bar 94. Moiseiwitsch takes the lower alto part of the right-hand third beat in the left hand (F-sharp and G).

Bar 155. Moiseiwitsch omits these notes. The 1948 recording confirms this.

Rachmaninoff Piano Concerto No. 2 in C Minor, op. 18

Two-piano score (figs. 2.1–2.6). A. Guthiel. Moscow.

London Philharmonic Orchestra, conducted by Walter Goehr, HMV Studio 1, Abbey Road, London, November 24, 1937.

Note 2.6. First movement, Moderato

Rehearsal 15. Moiseiwitsch takes the first two sixteenth-note Cs in the left hand and thereafter in groups of four, alternating right and left hands. The final top C is played in the left hand. (A solution taken by the author and surely many pianists!)

Note 2.7. Four bars after Rehearsal 16

Moiseiwitsch takes the fifth and sixth notes of the second group of sixteenth notes in the left hand. This eliminates an uncomfortable wrist twist.

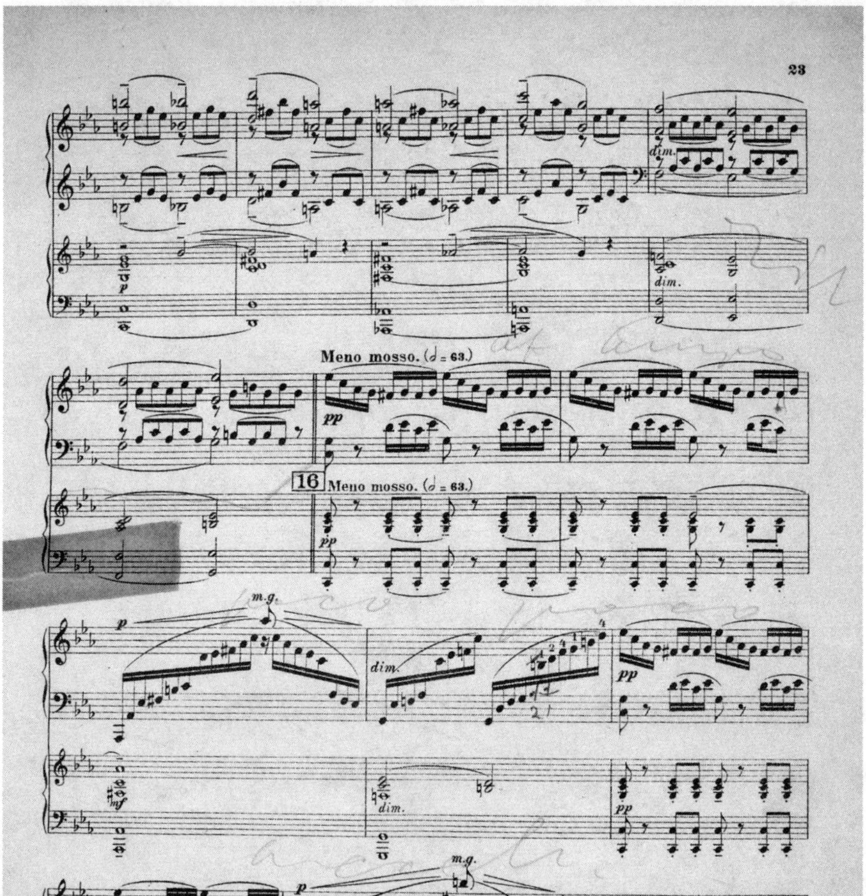

Note 2.8. Thirteenth bar after Rehearsal 16

Moiseiwitsch does some daring and effective recomposing here; see reproduction.

Note 2.9. Second movement, Adagio sostenuto

See reproduction. The following annotations after Rehearsal 20 illustrate Moiseiwitsch's free adaptation of Rachmaninoff's score. Since the two musicians were close friends and admirers, one can assume these suggestions would have met with the composer's approval!

Note 2.10. Third movement, Allegro scherzando

One bar after the piano's opening glissando, Moiseiwitsch takes the first G in the left hand then the next two eighth notes, D and G, in the right hand. The author assumes Moiseiwitsch would then take the following five eighth notes also in the right hand and the final four eighth notes in the left hand. The fingering from the second eighth note of that bar would then be: right hand 1, 3, 1, 2, 5, 3, 1 and left hand 1, 2, 5, 2 (1). This would neatly lead into the thumb starting the next bar.

Five bars after the piano's opening glissando, Moiseiwitsch takes the first sixteenth-note A-flat with the right-hand thumb and again two bars later. This gives a reliable emphasis on the A-flat; see illustration.

A. 8104 G.

Tchaikovsky Piano Concerto No. 2, op. 44.

Two-piano score. D. Rahter Leipzig (copyright 1928).

Liverpool Philharmonic Orchestra, conducted by George Weldon, Liverpool Philharmonic Hall, August 29, 1944. First movement cadenza recorded in HMV Studio 3, Abbey Road, London, October 19, 1944.

Figures 2.7–2.9 present three examples taken from the cadenza of the first movement. They illustrate the extent to which Moiseiwitsch went in his copious cuts and rewritings.

34
scen
do
sempre
cre
scen
do

These illustrations represent only a small part of the rich resource of material available in the Moiseiwitsch Archive. It was a great privilege to have been custodian of it for over thirty years. Although both Tanya and Sandra, Moisewitch's daughters, wished me to consider it as my own, I always felt that such a valuable archive should eventually be made available to the wider public. In 2003, I donated the collection to the British Library, London, and also the test pressings of his many recordings.

Illustrations are courtesy of Nicolas Bell, curator of Music Collections British Library London NW1 208. www.bl.uk.

Bibliography

This suggested reading list includes texts that either consist entirely of the subject of piano fingering or contain this material within a larger overall context. In the case of an anthology, both the general editor and the author of the reference on fingering have been listed. Also listed is a biography of Benno Moiseiwitsch, in connection with the article on his approach to piano redistributions that is included in the present book.

Bastien, James W. *How to Teach Piano Successfully*. San Diego, CA: Neil A. Kjos Music, 1988.

Beethoven, Ludwig van. *Sonaten für Klavier zu Zwei Händen*. Edited by Claudio Arrau and Lothar HoffmannErbrecht. Frankfurt, Germany: C. F. Peters, 1978.

Beethoven, Ludwig van. *Sonatas for Pianoforte*. Edited by Harold Craxton and Donald Francis Tovey. London: Associated Board of the Royal Schools of Music, 1931.

Beethoven, Ludwig van. *Sonatas*. Edited by Moritz Moszkowski. Paris: Heugel, n.d.

Beethoven, Ludwig van. *Sonatas for Pianoforte Solo*. Revised and fingered by Hans von Bülow and Sigmund Lebert. New York: G. Schirmer, 1894.

Beethoven, Ludwig van. *Sonatas for the Pianoforte*. Edited by Artur Schnabel. New York: Simon and Schuster, 1935.

Booth, Alice. "Vladimir de Pachmann." *Good Housekeeping*, February 1925, 52–53, 193.

Bowen, York. *The Simplicity of Piano Technique*. London: Augener, 1961.

Chopin, Frédéric. *Complete Works for the Piano*. Edited by Carl Mikuli. New York: G. Schirmer, 1934.

Ferguson, Howard. *Keyboard Interpretation from the 14th to the 19th Century: An Introduction*. Oxford: Oxford University Press, 1998.

Fielden, Thomas. *The Science of Pianoforte Technic*. London: Macmillan, 1934.

Gát, József. *The Technique of Piano Playing*. Translated by István Kleszky. London: Collet's, 1965.

Gerig, Reginald R. *Famous Pianists and Their Technique*. Bloomington: Indiana University Press, 1974.

Gilels, Emil. *Live in Moscow, Vol. 4*. Pleasantville, NY: Video Artists International, 2008, DVD. Originally filmed in 1978.

Hess, Myra. *Classical Music in the Forties*. London: Beulah, 2005, DVD. Originally filmed in 1942.

Horowitz, Joseph. *Conversations with Arrau*. New York: Alfred A. Knopf, 1982.

Horowitz, Vladimir. *At Carnegie Hall*. New York: Sony Classical, 2013, DVD. Originally filmed in 1968.

Hutcheson, Ernest. *The Literature of the Piano: A Guide for Amateur and Student*. Fingerings by Rudolph Ganz. New York: Knopf, 1966.

Kochevitsky, George. *The Art of Piano Playing: A Scientific Approach*. Evanston, IL: Summy Birchard, 1967.

Last, Joan. *The Young Pianist: A New Approach for Teachers and Students*. London: Oxford University Press, 1954.

Liszt, Franz. *Klavierwerke*. Edited by Emil van Sauer. Leipzig, Germany: C. F. Peters, n.d.

Liszt, Franz. *The Piano Music of Franz Liszt*. Edited by Earl Wild. New York: G. Schirmer, 1988.

Matthay, Tobias. *The Principles of Fingering and Laws of Pedaling*. London: Bosworth, 1908.

——. *The Visible and Invisible in Piano Technique*. London: Oxford University Press. 1947.

McLachlan, Murray. *Piano Technique in Practice*. London: Faber Music, 2015.

Moiseiwitsch, Maurice. *Moiseiwitsch, Biography of a Concert Pianist*. London: Frederick Muller, 1965.

Musafia, Julien. *The Art of Fingering in Piano Playing*. New York: MCA Music, 1971.

Neuhaus, Heinrich. *The Art of Piano Playing*. Translated by K. A. Leibovitch. London: Barrie and Jenkins, 1973.

Newman, William S. *The Pianist's Problems*. New York: Harper and Brothers, 1956.

Ortmann, Otto. *The Physiological Mechanics of Piano Technique*. New York: Dutton, 1929.

Pipa, Luís. *Fingering and Hand Position A Study of Some of the Implications of Fingering in Piano Performance*. Reading, UK: University of Reading, 1992.

Robert, Walter. "Fingering." In *Teaching Piano: A Comprehensive Guide and Reference Book for the Instructor*. Edited by Denes Agay. New York: Yorktown Music, 1981.

Rosenblum, Sandra P. *Performance Practices in Classic Piano Music*. Bloomington: Indiana University Press, 2007.

Sándor, György. *On Piano Playing*. New York: Schirmer, 1981.

Schick, Robert D. *The Vengerova System of Piano Playing*. University Park: Pennsylvania State University Press, 1982.

Slenczynska, Ruth. *Music at Your Fingertips*. New York: Cornerstone Library, 1968.

Taylor, Kendall. *Principles of Piano Technique and Interpretation*. Sevenoaks, Kent, UK: Novello, 1981.

Part II: Baroque Fingering and Interpretation: What Can a Modern Pianist Learn?

Nancy Lee Harper

Introduction
The Pianist's Dilemma

> The study of fingering is a treacherous path along which many have erred. For one thing, there is only one good system of keyboard fingering, and very few passages permit alternative fingerings.
>
> —C. P. E. Bach[1]

With the impact of the Baroque revival in the early twentieth century and Wanda Landowska displacing the harpsichord from the museum to center stage while proclaiming, "You play Bach your way; I'll play him *his* way,"[2] pianists everywhere have faced a dilemma. Shaken from nineteenth-century romanticized interpretations, pianists journeyed into new territory: to make intelligent and informed decisions regarding musicologically "correct" performance practice on an instrument that was not yet mainstream during this period. Their choices included

1. to play Baroque music on the modern piano in a "purist" fashion, imitating the practices of the harpsichord, clavichord, organ, or fortepiano, with little pedal;
2. to play Baroque music in a more sonorous and continuous legato although in a less romanticized manner, using the pedaling capabilities of the modern piano to their fullest;
3. to adopt a combination of the first two possibilities to emulate a historically informed performance on the modern piano;
4. to avoid playing any original Baroque works on the modern piano, opting instead for transcriptions of these works. Contrary to this idea is the viewpoint that any original Baroque work played on the piano is already indeed a "transcription."

This part of the book takes the third approach. It presents principles and concepts behind fingering choices in Baroque keyboard works (German, English,

French, Italian, and Iberian) as they may apply today--or not. It also aims to briefly describe the rich heritage that has shaped the Baroque repertoire without presenting an in-depth study of treatises and historical background related to fingering. To dispel contemporary pianist's reticence to perform music from this period, it acknowledges that some Baroque works were composed for the piano. Finally, the art of interpretation is intimately connected to fingering choices. This is equally true when performing on Baroque instruments and for modern pianists. For our purposes, the term "Baroque" encompasses the entire range of compositions from early to late in this period and also includes the Galant transition period to the Classical era.

Given the smaller keyboard range, restricted acoustic colors and dynamics, and a lack of sustaining pedals in Baroque keyboard music other than for the organ, the pianist must also acquire knowledge about agogic (flexible note lengths and/or tempi) and other rhythmic practices, vocal practices, stylistic considerations, articulation, and ornamentation (whose many rules have exceptions). Too, contemporary pianists will find that the clavichord technique of the bebung, or finger vibrato, makes no sense on modern instruments. And while the acoustics of current performance halls may differ from Baroque courts or cathedrals, choices regarding the relationship of the instrument to the venue and public remain equally valid for today.

On this fascinating journey, the pianist is encouraged to consult excellent translations of period treatises, including those for harpsichord, as well as aspects of phrasing and articulation found in wind instruction or string playing; critical editions, as well as facsimile editions and urtext editions; live and recorded performances on period instruments; bibliographic references available from the internet to private libraries; and, if possible, to study Baroque works on Baroque instruments, be they original or copies, in order to understand the acoustic properties of these instruments and how fingering relates to expression, and thus to interpretation.[3]

This work draws mainly from the musical examples of J. S. Bach and Domenico Scarlatti, although other composers are also mentioned. We will discuss fingering in light of the following:

- An overview of general baroque fingering concepts
- Some specific fingering exceptions
- Technical/musical challenges in choosing fingering
- Fingering and characterization
- Other stylistic considerations when choosing fingering

In this work, abbreviations used are RH for the right hand; LH for the left hand; the French terms D (*droit*) for right hand and G (*gauche*) for left hand; m. for measure; MSS for manuscript; and WTC for Well-tempered *Clavier.* Fingering is used where the thumb = 1 and the little finger = 5 in either hand, unless otherwise indicated. Musical examples contain the measure numbers on the score, unless they begin the movement or work. The terms "early piano," "fortepiano," and "pianoforte" are used interchangeably. The information give in brackets [ ] is my own and indicates additional information. The catalog numbers for the Domenico Scarlatti sonatas by Ralph Kirkpatrick (1911–1984) are used instead of those by Alessandro Longo (1864–1945), Giorgio Pestelli (b. 1938), or Emilia Fadini (b. 1930). Finally, most editions used are urtext.

My Interest in Baroque Fingering and Its Impact on My Playing

My interest in Baroque fingering is the outgrowth of my longtime desire, as a pianist, to understand J. S. Bach and his world so that when I played Bach on the piano, I could arrive at my own satisfactory and historically informed performances. I agree with Sandra P. Rosenblum that "the goal of historically founded performance practices is to reveal each composition to its fullest in a manner at once consonant with the composer's expectations (as best as we can discern them) and satisfying to the performer and the audience."[4]

My clavichord experimentation was brief, but I could appreciate how it became Bach's favorite instrument, with its delicate and expressive tone and bebung finger vibrato capable of producing what may be considered the eighteenth-century equivalent of "Debussy-like" shimmers. My studies of the pipe organ lasted a bit longer, but my inability to hear the center of the pitch of the pipe organ was disturbing and caused me to abandon it after only six weeks. The harpsichord caused me to have headaches after only ten minutes of study. The instrument was "colorless" and certainly did not possess the tonal or pedal capabilities of the piano. My first harpsichord teacher was a famous organist in London, who affirmed that pianists could not play the harpsichord. Having no time or instrument to practice with, I would sight-read my lessons to confirm his viewpoint. Years later, I fared somewhat better in my studies with a harpsichord player of French lineage. She was very liberal in her approach. Doubtless, I butchered the instrument. The third teacher, of Scottish lineage, was skeptical that she could teach pianists to play the harpsichord. Demanding and insistent, she would open to me a totally new sonorous world. My headaches stopped.

Around this same time during my doctoral studies in piano performance, I took a course on Baroque court dances, learning their steps and mannerisms. A similar course on Iberian Baroque dances would have been invaluable to interpret Domenico Scarlatti, whose own knowledge of these dances and pageantry was firsthand and adeptly conveyed.

Being hooked on Baroque by now, I commissioned a builder to construct a Flemish double harpsichord that was exquisitely decorated in French style, complete with lid and soundboard paintings by a faculty artist and his wife. Shortly afterward, I acquired a copy of a Stein piano, highly regarded by Mozart for its evenness and escape action, which allowed me to further explore the richness of the Classical style with its heavy and light execution and which is not dissimilar to some Baroque practices.[5] I was inspired by Daniel Gottlob Türk, author of the early *Piano School* (1789), who explained,

In a heavy execution each note must be played firmly (emphatically) and held out right to the end of its prescribed duration. Light refers to an execution in which each note is played with less firmness (emphasis) and the finger lifted from the key somewhat earlier than the duration of the note prescribes. In order to avoid a misunderstanding I must also remark here that the terms heavy and light generally refer more to the sustaining and separating of the notes than to their loudness and softness. . . . It can also be determined from the tempo whether one should choose a heavy or light execution."[6]

Türk's advice is right in line with the Baroque concept of agogic execution, of lengthening a note to linger a little, and of considering the tempo to convey the character, whether heavy or light (slow or fast). Today, I am happy to say that for any serious pianist who wishes to understand fingering concepts of early music, whether technically, aurally, intellectually, emotionally, and culturally, there is access to a wealth of reputable performances on period instruments, to the interpretation of Scarlatti sonatas by instrumentalists and dancers such as those illustrated by Luisa Morales and her troupe (see final chapter), and to the provocative claims made by fortepianist and scholar Malcolm Bilson (*Knowing the Score, I* and *II,* see bibliography).

Finally, as the first DMA in piano performance to serve on the music faculty in Portugal, during my twenty-one years of university teaching there from 1992 to 2013, I was privy to the wonderful Baroque world of music, architecture, manuscripts and collections, instruments, and graduate students who wished to pursue the gold mine that still exists in the Portuguese patrimony. I cannot imagine my Baroque interpretative life without these rich experiences.

Notes

1. C. P. E. Bach, *Essay on the True Art of Playing Keyboard Instruments*, trans. and ed., William J. Mitchell (New York: Norton, 1949), 41.

2. Wanda Landowska to Pablo Casals. Derek Watson, ed., *The Wordsworth Dictionary of Musical Quotations* (Ware, Hertfordshire, UK: Wordsworth Editions, 1994), 110.

3. J. J. Quantz, *On Playing the Flute*, trans. Edward R. Reilly (New York: Schirmer, 1966, first published 1752). Section 6 deals specifically "Of the Keyboard Player in Particular" (pp. 250–294). Quantz gives a lot of advice for realizing figured bass accompaniment. He contrasts the harpsichord with the piano, saying that even on the harpsichord the tone will vary from player to player (p. 259). Also, Leopold Mozart, *A Treatise on the Fundamental Principles of Violin Playing*, trans. Editha Knocker (London: Oxford University Press, 1948; repr. 1988), first published 1756.

4. Sandra P. Rosenblum, *Performance Practices in Classic Piano Music* (Bloomington: Indiana University Press, 1991), 1.

5. Copy after Johann Andrea Stein (1728–1792), Augsburg, Germany, five octaves, FF–f‴. On Mozart's piano preferences, see Otto Erich Deutsch and Peter Branscombe, *Mozart: A Documentary Biography* (London: Simon & Schuster, 1990), 167–168, quoted in Rosenblum, *Performance Practices*, 22.

6. Daniel Gottlob Türk, *Klavierschule oder Anweisung zum Klavierspielen für Lehrer und Lernende mit kritischen Anmerkungen* (Leipzig und Halle, 1789), quoted in Rosenblum, *Performance Practices*, 150–151.

3 An Overview of General Baroque Fingering Concepts

The art of piano fingering has its provenance from the lute, clavichord, clavicembulum (or early harpsichord), and organ practices of pre-Baroque eras, especially the Middle Ages. Renaissance keyboard collections, often for organ or clavichord, included guidance for fingering and performance.[1] Among the earliest are the English Robertsbridge Codex (1360), now housed in the British Library (manuscript no. 28550), with its lively estampie "Retrove"; the Italian *Codex Faenza* or Codex 117 (late fourteenth to early fifteenth centuries), cataloged as "I-FZc 117″ and housed in Faenza at the Biblioteca Comunale Manfrediana, contains keyboard and vocal music; and the German *Bucheimer Orgelbuch* or Buxheim Organ Book, a large collection of more than 250 original works (ca. 1460–70) by composers such as John Dunstable (ca. 1390–1453), Guillame Dufay (ca. 1397–1474), Gilles Binchois (ca. 1400–1460), Walter Frye (d. 1474?), and the blind Conrad Paumann (ca. 1410–1473), the latter of whose influence on the culture of organ playing and composition culminated with J. S. Bach.[2]

Keyboard fingering underwent experimental changes from the sixteenth to seventeenth centuries. Fingers were considered as "good" (preferred) or "bad" (not preferred and generally to be avoided). These were not always what today's pianists would deem "strong" or "weak" fingers, although they could have been. "Good" fingers in the sixteenth century did permit the use of the thumb, although this was not a prevalent practice. The sixteenth century "good" fingers varied from second and fourth in the Italian and German schools to first, third, and fifth for the English virginalists.

The seventeenth century provided us with many fingering notions until fingering became more or less as we know it today. Attempts at sequential fingering from 1–10 were made by Christian Erbach (1568–1635). Henry Purcell (1659–1695) experimented with a system whereby the left-hand fifth finger = 1, while the right-hand thumb = 1. Alessandro Scarlatti (1660–1725) developed a notational system with symbols for each finger. None of these systems ever became mainstream.

Hand and body positions over the centuries also gradually changed. Hand positions went from a "cat hand" (figs. 3.1 and 3.4) to a more level wrist, then to a slightly inclined one. The body position changed from an incline to the right to a more centered one, as can be seen from the figures here. The fifteenth-century practice of a low wrist on an instrument with narrow keys and shallow key bed (fig. 3.1) would result in a "cat hand" and seem unnatural today. Sixteenth-century iconographic evidence shows contrasting hand positions, if they are to be believed. The first (fig. 3.2) seems to imply the technique of "crossing over" and "turning under" of fingers with high wrists, while the second approximates what would be considered today to be a more natural hand position (fig. 3.3). These differing hand and finger positions are demonstrated in figures 3.4, 3.5, and 3.6. Today's hand position on the modern piano would be closer to that of the late sixteenth century through the eighteenth century (figs. 3.3 and 3.6), unless a flat-finger technique is employed. Today's body positions may vary from sitting high or low and close or far from the keyboard, depending on different perspectives, body types, and instruments, among other considerations.

Figure 3.1. "Angel Playing the Organ" (1432) from *The Ghent Altarpiece* by Jan van Ecyk (1390–1441). Used with kind permission from Saint-Bavo's Cathedral; www.lukasweb.be, Art in Flanders vzw, photo Hugo Maertens.

Figure 3.2. "St. Cecilia" by Hendrick Goltzius (1558–1617). © The Trustees of the British Museum and used with kind permission.

Figure 3.3. Titian's "Venus with a Musician" or "Venus with Organist and a Dog," 1550, Prado Museum, Madrid. Museo Nacional del Prado, used with kind permission.

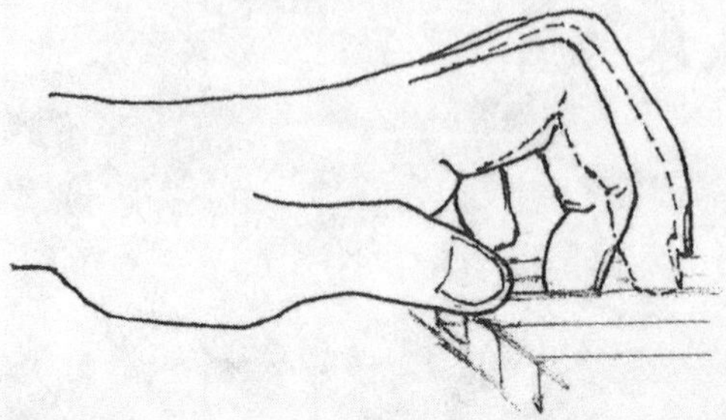

Figure 3.4."Cat hand." Hand position of late Renaissance and early Baroque periods (ca. sixteenth century), originating from lute principles. Used with kind permission from Luca Chiantore.

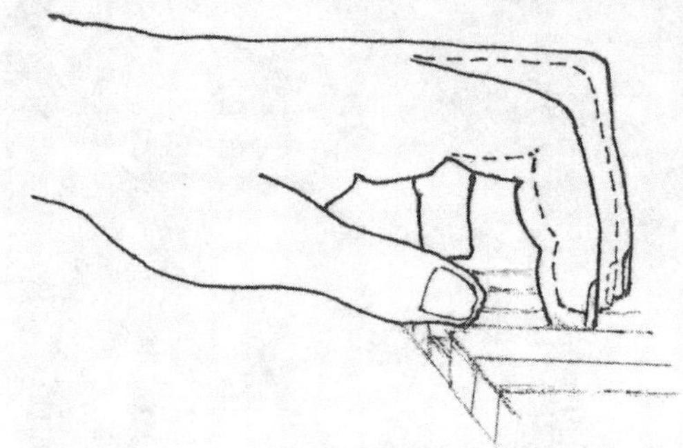

Figure 3.5. Hand position during late sixteenth and first half of seventeenth century. Used with kind permission from Luca Chiantore.

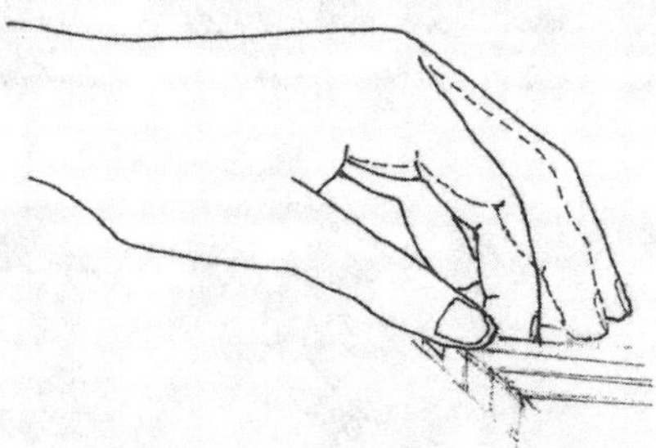

Figure 3.6. Hand position of late seventeenth and eighteenth century. Used with kind permission from Luca Chiantore.

From its inception, the Baroque French school emphasized beauty and elegance of tone and style. From it came the relevant concepts of *main morte* ("dead hand") and *jeu perlé* (pearly touch). Jean-Philippe Rameau (1683–1764) advised, "No great movement is ever made when a smaller one will suffice. The fingers are guided by the hand, the hand by the wrist and the wrist by the elbow."[3] He urged to think of the fingers "as springs attached to the hand by means of hinges which leave them complete freedom of movement."[4] François Couperin's (1668–1733) use of fingering varied from the old to the modern. His use of the thumb was adopted by J. S. Bach, who incorporated many French elements into his performance and works.

The Italian Baroque school produced two unusual musicians who contributed greatly to the keyboard through glorious music and a pedagogical objective: Alessandro Scarlatti and his son Domenico. While Domenico's keyboard contributions are well known today and will be discussed later, his father's unique fingering system, which he applied to some of his compositions, became lost in obscurity. This author speculates that it may have been invented to use with children, as it is a kind of musical shorthand. However, the system could have facilitated fingering notation for more advanced harpsichordists as well. The symbols are uniform from hand to hand. For example, for fifth fingers a triangle was indicated, a slur for fourth fingers, a horizontal cross for third fingers, a dash for second fingers, and an asterisk for thumbs (fig. 3.7). Alessandro's scale fingerings and unique notational system (fig. 3.7) not only combine both old (crossing over of 3–4) and new schools (sequential 5–4–3–2–1)—the latter of which is quite comfortable in the descending parallel scale—but also aim for virtuosity. Ease of hand is found in his first Toccata (ex. 3.1). This example reveals how what has come to be "traditional" fingering today was already in use for broken or arpeggiated chordal passages. Alessandro's exact fingering has been given in the following example (ex. 3.2), a good illustration of which is found his scale fingering system in mm. 18–19. He makes an exception to his own rules in m. 37 (ex. 3.3) in the descending passage, where twice finger 3 crosses over finger 2, thereby forcing finger 2 to begin the next measure, which becomes a kind of phrasing tool. A similar gesture is found going from m. 48 to m. 49 (ex. 3.4). The question arises in this example as to why he would use fingers 2 and 5 in such close proximity, such as D-sharp to F-sharp and E to G. Since both of these examples (m. 48, ex. 3.4) are followed by finger 3, it would seem that the composer is aiming for a supple wrist. For fun, try placing the correct symbol below each note to correspond with the fingering given.

Figure 3.7. Alessandro Scarlatti's scale fingerings and notational system.[5]

Example 3.1. Alessandro Scarlatti, *Toccata Primo*, Shedlock edition, mm. 1–7, original notation and realized.[6]

Example 3.2. Alessandro Scarlatti, *Toccata Primo*, Shedlock edition, mm. 17–19. [7]

Example 3.3. Alessandro Scarlatti, *Toccata Primo*, Shedlock edition, Right hand.[8]

Example 3.4. Alessandro Scarlatti, *Toccata Primo*, Shedlock edition, Right hand, mm. 48–49 (first two beats).[9]

It is not out of the realm of accepted performance practice today to play the keyboard toccatas of Alessandro on the modern piano. More than one scholar has speculated that Toccata VII was specifically composed for the early forte-piano.[10] Note the broken chord and scale passages in the Presto movement that work well with traditional fingering for those figures (ex. 3.5). In the Cantabile movement (ex. 3.6), the same may be especially said for mm. 3–5 (ex. 3.6).

The great keyboard miniaturist Domenico Scarlatti (1685–1750) became one of the most discussed, researched, and performed musicians of the Baroque. For

Note: The right-hand chords are as given in several other sources. In the Neapolitan manuscript the three chords are c^2-f^2-a^2, b-flat^1-d^2-f^2 and b^1-d^2-f^2.

Example 3.5. A. Scarlatti, Toccata VII, Presto, mm. 18–21.[11]

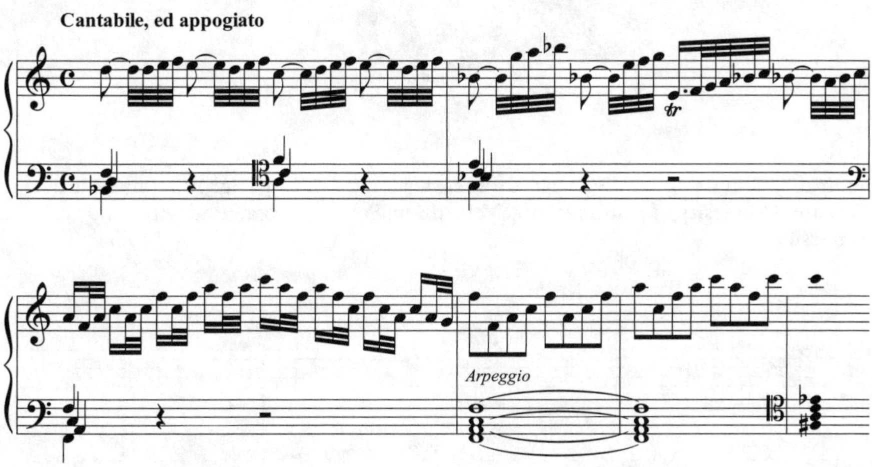

Example 3.6. A. Scarlatti, Toccata VII, Cantabile, ed appogiato, mm. 1–6.[12]

all his fame, he remains a mystery both as a composer and as a person. From 1719 until his death, he was in service to the Portuguese King John V (1689–1750), whose wealth featured the best libraries and musicians and, in whose court, the early fortepiano was frequently heard. One of Scarlatti's prime functions was to educate the king's children, including the future Queen of Spain, the gifted Maria Bárbara (1711–1758). Figure 3.8 is a copy of one of the early fortepianos constructed by Manuel Antunes in 1767, modeled on a Cristofori piano. The piano is still in playable condition and has been recorded on in recent times. Although Domenico Scarlatti would not have played upon it, he would have known similar instruments at King John's court and later during his sojourn in Spain. His Sonata in G Minor, K. 88, clearly reflects its appropriateness on the fortepiano (ex. 3.7), even though the sonata may have been intended for solo instrument and continuo.

King John V also underwrote the publication of the first piano sonatas, Lodovico Guistini di Pistoia's (1685–1743) twelve *Sonate de Cembalo di Piano, e Forte detto volgarmente di martelletti, op. 1* (Firenze, 1732), dedicated to the

Figure 3.8. Grand piano by Manuel Antunes, Lisbon, 1767. Copyright National Music Museum, University of South Dakota, Vermillion, South Dakota, used with kind permission.[13]

Example 3.7. Domenico Scarlatti, Sonata in G Minor, K. 88, mm. 1–3.

king's younger brother, Dom António Francisco de Bragança (1695–1757).[14] Here follows an example in Guistini's Sonata in G Minor, no. 1, of the use of the dynamic markings (fig. 3.9) of piano (m. 22) and forte (m. 24), which the early pianoforte was able to express, unlike the harpsichord unless through coupling registers or using a lute stop, both of which are awkward, if not impossible, in the middle of a phrase.

Figure 3.9. Lodovico Guistini di Pistoia, Sonata in G Minor, no. 1, mm. 22–25.[15]

Shortly on the heels of Guistini's sonatas for the new hammer instrument came Domenico Scarlatti's *Essercizi per gravicembalo* (1738–1739) with its "ingenious jesting," as Scarlatti himself described them in his preface. This collection may be regarded as the first virtuoso studies for the piano, according to Jacqueline Ogeil, who also describes it as the first great piano music.[16]

Besides being a brilliant harpsichordist, Domenico Scarlatti was also a virtuoso singer.[17] Some of the vocal qualities were incorporated into his sonatas, such as the "breath vibrato" or tremolo. It has been speculated that during his frequent and long absences from Portugal, he served as a musical agent for the king, observing what was happening in other European musical courts. Domenico bestowed a rich legacy of a kind of musical-cultural reportage of his new Iberian homelands that was mixed, at times, with characteristics from his native homeland of Italy.[18] The result was a unique blending of Ibero-Italian elements in some of the sonatas. Yet in more than 560 keyboard sonatas, he left only two explicit fingering indications (although he implied others). These are discussed later. No manuscript in Scarlatti's hand exists except for a letter of 1752.[19]

J. S. Bach is considered by some to be the "father" of modern piano technique, while his son C. P. E. Bach may be viewed as the "father" of modern piano fingering. J. S. Bach offered some liberal ideas and presented a model for technical mastery through a still hand and total control of all performance elements. His keyboard works provide ample testimony to his pedagogy and mastery of Baroque keyboard technique. He left only a few specific fingerings from the *Clavierbüchlein vor Wilhelm Friedemann Bach*, 1720:

- "Aplicato," C Major, BWV 994
- "Præambulum," G Minor, BWV, 930 (no. 11 of the *Twelve Little Preludes*), most likely for clavichord
- "Praeludium und Fughetta," C Major, BWV 870a (an early version of WTC, II, no. 1), most likely for harpsichord

Example 3.8. J. S. Bach "Aplicato," C Major, BWV 994, *Clavierbüchlein vor Wilhelm Friedemann Bach*, mm. 1–4.[20]

In the excerpt in example 3.8, Bach maintains a preference for crossing over fingers (RH 3–4, LH 2–1). From an analysis of the three excerpts shown in example 3.9, we can infer the following:

Example 3.9. J. S. Bach "Praeludium," C Major, BWV 870a: (a) mm. 1–2; (b) 4–5 (RH); and (c) 3–6 (LH).[21]

- In (a) chordal shapes form the basis of the fingering.
- In (b) repeated usage of 1–1 on adjacent notes in the alto voice gives rhythmic vitality to this section.
- In (c) use of 5–4 on large intervals obliges separation of the notes.

Example 3.10. J. S. Bach "Praeludium," C Major, BWV 870a, mm. 12–15 (RH).[22]

In example 3.10, the concept of contraction-expansion of the hand features a rare finger 5 (in m. 12, third beat) on a black key (C-sharp). Notice the change of fingering on the same notes in the alto voice, which not only works for independence of the fingers but also for the expressivity of the voices. Successive thumbs or fifth fingers provide rhythmic character.

Example 3.11. J. S. Bach "Fughetta," C Major, BWV 870a, mm. 5–7 (RH).[23]

In example 3.11, Bach advocates for equivalent fingering for melodic sequences. Notice also the 1–1 usage for the fourth in the alto voice in m. 6.

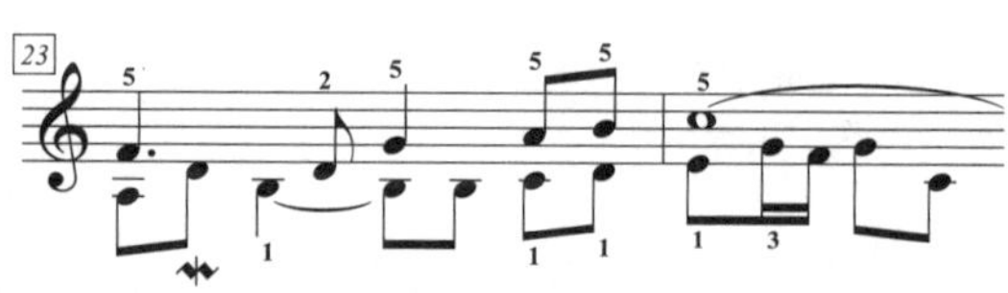

Example 3.12. J. S. Bach "Fughetta," C Major, BWV 870a, mm. 23–24 (RH).[24]

Chordal fingering prevails in example 3.12. The successive 1–5, 1–5, 1–5 across the bar line gives rhythmic vitality and is a very natural fingering.

Example 3.13. J. S. Bach "Fughetta," C Major, BWV 870a, mm. 31–34 (RH).[25]

This most curious of these examples (ex. 3.13) shows no finger substitution as would be expected, but portrays a rather boisterous and hardy character.

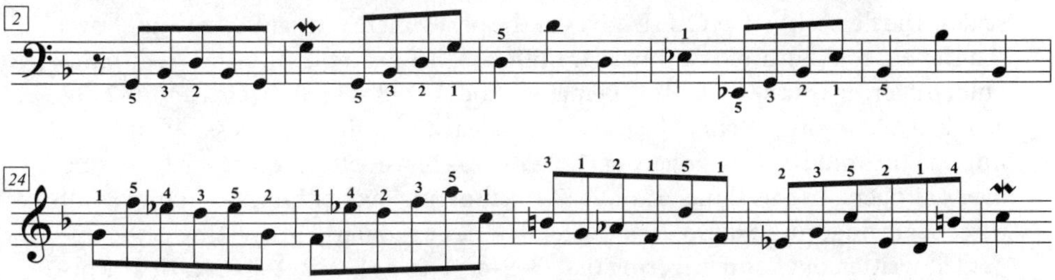

Example 3.14. J. S. Bach "Præambulum," G Minor, BWV 930, *Clavierbüchlein vor Wilhelm Friedemann Bach*, a) mm. 2–6 (LH) b) 24–28 (RH).[26]

Bach combines older fingering (as seen at the beginning of the "Aplicato," ex. 3.8) and more modern fingering ("Praeambulum," m. 23, left hand, ex. 3.14), which shows his extensive technical command.[27] Bach's fingering is predicated on chordal shapes and ease of hand, in spite of what might at first glance seem uncomfortable in m. 24 with the 3–5 fingering on D–E-flat. A slight inclination of the hand solves any potential problem on whatever keyboard it is played.

Example 3.15a. J. S. Bach, "Aplicato," C Major, BWV 994, *Clavierbüchlein vor Wilhelm Friedemann Bach*, mm. 5 (from Dolmetsch, *Interpretation*, 413).

Example 3.15b. J. S. Bach, "Præambulum," BWV 930, *Clavierbüchlein vor Wilhelm Friedemann Bach*, mm. 22–23, 5th under 3rd hand shifts.

The right-hand fingering in Bach's "Aplicato" in example 3.15a provides again uses finger crossings, this time of descending 3–2, 3–2. It is unlikely that a lift between the first group of eighth notes and the second would be appropriate, especially given the harmony of the LH. Again, the right-hand fingering in example 3.15b is a similar concept—that of crossing over (m. 22 to m. 23). These two measures require a very flexible wrist in order to navigate the expansion-contraction inherent in the melodic shape.

C. P. E. Bach's Approach to Fingering Technique

C. P. E. Bach's *Essay on the True Art of Playing Keyboard Instruments-- Versuch über die wahre Art das Clavier zu spielen*, H. 868, H. 870 of 1753 (Part 1) and 1762 (Part 2) has become the basis for modern piano fingering, including scales. The flexibility that C. P. E. gives to the performer is enlightening and shows that he accepts both old and new traditions.[28] In example 3.16 the right-hand outer fingerings of the ascending G major scale (1–2–3–1–2–3–4, etc., and 1–2–3–4–1–2–3, etc.) would seem to be the most logical and utilize the crossing under of fingers. The middle scale fingering (1–2–3–4–3–1–3–1, etc.) requires the crossing over of fingers. In this same example (3.16), crossing over of fingers is found in all three scale fingering examples of the left hand. Particularly interesting is the upper left written out hand fingering of 4–3–2–1–4–3–2–1–3–2–1–4–3–2–1. The orderly German mind is at work. In the descending G major scale of example 3.17, the bottom right-hand fingering and the top left-hand fingering constitute the traditional scale fingering used today. In the other possibilities, the right hand uses the crossing over of fingers. However, the left hand is found to both cross under (middle scale) and to cross over (bottom scale).

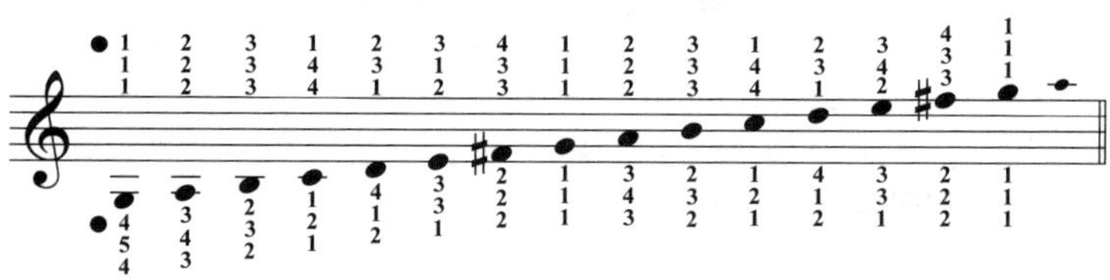

Example 3.16. C. P. E. Bach, G-major scale fingering, ascending (RH, LH).

Example 3.17. C. P. E. Bach, G-major scale fingering, descending (RH, LH).

C. P. E. paved the way to the Classical era and foreshadowed the Romantic period by breaking away from the polyphony of his father and developing his *em-*

findsamer Stil ("sensitive style"). His innovation, the gigue-like *Clavierstücke für die Rechte oder Linke Hande Allein* ("Keyboard Piece for the Right or Left Hand Alone"), published in 1770, is considered to be the first one-hand keyboard piece. Fingering would follow the chord shapes, with the sitting position more inclined to the right when playing with the left hand (ex. 3.18).

Example 3.18. C. P. E. Bach, *Clavierstücke für die Rechte oder Linke Hande Allein* ("Keyboard Piece for the Right or Left Hand Alone," 1770), the first known one-hand keyboard piece.[29]

Mention of Baroque Women's Contributions

In addition to the Bachs' contributions to Baroque fingering, tribute must also be made to the era's women composers. While there are no known treatises by women composers during this period, there are significant contributions by them, including Elisabeth-Claude Jacquet de la Guerre (1665–1729); Maria Teresa Bárbara de Brangança (1711–1758), Domenico Scarlatti's pupil for whom were composed his sonatas; Elisabetta de Gambarini (1731–1765); and, to stretch a bit, Ana Lucia Boni (b. 1738–179?). Although there is not space here to devote to these marvelous musicians, our focus is on one in particular: the French composer Elisabeth-Claude Jacquet de la Guerre.

Elisabeth-Claude Jacquet de la Guerre, a child prodigy who was called "the marvel of our century," became a famous harpsichordist and organist adept at improvisation, as well as a composer.[30] She was a favorite at the court of Louis XIV. She had many "firsts":

> The first known woman composer of harpsichord pieces; the first to have solo keyboard works and violin sonatas published; and the only French harpsichord composer to have compositions published before and after the turn of the eighteenth century. Jacquet de la Guerre is also considered to be the first French woman composer to have written sacred cantatas and have them published, for sacred compositions of considerable size were rarely published in her day. She was the first woman to compose a *tragédie en musique* (*tragédie lyrique*). Her *Jeux à l'Honneur de la Victoire,* published c. 1691–1692, was among the earliest *opera ballets.* And she was the first women to have an opera performed at the *Académie Royale de la Musique,* the acme of performance venues in Paris.[31]

Facing, above, and following page Examples 3.19a, 3.19b, and 3.19c. Jacquet de la Guerre, *Pieces de la Clavessin*, Suite no. 1, Prelude from Suite in D Minor.

Similarity with Louis Couperin's (1626–1661) unmeasured Preludes is noted in Jacquet de la Guerre's first Prelude, from her first Suite (exx. 3.19a and 3.19c).[32] The charming measured middle section (ex. 3.19b, beginning in m. 8) balances well the freer outer sections. Doubtless, no two performances of this prelude would be the same, so broad is the freedom of interpretation given to the performer.

Several technical/musical practices are found in this Prelude, most of which will be addressed in upcoming chapters The following may be useful whether performing the work on harpsichord or piano:

1. Finger slides from a raised key to a lower one for legato purposes
2. Finger substitution on the first ornamented note, in order to change the hand position and maintain legato
3. Chordal fingering in the unmeasured part unless the notes are filled in, in which case sequential fingering would apply
4. Crisp articulation: in the bouncy measured part of the prelude: the first three thirds in the right hand at the beginning of this part might be fingered 1–3, 1–3, 2–4, thus permitting the ornament to be easily realized on the first third and a smooth connection of the sixteenth notes of the second beat
5. Arpeggiated chords, in mm. 8–10 of the measured part, rolled downward or upward according to the whim of the performer.

Pianists will also find this repertoire rewarding. Just as Rameau and Couperin are today performed on the modern piano, so too the works of Jacquet de la Guerre and other Baroque women composers deserve experimentation in this way.

Summary: Axioms for Baroque Fingering

By now, after having very briefly explored some general Baroque fingering concepts in different countries—Italy, France, Iberia, England, and Germany—the reader is becoming aware that fingering is much more than just that. Clearly, the concepts of breathing, phrasing, and articulation, as well as choice of instrument, are inseparably intertwined in one expression when choosing a fingering.

In general, the basis of Baroque fingering may be broadly summarized as a reflection of three axioms that follow. As this works unfolds, the reader will find ample examples of these three axioms.

1. The choice of the best or final fingering was never an isolated event but was always linked to musical expression (*doigté de l'expression*, as opposed to the practice of pure technique, *doigté du mécanisme*).[33]
2. Fingering, in part, depended on the instrument (clavichord, harpsichord, fortepiano, or organ), or as C. P. E. Bach said, "the shape of an instrument," which depended, in part, on the acoustic environment in which the music would be performed (intimate spaces to grand halls). The shape of the keyboard and of the hand reveal the best fingering (the hand has three long fingers, two shorter ones, just as keyboard has longer and shorter keys).[34]
3. Fingering was derived or influenced by other aesthetic principles, including the affections and principles of singing, string and wind playing, stylistic considerations (dance characteristics, vocal qualities), and harmonic development.

Notes

1. According to François-Joseph Fétis (1784–1871) and Ignaz Moscheles (1794–1870) in their *Méthode des Méthodes de Piano* (Paris: Schlesinger, 1837), 2, the harpsichord was born from an application of lute principles. The lute was considered the "king of instruments" during the Renaissance; see Luca Chiantore, *Historia de la técnica pianística* (Madrid: Alianza Música, 2001), 46–47. For a more comprehensive list of instruments that includes organ, positive, portative, regal, echiquier, clavichord, harpsichord, virginals, spinet, fortepiano, and pianoforte, see Howard Ferguson, *Keyboard Interpretation from the 14th to the 19th Century* (Oxford: Oxford University Press, 1998), chapter 1.
2. For more on the Robertsbridge Codex and Codex Faenza see Chiantore, *Historia*, 33.
3. Margery Halford, ed., *The Harpsichord Manual: An Introduction to the Technic, Ornamentation and Performance Practices* (Sherman Oaks, CA: Alfred, 1980), 6.
4. Halford, *Harpsichord Manual*, 6.
5. Alessandro Scarlatti's scale fingerings and notational system. Alfredo Casella, *Il pianoforte* (Rome: Ricordi, 1937), 144.
6. Alessandro Scarlatti, *Toccate per Cembalo*, ed. J. S. Shedlock (London: Bach, 1908), 6. According to this edition, the drawing of the hands pictured above were most likely those of Alessandro Scarlatti.
7. Chiantore, *Historia*, 69.

8. Chiantore, *Historia*, 69.

9. Chiantore, *Historia*, 69.

10. An interesting proposal by Jacqueline Ogeil in her PhD dissertation, "Domenico Scarlatti: A Contribution to our Understanding of his Sonatas through Research and Performance" (University of Newcastle, Australia, 2006), 70–71, is that Alessandro's Toccata no. 7 (ca. 1723) may have been composed for the early piano (Cantabile, ed appogiato [at ease; singable and leant upon]; Presto).

11. Ogeil, "Domenico Scarlatti," 70–71.

12. Ogeil, "Domenico Scarlatti," 70–71.

13. Grand Piano by Manuel Antunes, Lisbon, 1767, NMM 5055, used with kind permission from the National Music Museum, University of South Dakota, Vermillion, SD.

14. The Guistini sonatas have been recorded on an early Portuguese fortepiano (Manuel Antunes, 1767), a Cristofori-type four-octave piano with hand operated *una corda* that is housed in the National Music Museum at the University of South Dakota, by the Portuguese musician, Cremilde Rosado Fernandes. This early fortepiano has a range of Cd‴. It looks and sounds remarkably like a harpsichord with hammers. It is cataloged as NMM 5055, as Grand Piano by Manuel Antunes, Lisbon, 1767, Augusto Carvello Monteiro, Lisbon, Rawlins fund, 1990; see http://nmmusd.org/Collections.

15. Mieczysław Horszowski (1892–1993) has recorded this sonata and others on the 1720 Cristofori Pianoforte at the Metropolitan Museum of Art. Mieczyslaw Horszowski, *The Christofori Pianoforte 1720: Sonatas for Pianoforte (No. 1 in g minor, No. IV in e minor, No, VII in G Major, No, X in f minor) by Lodovico Giustini*, (New York: Musical Instruments in the Metropolitan Museum of Art) recorded 1977–78, Titanic, TI-78, 1980.

16. Scarlatti's preface, "lo scherzo ingegnoso delll'Arte. . . ." See Jacqueline Ogeil, "Did Domenico Scarlatti Compose the First Great Piano Music?," in *Domenico Scarlatti Adventures, Essays to Commemorate the 250th Anniversary of His Death*, ed. Massimiliano Sala and W. Dean Sutcliffe (Bologna: Ut Orpheus Edizioni, 2008), 343–367.

17. Gerhard Doderer, "Aspectos novos em torno da estadia de Domenico Scarlatti na corte de D. João V (1719–1727) / New Aspects Concerning the Stay of Domenico Scarlatti at the Court of King John V (1719–1727)" in *Libro di tocate per cembalo:* Faksimile-Nachdruck: *Domenico Scarlatti* (Lisboa: Instituto Nacional de Investigação Científica, 1991), 10.

18. See João Pedro d'Alvarenga, "Domenico Scarlatti in the 1720s: Portugal, Travelling, and the Italianisation of the Portuguese Musical Scene," in *Domenico Scarlatti Adventures*, ed. Massimiliano Sala and W. Dean Sutcliffe, 17–68.

19. To Don Fernando de Silva y Alvarez de Toledo, Duke of Huescar. See Ralph Kirkpatrick, *Domenico Scarlatti,* rev. ed. (Princeton, NJ: Princeton University Press, 1983), 344.

20. Chiantore, *Historia*, 74.

21. Chiantore, *Historia*, 75.

22. Chiantore, *Historia*, 75.

23. Chiantore, *Historia*, 75.

24. Chiantore, *Historia*, 75.

25. Chiantore, *Historia*, 76.

26. Chiantore, *Historia*, 76.

27. (a) Arnold Dolmetsch, *The Interpretation of the Music of the Seventeenth and Eighteenth Centuries* (Seattle: University of Washington Press, 1969), 413; and (b) Dolmetsch, *Interpretation*, 415.

28. C. P. E. Bach, *Essay on the True Art of Playing Keyboard Instruments*, trans. and ed. William J. Mitchell (New York: Norton, 1949), 49. First published 1753.

29. C. P. E. Bach, *Essay*, 50.

30. Edith Borroff, "Elisabeth-Claude Jacquet de la Guerre," in *The Norton/Grove Dictionary of Women Composers*, ed. Julie Anne Sadie and Rhian Samuel (New York: Norton, 1995), 236.

31. Cecilia Hopkins Porter, *Five Lives in Music: Women Performers, Composers, and Impresarios from the Baroque to the Present* (Urbana: University of Illinois Press, 2012), 75.

32. Elisabeth-Claude Jacquet de la Guerre, *Pieces [sic] de Clavecin*, ed. and typeset Steve Wiberg, based on a facsimile of the first printing, 1687 (Nashville: Due West Editions, 2011).

33. Frederick Neumann, *Performance Practices of the Seventeenth and Eighteenth Centuries*, prepared with the assistance of Jane Stevens (New York: Schirmer, 1993), 254.

34. C. P. E. Bach, *Essay*, 41.

4 Articulation (Attack, Decay, Lifting, Slurring, *Affekt*)

"The musical term 'articulation' comes originally from linguistics," where it refers to enunciation.[1] Musical articulation has four main aspects: (1) attack, or how to start a tone; (2) how to hold the tone; (3) decay, or how to end the tone; and (4) how to connect it with the following tone.[2] The intelligent pianist will be cognizant of all four aspects. The sustaining pedal has a big role to play, just as do the ear and fingers, in creating either a perfect legato or at least giving the illusion of connecting or holding tones.

Attack and Decay

Attack and decay also involve the brain, ear, feet, and fingers. In some cases, the pianist will want to use the damper pedal before starting the first note or chord. Here are two possible ways of beginning the opening of Bach's C-minor Partita: (1) "decisive" or rhythmic, in which the pedal simultaneously is lowered as the notes are played with arpeggiation (ex. 4.1); (2) more melodic, with a quick roll simultaneously in both hands, with the pedal depressed before playing (ex. 4.2). Arpeggiation may help to define the character by being drawn out or performed quickly. Similarly, the pianist will also have to determine how to execute the first chord of Bach's Italian Concerto--together or quickly rolled, to give another example (ex. 4.3). There are many examples of this kind of decision to be made, whether at the beginning or within the context of a phrase.

Example 4.1. "Militant" interpretation. J. S. Bach, Partita, no. 2, BWV 826, mm. 1–2.

Example 4.2. Arpeggiated interpretation. J. S. Bach, Partita, no. 2, BWV 826, mm. 1–2.

Example 4.3. Opening chord. J. S. Bach, Italian Concerto, BWV 971, m. 1.

A good release on the final notes of a piece, be it slow or fast, is also enhanced by the coordination between hands, feet, and ear. A harpsichordist, by virtue of having to always tune the instrument, becomes sensitized to listening to ends of phrases and how quickly the vibrations of the strings decay. Pianists can benefit from this valuable skill. Some pianists do a kind of clavichord bebung touch at the end of a piece, an effect that makes absolutely no difference to the sound whatsoever on the modern piano, but if it helps the pianist to listen, then it will have served an important function.

The notion of articulation is somewhat bound up with the concept of attack and decay. The German American performer and music scholar Erwin Bodky (1896–1958), after an extensive study of Baroque works, summarized the usage of the articulations of non-legato, staccato, and legato in varying tempi.[3] For his premise, he relied on the music itself to suggest the kind of articulation to be used. Although broad in scope, these may be of assistance to pianists (table 4.1).

Table 4.1. General Baroque articulation guidelines[3]

Tempo	Articulation
Allegro	Non-legato, staccato
Adagio	Legato
Moderato	Small intervals slurred (seconds, thirds); large intervals detached

In another performance practice generalization, pianists from the Russian tradition of Bach playing often play fast notes detached and slower ones connected. Harpsichord performance was not a tradition in Russia during the Baroque period; rather, the organ was.

Wanda Landowska, a Baroque performer on harpsichord and piano, gave this advice that may be appropriate for pianists:

> It has been said that my touch is a perpetual *staccato*. This is a fundamental misunderstanding. The great precision required to strike the keys at the harpsichord is sometimes misconstrued for *staccato* touch. This error also stems from the elasticity of my bouncy touch, with its precise and neat outlines. I use perfect *legato*, however, as harpsichord touch requires. This is a condition *sine qua non*. Even when staccato is required for certain effects, the basis of harpsichord touch remains the *legato*.[4]

Figure 4.1. Wanda Landowska's "cat hand position" performing on a double manual harpsichord, with a cat observing. Photographer Philippe Halsman/Magnum Photos, used with kind permission.

Landowska's hand position (see figure 4.1) would hardly suit modern pianists.

During the nineteenth century, the idea of continuous legato was the predominant approach to Baroque performance on the piano. It was Ferruccio Busoni (1866–1924), at the end of that century, who raised an objection to the ideal of the smooth and supple romantic legato. He subscribed to the distinct execution, the non-legato touch, which, he believed, suited Bach's style best.[5] The sign ' over a note in Bach's time indicated staccato, not staccatissimo. This sign evolved into the later dot over or under a note to indicate staccato.[6]

Lifting

In Bach's Fugue 21, WTC, BWV 866, the pianist may change the fingering according to the chosen articulation.[7] In the Czerny edition (ex. 4.4a), the right-hand fingering 2–1, with a lift on the thumb to prevent an accent, will give the desired articulation. By using the same fingering on neighboring notes, the right-hand fingering 1–1 in the Busoni edition (ex. 4.4b) will give the exact articulation indicated.[8]

Example 4.4a. J. S. Bach, Fugue 21, WTC, BWV 866, mm. 1–3, Czerny edition.

Example 4.4b. J. S. Bach, Fugue 21, WTC, BWV 866, mm. 1–3, Busoni edition.

In Domenico Scarlatti's Sonata in A Minor, K. 175 (ex. 4.5) showing right-hand fingering, lifting becomes imperative on beat two (m. 1 and m. 3) to ensure clarity.

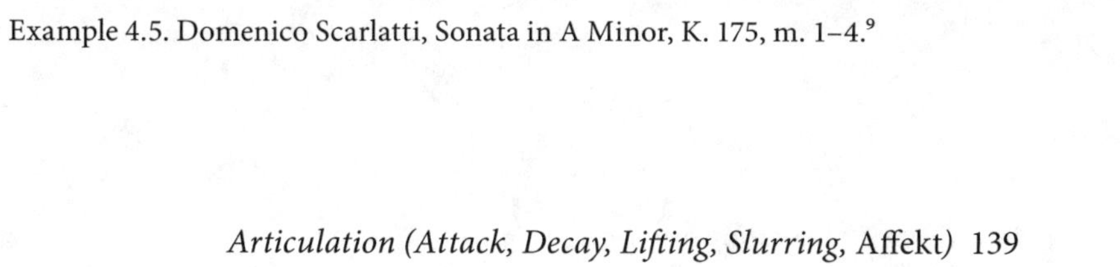

Example 4.5. Domenico Scarlatti, Sonata in A Minor, K. 175, m. 1–4.[9]

The Doctrine of Affections (*Affekt*)

In trying to arrive at an acceptable historically informed performance on the modern piano while contemplating articulation, it's useful to consider the Baroque philosophy of the Doctrine of the Affections. These include Admiration, Love, Hatred, Desire, Joy, Sorrow, Sadness, Anger, Jealousy, and so on. Surprisingly, the affections are not emotions but the power and obligation of music to move the emotions. As the early music scholar Claude V. Palisca (1921–2001) explained:

> Behind the traits that mark music as baroque, then, are their reason for being: the passions, or as they were more often called then, the affections. Affections are not the same as emotions. A sixteenth-century poetic critic, Lorenzo Giacomini, defined an affection as "a spiritual movement or operation of the mind in which it is attracted or repelled by an object it has come to know." The most comprehensive study of the affections up to its time was the treatise of René Descartes, *The Passions of the Soul* (1649), in which this pioneer of rationalism elaborated . . . upon the theory.
>
> Johan Mattheson at the end of our period in his *Der vollkommene Capellmeister* (The Perfect Musical Director, 1739) still theorized at length about the affections and their representation in music. . . . If, then, there is any common thread that unites the great variety of music within the period that we call baroque, it is an underlying faith in music's power, indeed, its obligation, to move the affections.[10]

Thus, the art of choosing an appropriate fingering for the performer—who in turn has to be able to express the music in order to move the affections—is not to be underestimated. To find a suitable fingering, the performer might wish to follow these steps:

1. Sing the passage.
2. Imagine it as a string player would bow it or as a wind player would tongue it.
3. Look at its harmonic shape.[11]
4. Look for dancelike qualities and vocal lyricism.
5. Determine the character or *Affekt*.

Ralph Kirkpatrick's observation may also be helpful: "The earliest methods of fingering all operated two by two, like stepping. . . . Out of this development came early keyboard fingering, which also proceeds in units of two, like stepping, except for the use of several pairs of fingers. For all its efficiency, our full ten-finger system has a tendency to divorce us from the real feeling of what we are playing. We have never really learned to move in units of ten."[12]

Example 4.6. Domenico Scarlatti, Sonata in A Major, K. 24, m. 1–3, with upbeat.

"Hopping" displays the *affekt* of "joy." Here (ex. 4.6), Scarlatti in his Sonata in A Major, K. 24, indicates to begin with the left hand for the first four notes, then alternate hands. Possible choices are as follows:

1. Use fingers 3 in both hands until m. 2.
2. Use arpeggio fingering in both hands.
3. Use arpeggio fingering in the left hand and finger 3 in the right hand.

Example 4.7 from J. S. Bach's C-sharp Major Fugue, BWV 848, highlights typical Baroque fingering practices for good articulation and expression of the *affekt*, a fingering that at first may seem unnatural, even uncomfortable. The left-hand fingering shifts not only provide precise phrase articulation but also rhythmic control. Pianists may find it useful to implement.

Example 4.7. J. S. Bach, WTC, I, C-sharp Major Fugue, BWV 848, mm. 24–25, left hand.[13]

Slurring

"From surviving examples of early keyboard fingering it is clear that the music of the 16th, 17th, and early 18th centuries was broken up in performance into much smaller units than is customary with the late 18th- and 19th-century music."[14] This kind of articulation resulted in a less smooth-sounding performance than is customary today on the piano.

Bach's Italian Concerto, I (ex. 4.8), composed in 1735, could have been played on an early piano, which was capable of the *forte* and the *piano* he indicated (m. 30). A similar effect could also have been achieved on a double-manual harpsichord. A possible solution on the piano would be the repeated right-hand fingering of 3–2 (m. 36) and 4–3–2 (mm. 37–38), lifting after each figure.

Example 4.8. J. S. Bach, Italian Concerto, I, BWV 971, mm. 36–39, Bach Gesellschaft Edition.

It is not uncommon to find a slurring notation that resembles a bowing mark for a stringed instrument, such as the violin (ex. 4.8). This kind of slurring would also indicate to the keyboard player the correct articulation. On the piano, it would not be outside the realm of good technique to use the thumb on the first note of every other slurred group (ex. 4.8, m. 36 and m. 38). Bach's E Major French Suite is a clear example of string bowing in a keyboard work (ex. 4.9). A few other Bach examples of his slurring are shown in table 4.2. There are many others in his output.

Example 4.9. J. S. Bach, E Major French Suite, BWV 817, Allemande, Bach Gesellschaft Edition, mm. 1–3.

Table 4.2. Selected examples of Bach's slurring

Work	Movement	Description
French Suite in C minor	Menuet	Almost every RH measure is slurred; only melodic entrances are indicated in LH
English Suite in A minor	$\frac{3}{2}$ Courante	Four-note slurs sometimes occur in both hands; a two-note slur occurs in LH three measures before end
English Suite in A minor	Sarabande	Slurring on sixteenth notes in m. 2, in m. 9–11 in first half, and in m. 15–19 and m. 25–27

Caution is advised for the pianist not to exaggerate either the legato or the separations. It is a fine line that will have to be controlled by fingers, feet, and the ear and of course will also depend on the instrument and its capabilities.

Notes

1. Frederick Neumann, *New Essays on Performance Practice* (Rochester, NY: University of Rochester Press, 1989),187.
2. Neumann, *Performance Practices*, 187.
3. Erwin Bodky, *The Interpretation of Bach's Keyboard Works* (Cambridge, MA: Harvard University Press, 1960).
4. Reginald R. Gerig, *Famous Pianists and Their Technique*, new ed. (Bloomington: Indiana University Press, 2007), 31.
5. George Kochevitsky, *Performing Bach's Keyboard Music* (White Plains, NY: ProAm Music Resources, 1996), 38.
6. Kochevitsky, *Performing Bach's Keyboard Music*, 40.
7. Kochevitsky, *Performing Bach's Keyboard Music*, 42; my fingerings.
8. Kochevitsky, *Performing Bach's Keyboard Music*, 42.
9. Domenico Scarlatti, *Sonatas for the Keyboard II*, ed. Maurice Hinson (Van Nuys, CA: Alfred Publishing, 1996), 6. Rafael Puyana may be heard playing Sonata in A Minor, K. 175, on a three-manual German Hass harpsichord in a video recording available on YouTube, uploaded August 25, 2008, https://www.youtube.com/watch?v=6Gubohd0nO8&feature=emb_logo.
10. Claude Palisca, *Baroque Music*, 3rd ed. (Englewood Cliffs, NJ: Prentice-Hall, 1991), 3–4.
11. Howard Ferguson, *Keyboard Interpretation from the 14th to the 19th Century* (Oxford: Oxford University Press, 1998), 59.
12. Ralph Kirkpatrick, *Interpreting Bach's* "Well-tempered *Clavier": A Performer's Discourse of Method* (New Haven: Yale University Press, 1984), 59.
13. J. S. Bach, *Das Wohltemperierte Klavier, Teil 1*, urtext edition, ed. Otto von Irmer and fingered by Walther Lampe (Munich: Henle, 1995), 15.
14. Ferguson, *Keyboard Interpretation*, 57.

5 Hand Splitting or Redistribution, Stemming, and Cross Hands

In this short chapter, salient examples are given to address the simple questions of which hand to use and when. While these issues normally arise in repertoire spanning more than the typical five octaves of Baroque keyboards, the same questions can equally apply to certain aspects of Baroque pieces. This is especially true when performing these works on the piano and particularly may apply in polyphony when melodic voicing becomes a challenging concern.[1] In this chapter, discussion ensues around hand splitting or redistribution of passages between the hands, around the notion of notational stemming as an indicator for which hand to use, and around cross-hand passages, regardless of whether they are explicitly indicated.

Hand Splitting or Redistribution

The technique of dividing passages between the hands (hand splitting or redistribution) works well in some Baroque passages. Pianists may wish to use this technique to maintain the lyrical legato of upper or inner voices.

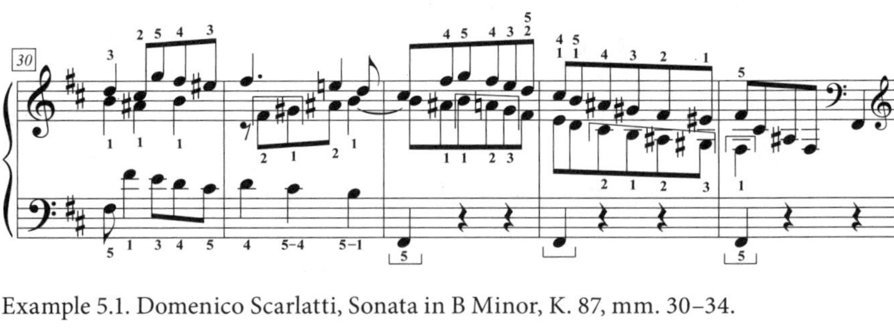

Example 5.1. Domenico Scarlatti, Sonata in B Minor, K. 87, mm. 30–34.

One possibility of fingering in Domenico Scarlatti's organ-like Sonata in B Minor, K. 87 (ex. 5.1), would be to maintain the descending sixths in the right hand by using finger substitution as necessary (ex. 5.1, m. 31) and ample pedal. However, the possibility of dividing the passage between the hands will facilitate a legato execution that would not easily be had otherwise (ex. 5.1, mm. 32–33).

Example 5.2. Domenico Scarlatti, Sonata in E Major, K. 264, mm. 127–135.

In another example, the Scarlatti Sonata in E Major, K. 264 (ex. 5.2), a wealth of harmonic activity enhances the musical interest. However, it may be challenging for the performer to find comfortable fingering. Fingering is chosen to outline the sequences (m. 128, m. 130, m. m. 132, m. 134). If the pianist's right hand does not accommodate the suggested fingering in m. 130 (4–3–4), an alternative is given that forces a small breath or break if the right-hand 5 ends m. 130 and begins m. 131. This solution, which will seem disjunct to pianists, creates a lovely clarity of the sequences that also coincides with the key change in m. 131. With this passage, the performer may desire to take the alto voice in the right hand with the left as noted in brackets. The same would apply in m. 135.

Example 5.3. J. S. Bach, *Goldberg Variations*, BWV 988, Sinfonia 15, mm. 26–28.

In the Sinfonia of J. S. Bach's Goldberg Variations BWV 988 (ex. 5.3), the performer will have many choices of redistributions. Depending on hand size and instrument, one possible solution would be to take the D in the alto voice on the second beat in m. 26 with the left hand, if it is not possible to play it in the right hand. In the following measure, m. 27, the left hand could take the inner voices. This allows the right hand, if played on the piano, to sing. If it is played on harpsichord, this approach allows the right hand to easily use finger substitution in preparation for the following legato upper sequence. The left hand continues with the alto voice in m. 28.

Stemming

Stemming in Baroque notation could indicate "handing," or rather, which hand was to be used: stems up = right hand and stems down = left hand. In the original manuscript of the Gigue of Bach's Partita, no. 1, BWV 825 (exx. 5.4 and 5.5), these stems show that long notes are to be played by the right hand and triplets with the left hand.[2] Some pianists may prefer the opposite handing, a practice that may have originated with Czerny's edition.[3] Try this passage on the piano in both ways and it will become clear why pianists prefer to play the long notes with the left hand.

Example 5.4. J. S. Bach, Partita, no. 1, BWV 825, Gigue, manuscript facsimile, mm. 1–6, showing long notes to be played by right hand and triplets with left hand.

Example 5.5. J. S. Bach, Partita, no. 1, BWV 825, Gigue, mm. 23–28.

Other possible interpretations of stemming are to define phrasing, to make the score easier to read, or to indicate interchangeability of the hands to ensure a good technical development.

In J. S. Bach's Toccata in G Major, BWV 916 (ex. 5.6), stemming of the scale passage would indicate a possible fingering of right hand 5–4–3–2; left hand 2–3–4 or right hand 4–3–2–1. Using the left hand 1–2–3 would be less good because of potential unwanted accents by the thumbs on weak beats.

Example 5.6. J. S. Bach, Toccata in G Major, BWV 916, mm. 1–3.[4]

Cross Hands

Domenico Scarlatti's sonatas are full of virtuoso cross-hand technique, which he designates in his scores when it is obligatory. Some examples follow (5.7 and 5.8).

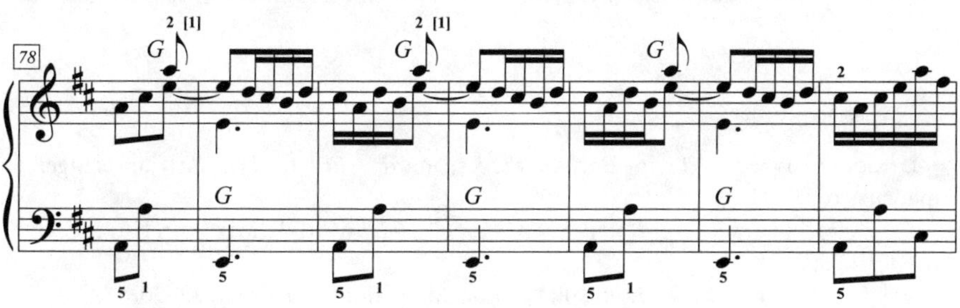

Example 5.7. Domenico Scarlatti, Sonata in D Major, K. 96, mm. 78–84, cross hands.

Example 5.8. Domenico Scarlatti, Sonata in B Minor, K. 27, *Essercizi*, mm. 4–6.

Two fingering possibilities are presented in Domenico Scarlatti's popular D Major Sonata, K. 96, which opens with horn calls (ex. 5.9). Although not indicated, cross hands may facilitate the opening passage. If it is begun with the left hand, then the right hand would play notes A and E while the left hand danced over it. This leaves the right hand stationary and ready to play the trills in m. 6, m. 8, and m. 10. If the performer does not feel comfortable with that solution, then as an alternative the lower voice could be taken with the left hand. Of course, the entire passage could be played with only the right hand, avoiding any crossing at all. Just as Scarlatti's works are rich in imagination, so too the performer should feel free to find alternative fingering solutions that permit the desired execution of the work. This example is further discussed in chapter 7.

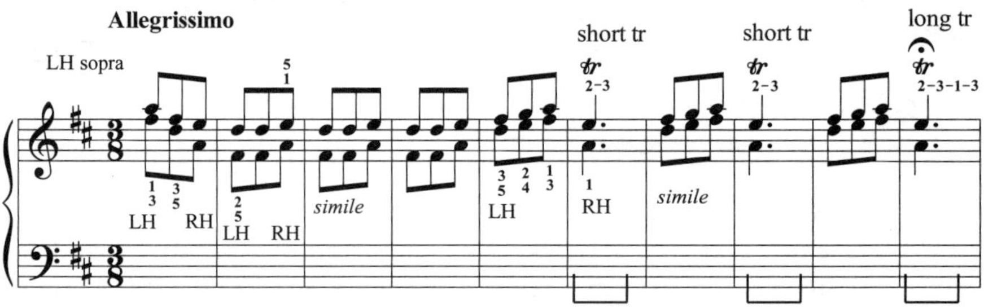

Example 5.9. Domenico Scarlatti, Sonata in D Major, K. 96, mm. 1–10, cross hands and with short and long trills.

Notes

1. Richard Troeger, *Playing Bach on the Keyboard: A Practical Guide* (Cambridge: Amadeus, 2003), 216.
2. J. S. Bach, *Partita, No. 1, in* B-flat *Major*, ed. Willard A. Palmer (Van Nuys, CA: Alfred, 1971), 7.
3. J. S. Bach, *Partita, No. 1, in* B-flat *Major*, ed. Willard A. Palmer, 29–30.
4. J. S. Bach, *Toccata in G Major*, Bach-Gesellschaft *Ausgabe*, vol. 36, ed. Ernst Naumann (Leipzig: Breitkopf und Härtel / Bach, 1890).

6 Crossing and Turning of the Fingers

"In the early fingering systems, the thumb was rarely used as a pivot over which the fingers could pass either up or down the scale––and then virtually only in the left hand. Lateral movement of the hands was most often achieved by passing one of the middle fingers (usually the long third) over one of its neighbors. In the right hand, the third finger would be slipped over the fourth when ascending and over the second when descending; in the left hand vice versa."[1] In other words, the process would be reversed.

Howard Ferguson's explanation at the beginning of this chapter points out three important usages of the hand and fingers in the early systems. First, the hand generally moved laterally, inferring that lateral motion or a relatively "still" hand was the preferred hand technique. Secondly, the thumb was rarely used and, when needed, turned under the hand in ascending or descending passages as a pivot for the other fingers, although it is conceivable that in certain passages where a slight space, breath, or non-legato would be musically appropriate that the thumb could be laterally moved without having to turn under the fingers. Finally, the middle fingers of either hand were used to cross over neighboring fingers, usually the middle finger but not exclusively. These practices would have also included the concept of "good" and "bad" fingers, as briefly mentioned in chapter 3, even though it varied from country to country, time period to time period.

As keyboard instruments evolved, notably with the invention of the piano, fingering concepts changed. The thumb eventually became a finger equal to the others and not just the odd stepchild to be included occasionally. In Germany, J. S. Bach, who already knew some of the early pianofortes, was a champion of the use of the thumb. It has been seen from chapter 3 in C. P. E. Bach's fingering examples (3.16 and 3.17) that both the old (crossing and turning of fingers but with little use of thumb) and new (traditional scale fingerings used today) fingering systems were accepted. As the piano developed, the weight of the keys and keyboard action became heavier, and gradually the notion of finger independence became the ideal technique, a notion that prevails today among most pianists and pedagogues.

Of the two Baroque techniques—crossing over and turning under of fingers—the first is little used today among pianists, while the second is commonplace in pianistic repertoire and traditional scale fingerings. Crossing over of the fingers may be uncomfortable for some hands, but other conditions may require its implementation (exx. 6.4, 6.5, and 6.6). Occasionally, crossing over of fingers will be found in the repertoire performed today, as in Chopin's Étude in A minor, op. 10, no. 2 (published 1833, ex. 6.1). This Chopin study may have been inspired in contrast to Ignaz Moscheles's (1794–1870) Étude in G Major, op. 70, no. 3 (published 1827) that prefers the turning under usage.

Example 6.1.
Chopin, Étude, op. 10, no. 2, mm. 1–3.

In J. S. Bach's Two-part Invention in D Minor, BWV 775 (ex. 6.2),[2] several different right-hand possibilities exist for the opening motive that use crossing over or turning under. Depending upon the shape of the hand and its size, the first option for both hands (crossing over) may be the most comfortable.

Example 6.2. J. S. Bach, Two-part Invention in D Minor, BWV 775, mm. 1–4.

1. 1–2–3–4–5–4 (cross over)
2. 2–3–4–2–3–4 (cross over)
3. 2–1–2–3–4–5 (turn under).

For m. 3, here are some possibilities for the left hand:

1. 5–4–3–2–1–2 (paralleling the first example of the right hand)
2. 3–2–1–3–2–1 (cross over)
3. 4–3–2–1–2–1 (cross over, thumb on black key)

In Bach's G Minor English Suite, BWV 809 (ex. 6.3), there are many possibilities of fingering. Remembering that comfort, security, phrasing, and expression are the guiding principles when choosing a fingering, several options are presented. These include the turning under of the fingers as well as redistributions that the pianist may want to try in m. 2, 8, 10, and 12 in concert tempo, since almost any fingering will work in a slow tempo. Unwanted accents should be avoided. However, the concept of light and heavy execution, previously mentioned in the introduction, could apply here and is indicated in mm. 1–2 by the upward and downward arrows, similar to bowing practices. From mm. 15–16, a lift is automatically ensured by the fingering suggested.

Example 6.3. J. S. Bach, English Suite in G Minor, BWV 808, mm. 1–16.[3]

With aging, focal dystonia, or other problems, the Bach fingerings in selections from the *Well-Tempered Clavier*—the Prelude in C Minor, BWV 847 and the Prelude and Fugue in E Minor, BWV 855, and Fugue in E♭ —by the Ukrainian-German pianist-pedagogue Heinrich Neuhaus (1888–1964) show how some alternate turning solutions helped him continue to play in spite of the "sluggish" condition of his hand.[4] Neuhaus commented on these fingering changes: "I would point out in these three examples, how much more beautiful, economic and simple was the first fingering (the old) than the second (the new). But what can I do? At present the second fingering is more useful to me because it requires a greater swing in the rotating movements and a more frequent use of the thumb and second finger. One must make do with what one has."[5]

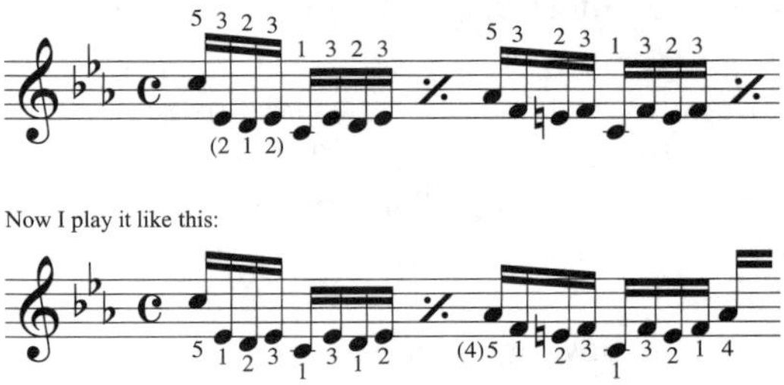

Example 6.4. J. S. Bach, Prelude in C Minor, WTC I, BWV 847, Neuhaus fingering: (a) fingering as young man; (b) fingering as older man with focal dystonia, mm. 1–2.[6]

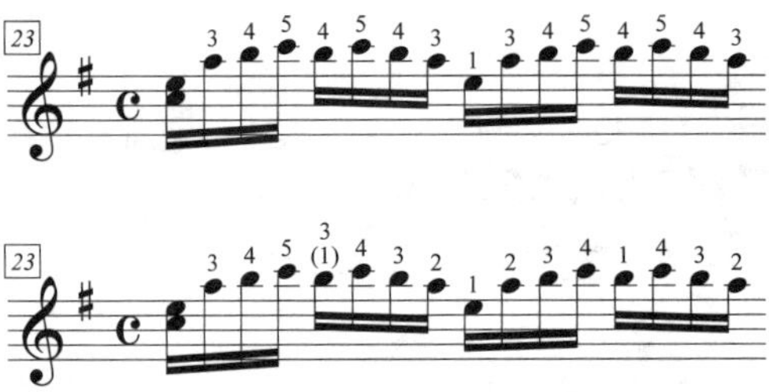

Example 6.5. J. S. Bach, Prelude in E Minor, WTC I, BWV 855 (Presto), Neuhaus fingering: (a) fingering as young man; (b) fingering as older man with focal dystonia, m. 23.[7]

In the Fugue in E minor (No. 10), which follows this Prelude, I used, of course, to play the subject thus:

But now I play it like this:

Example 6.6. J. S. Bach, Fugue in E Minor, WTC I, BWV 855, Neuhaus fingering: (a) fingering as young man; (b) fingering as older man with focal dystonia, mm. 1–2.[8]

In all three of the alternative solutions (exx. 6.4, 6.5, and 6.6), Neuhaus presents a hand that is unusually contracted. Most pianists would not find these solutions to be helpful under normal circumstances.

With the possibility of equal temperament, modern pianistic technique naturally evolved. In this example of Domenico Scarlatti's scale passages where the fingers cross over the thumb (ex. 6.7), traditional scale fingering is a comfortable solution. Because of the key in which this sonata is written, these passages could clearly not be performed as glissandi. They could theoretically be redistributed between the hands, but it would seem that Scarlatti wishes the performer to show off virtuoso technique.

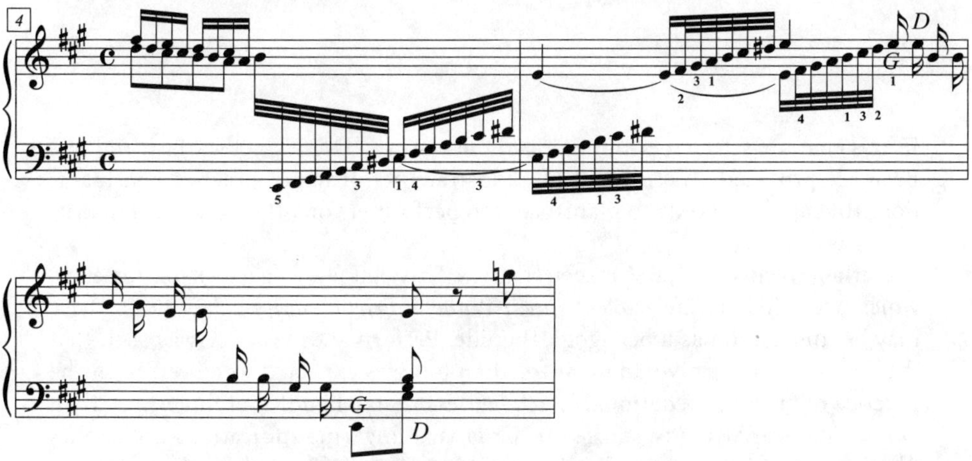

Example 6.7. Domenico Scarlatti, Sonata in A Major, K. 24, mm. 4–6.

Notes

1. Howard Ferguson, *Keyboard Interpretation from the 14th to the 19th Century* (Oxford: Oxford University Press, 1998), 67.
2. J. S. Bach, "Two Part Inventions," in *Keyboard Music* (from the Bach-Gesellschaft-*Ausgabe* edition), ed. William Rust. New York: Dover, 1970, 274.
3. J. S. Bach, *Englische Suiten, BWV 806–811*, urtext edition, ed. Rudolf Steglich, fingered by Hans-Martin Theopold (Munich: Henle Verlag, 1971). Additional fingering is suggested by the author in measures 1–3 and in brackets.
4. Heinrich Neuhaus, *The Art of Piano Playing*, 2nd ed. (London: Kahn and Averill, 1993), 149.
5. Neuhaus, *The Art of Piano Playing*, 150.
6. Neuhaus, *The Art of Piano Playing*, 148.
7. Neuhaus, *The Art of Piano Playing*, 143.
8. Neuhaus, *The Art of Piano Playing*, 149.vv

7 Repeated Notes, Glissandi, and Implied Fingering through Musical Figures

In this chapter, selected examples from the works of Domenico Scarlatti and J. S. Bach are provided. These succinctly illustrate performance practice considerations that apply not only to pianists but to performers on other keyboard instruments as well.

Earlier, in chapter 2, it was seen that J. S. Bach left few fingerings for posterity, which occur in his *Clavierbüchlein vor Wilhelm Friedemann Bach* of 1720. These may be understood as a pedagogical guide. Performance practice was such that the performer not only had great freedom but was expected to be versed in the practice of tasteful execution. If Bach left less than a handful of fingerings, then Domenico Scarlatti left even fewer. Only two fingering indications are explicitly found in Domenico Scarlatti's over 560 sonatas (for harpsichord, clavichord, organ, and fortepiano). Of these two, one indicates that the fingers should be changed on repeated notes and the other gives a rapid glissando to be played by one finger in a scale passage. In the latter, Scarlatti does not specify which finger to use but rather leaves the choice to the performer. These examples follow (exx. 7.1 and 7.3).

Repeated Notes

The practice of fast repeated notes in the works of Domenico Scarlatti is frequently found in the context of imitating the guitar's light punteado (plucking) touch, which is not an easy feat for pianists on the heavier and slower-action modern piano. In Scarlatti's Sonata in D Major, K. 96 (ex. 7.1), the Neapolitan composer urges *Mutandi i deti*,[1] or "changing the fingers," but does not hint at which he prefers. Given the brisk tempo, logical fingerings would be right-hand 3–2–1 or 4–3–2. The former has been effectively used by Hungarian piano virtuoso György Cziffra (1921–1994).[2] If preferred, the fingers 2–1 or 3–2 may be used to execute duple groupings that pair up with the left hand. The dangers inherent in this choice could be unwanted sluggishness and accents and the inability to easily maintain longer phrase lines.

Example 7.1. Domenico Scarlatti, Sonata in D Major, K. 96, "Mutandi i deti," mm. 33–38.

In a similar passage in Scarlatti's Sonata in D Minor, K. 141 (ex. 7.2), pianist Martha Argerich (b. 1941) can be seen using repeated right-hand 3–2–1.[3] With her extraordinary speed, she uses a small in-out motion of the forearm. This example is also one of guitar imitation of the punteado touch.

Example 7.2. Domenico Scarlatti, Sonata in D Minor, K. 141, mm. 1–9.

Glissandi

In Scarlatti's Sonata in F Major, K. 379 (ex. 7.3), he employs a bristling glissando on the white keys, indicating, in Spanish, that it should be played "with one finger" ("con dedo solo" [*sic*]).[4] By using the right-hand second finger, this fingering allows a natural and comfortable transition to the thirds (right-hand 1–3) that follow.[5]

Example 7.3. Domenico Scarlatti, Sonata in F Major, K. 379, "Con dedo sólo," mm. 33–34.

Musical Figures Dictating Fingering

Beyond Scarlatti's own explicit fingering indications, he implies fingering with musical figures. A sequential fingering would be the most logical fingering to be used in examples 7.4 and 7.5. The effect in Scarlatti's Sonata, K. 3 (*Essercizi*; ex. 7.4), given its presto tempo, is quasi glissandi. An alternative would be to use cross hands: left hand (1–2–3–4–5); right hand (5–4–3–2–1); left hand (1–2–3–4–5) in the opening.

Example 7.4. Domenico Scarlatti, Sonata, K. 3 (*Essercizi*), mm. 1–9.

Another implied fingering is found in Scarlatti's Sonata in B-flat Major, K. 228 (ex. 7.5, m. 116), where the hand is forced to lift after the five-note pattern. The same could be true if the performer chose the right-hand fingering of 1–2–3–4–5 in m. 2 instead of 2–1–2–3–4.

Example 7.5. Domenico Scarlatti, Sonata in B-flat Major, K. 228, mm. 113–118.

It is curious that there is no reference in contemporary treatises of Scarlatti's time that deal with his hand-crossing technique or his fingering indications, whether explicit or implicit. This absence should not imply that the single movement Scarlatti sonatas were not known outside of the Iberian Peninsula.

No doubt that the publication of Scarlatti's *Esssercizi* (1738–1739) gave impulse to the spread of his works as will be seen below. Too, the fact that they do not occur as suites, which were popular at the time, does not mean that they were not widely dispersed or intended to be performed in groups. One scholar-cataloger, Ralph Kirkpatrick, maintains that many of the bipartite sonatas were to be performed in pairs and a few in triptychs.[6] The so-called Coimbra manuscript MSS 58 (see chapter 12, table 12.1) consists of four Scarlatti sonatas in the same key, which some musicologists speculate should be performed together.

According to the German Austrian musicologist Eva Badura-Skoda, "C. P. E. Bach obviously had the opportunity to study Scarlatti's *Essercizi*."[7] This statement clearly contradicts Kirkpatrick's contention that the sonatas were little known outside of Spain and England.[8] Some of the same devices (double trills; alternating distribution of notes between the hands; passages with thirds, sixths, and octaves in one hand; chords with added notes; trills on final note of piece) found in the *Essercizi* are also found in C. P. E. Bach's keyboard sonatas of a few years later, namely his Prussian and Würtemberg sonatas of the 1740s.[9] Even J. S. Bach acquired a copy of the printed version in Leipzig, which would also have been available in Berlin and Vienna.[10] Scarlatti's growing influence in his lifetime expanded later to such composers as Johannes Brahms (1833–1897), Manuel de Falla (1876–1946),[11] Enrique Granados (1867–1916),[12] and others.

J. S. Bach, like Scarlatti, may imply fingering through musical figures. Two such examples follow from the Italian Concerto, BWV 971, in the second movement. In the opening of this movement (ex. 7.6), the pianist might be tempted to take the ascending figures with the right hand in order to maintain the legato while using an abundance of pedal. This would merge the two motives that are clearly indicated by Bach into one and completely change their character, annulling the inherent character and defeating the sense of breathlessness required not only in the return (recapitulation) of the main motives but elsewhere.

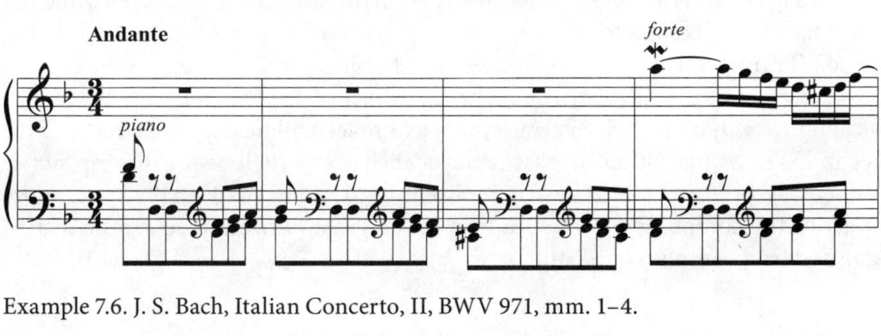

Example 7.6. J. S. Bach, Italian Concerto, II, BWV 971, mm. 1–4.

A different musical figure in the same movement (ex. 7.7) forces the performer to lift or breathe between short motives. As such, it becomes necessary to change fingering on the repeated notes in order to get the maximum expressivity possible (m. 23–24; m. 24–25). The contrast between the expressive legato right-hand melody offsets and provides ample contrast to the pulsating left hand. The pianist who wishes to portray the pulsating left hand will use the pedal judiciously and in some instances with half pedal, constantly listening to get the desired effect.

Example 7.7. J. S. Bach, Italian Concerto, II, BWV 971, mm. 23–28.

By setting up the left hand in the second movement as he did, Bach created a magical prenocturnal element that unifies the movement. If the performer keeps a steady tempo for the left hand and allows the right hand to meander in an expressive quasi-improvisation, this movement may be said to foreshadow the performance practice of both Wolfgang Amadeus Mozart (1756–1791) and Frédéric Chopin (1810–1849)—the former who declared, "My keeping so accurately in time . . . causes surprise, the left hand being quite independent in tempo rubato of an adagio," and the latter whose steady left hand was likened to a tree while the right hand was likened to the "tops of trees blown hither and thither by a strong wind" (Franz Liszt, 1811–1886, describing Chopin's playing of tempo rubato).[13]

Performers will find numerous other examples of implied fingering that a musical figure will dictate. Sometimes these examples will be decisions that involve technical decisions; other times, the musical character will be the driving factor. Either way, performers will have to be attentive to small details that will get at the heart of the composer's wishes. In this way, a great performance can be distinguished from simply a good one.

Notes

1. An old Italian term.
2. "Scarlatti: Sonate in D Major, K. 96, La Chasse," performance by György Cziffra, video, 4:10, August 17, 2013, https://www.youtube.com/watch?v=AxAEnKFeofM.
3. "Scarlatti Sonata in D minor, K. 141 by Martha Argerich (2008)," March 27, 2008, video, 3:28, July 28, 2011, https://www.youtube.com/watch?v=wjghYFgt8Zk.
4. The correct Spanish would read "con dedo sólo."

5. Barbara Sachs, "Scarlatti's *tremulo*," *Early Music* 19, no. 1 (February 1991): 91. This term corresponds to Pasquali's terminology (*Art of Fingering the Harpsichord*, 1757, published in the year of Scarlatti's death) for slurred notes to be played by one finger, which he called *sdrucciolato*.

6. For more on that subject, see Kirkpatrick and the two volumes of his edition of the Scarlatti Sonatas: Domenico Scarlatti, *Sixty Sonatas in Two Volumes*, ed. Ralph Kirkpatrick (New York: Schirmer, 1953).

7. Eva Badura-Skoda, *The* Eighteenth-Century *Fortepiano and its Patrons from Scarlatti to Beethoven* (Bloomington: Indiana University Press, 2017), 246.

8. Eva Badura-Skoda, *The* Eighteenth-Century *Fortepiano*, 246.

9. Eva Badura-Skoda, *The* Eighteenth-Century *Fortepiano*, 246.

10. Eva Badura-Skoda, *The* Eighteenth-Century *Fortepiano*, 246.

11. Falla's Harpsichord Concerto, III, is composed in a Scarlattian style. Several other Falla's mature works bear the Scarlattian stamp.

12. Enrique Granados transcribed twenty-four Scarlatti sonatas (two other sonatas are by other composers whom he mistook for Scarlatti) for modern piano as *Veintiséis Sonatas Inéditas para Clave, compuestas in España para la Familia Real (1729–1754), transcriptas libremente para Piano*. Madrid: Sociedad Editorial de Música (n.d.). Originally the set was published in 1905 with an "Estudio-biográfico-bibliográafico-crítico" by Felipe Pedrell in Barcelona: Vidal Llimon y Boceta.

13. *The Letters of Wolfgang Amadeus Mozart (1769–1791)*, trans. from the collection of Ludwig Nohl, vol. 1 (New York: Kurd and Houghton; Philadelphia: Frederick Letpoldt, 1866), https://archive.org/stream/lettersofwolfgan01moza/lettersofwolfgan01moza_djvu.txt; and Jean-Jacques Eigeldinger, *Chopin: Pianist and Teacher: As Seen by His Pupils* (Cambridge, UK: Cambridge University Press, 1986), 51.

8 Fingering in Ornamentation

If the pianist or performer finds the subject of ornamentation confusing, it will be remembered: "More than 200 books and tables dealing with ornaments were written and compiled between 1600 and 1800."[1] Ornamentation, while having established rules, often deals with the exceptions to the rules. The act of embellishing is an act of improvisation, to some extent. Ornamentation can be subjective and is affected by various factors: the instrument, the environment or acoustics of the hall, the tempo chosen, the edition used, and the mood and stylistic perception of the performer. The keyboard player may make different choices for ornamentation when performing with other musicians.

Jean-Henri d'Anglebert's ornamentation table served as a guide for J. S. Bach and his pupils. Sometimes Bach wrote out ornaments as he wished them to be played in a particular work. A good example of this practice is the Sarabande of his A-minor English Suite, BWV 807. Other times, Bach notated ornament symbols as a kind of musical shorthand. The performer could assume that those same ornaments might be executed at similar places in the score even though they were not indicated.

These general rules apply for Bach's ornaments:

- They are played, almost without exception, *on* the beat, thus taking their time from the following note.
- They are mainly diatonic (as opposed to chromatic).
- They should not change or blur the melodic outline of a composition.
- They should not alter the harmonic structure of a composition.
- They should not, as C. P. E. Bach warned, "[corrupt] the purity of voice leading."[2]
- All ornaments should be interpreted *in context*.[3]

Bach mostly used the trill, turn, and slide as melodic ornaments. Harmonic ornaments are the appoggiatura, the acciaccatura, and the broken chord. The rhythmic ornaments are mostly the mordent and the inverted mordent.[4] Fingering in Bach's ornaments is determined by their function, whether to emphasize the melodic, harmonic, or rhythmic nature of the note(s). In whatever situation, ornaments should not get in the way of any of these functions, or impede or cover voice leading.

Pianists should chose a good fingering for Bach's ornaments that will ensure a smooth and/or rhythmic execution. In general, ornaments are played with consecutive fingers; however, Bach did indicate trills with 3–5. C. P. E. Bach admits that trills are the most difficult of all the ornaments and that not all performers are successful playing them. He adds, "No one can succeed without a minimum of two good trills in each hand."[5] He gives indications for their performance and "intelligent practice" by all fingers, even though not all fingers will be able to trill well because there are natural differences between them.[6] If double trills are to be performed, C. P. E. Bach suggests alternate fingers and in some cases the crossing over of fingers.[7] In an example of turning under, he says that it would not be incorrect to use a 2–1 fingering in the left hand for an E-flat–D descending trill.[8]

In Bach's Sonata in A Major for flute and cembalo, BWV 1032, Largo e Dolce (ex. 8.1), the preferred right-hand beginning note fingering choices are 3 or 4. In either case, a small wrist rotation helps to emulate the flute line as well as to breathe with the flutist.

Example 8.1. J. S. Bach, Sonata in A Major for flute and cembalo, BWV 1032, Largo e Dolce, m. 1.

Terminations of trills often present problems in chamber music. Secure fingering is a must, which means measuring the alternations of the trill notes. At the ending of the first movement of Bach's First Sonata for Gamba and Clavier, BWV 1027 (ex. 8.2), both violinist and keyboardist play the exact number of alterna-

Possible realization for gamba trill in m. 26

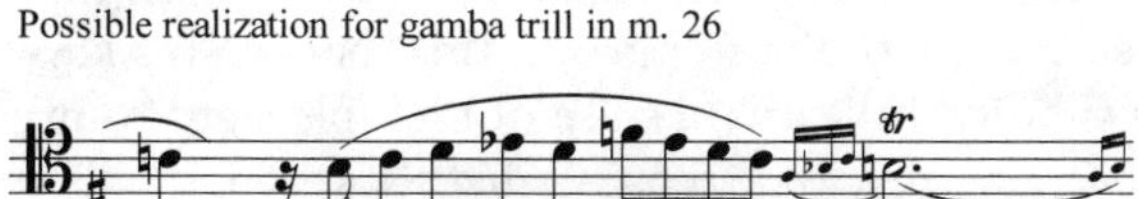

Example 8.2. J. S. Bach, First Sonata for Gamba and Clavier, BWV 1027, ending of first movement, mm. 26–28.[9]

tions. Although Bach's preferred trill fingers 3–5 work best on black-white notes (as on modern keyboards), a better fingering in this example would be to start the trill preparation with 2 and trill with 1–3, terminating with 2–3–2.

The string or voice tremolo is associated with the Italian *trillo* with its "repeated and accelerated repercussions on the same pitch."[10] In Domenico Scarlatti's works, the tremolo sign may mean that repeated notes should be played. The tremolo in wind music was equated with "breath vibrato" or repeated notes.[11] In texted music, this kind of tremolo was associated with shivering, which would imply "cold, fear, awe, death, grief, sleep, and weakness."[12]

The Austrian American musicologist and violinist Frederick "Fritz" Neumann (1907–1994) notes: "J. S. Bach uses the wavy-line symbol with unquestionable vibrato meaning a few times for the voice and for melody instruments. It will be remembered that the symbol has the meaning of an extended trill only for his keyboard works."[13] Although the tremolo sign is not given in this first edition of Bach's transcription of Marcello's Oboe Concerto (ex. 8.3), the slow repeated notes in the first measure, followed by the repeated note dissonances of the second measure and continued by the pulsating chordal accompaniment, indicate the nature of the *affekt.* To portray this the pianist may wish to finger the passages in strong-weak ("good-bad" fingers, such as right-hand 3–2) groups of two while amply using pedal to carry the long phrases.

Example 8.3. Bach keyboard transcription of Marcello's Oboe Concerto, BWV 974, II, mm. 1–6.

Scarlatti's Trills and Tremolo

Trills in the works of Domenico Scarlatti are generally begun on the main note, followed by the upper auxiliary note. Of course, there can always be exceptions. The context has to be carefully considered. The guiding rule for any trill is to embellish the melodic line, not to impede it. Like Bach, Scarlatti's trills are usually performed *on* the beat. Later, we will see an unconventional application of a final trill on the modern piano (ex. 8.12).

Music scholars have made several interesting speculations about the nature of Domenico Scarlatti's tremolos. As we've mentioned, the term *tremolo* may indicate "repeated and accelerated repercussions on the same pitch."[14] Given that Scarlatti was a virtuoso singer, the use of the tremolo in this sense in his keyboard works may have some validity. In Scarlatti's use of multiple signs to indicate the right-hand tremolo (trem., tre., and so on)—what Kirkpatrick calls a "puzzlingly consistent distinction"—most performers (pianists and harpsichordists alike) play a trill.[15]

Citing Pasquali's *Art of Fingering the Harpsichord* (completed in 1757, the year of Scarlatti's death), Barbara Sachs makes a strong case for the repeated-note tremolo. The possible fingering combinations for the repeated-note tremolo (right hand only) would be 4–3–2, 4–4–3, 5–4–3, 3–3–2, 3–2–1. Most pianists use a long trill, which is much more difficult than the "bouncing ball" effect of the repeated-note tremolo.

The tremolo is found in Scarlatti's sonatas on single notes, on long notes, in chords, and as a compound ornament. Particularly pertinent in this respect are sonatas K. 96, K. 118, K. 119, and K. 141, some of which are given here.

Example 8.4. Domenico Scarlatti, Sonata in D Major, K. 96, tremolo on long notes, mm. 11–16.

In Scarlatti's Sonata in D Major, K. 96 (ex. 8.4), the fingering is for the repeated-note tremolo in the upper voice, or *tremulo di sopra*, as is indicated. Although the tremolo is not indicated over the other right-hand notes, it would seem to be implied, and the performer may wish to continue the passage in a manner similar to the opening. If the pianist opts to play a trill instead, and many do, an alternate fingering may be used (ex. 8.5). The trill would be started with right-hand fingers 2–3. It would continue in m. 3 using 1–2, in order to allow the fourth finger to play the single note F-sharp. The lower trill continues with fingers 1–2 on D and E, while fingers 4 and 5 strike the F-sharp and A in m. 15.

Example 8.5. Domenico Scarlatti, Sonata in D Major, K. 96, alternate fingering when playing a trill, mm. 11–15.

Other realizations are suggested in Scarlatti's Sonata in A Minor, K. 175 (ex. 8.6), and Sonata in D Major, K. 118 (exx. 8.7, 8.8, 8.9, and 8.10.).

Example 8.6. Domenico Scarlatti, Sonata in A Minor, K. 175, right-hand written trill, followed by tremolo (repeated notes) in chords, mm. 25–26 and mm. 29–30.

In K. 175 (ex. 8.6), the symbol given is a trill in m. 25, which is then followed in the next measure by a tremolo. A similar incidence occurs at a higher pitch in m. 29, followed by a tremolo in m. 30. Actually, in this harmonically dense pas-

Example 8.7. Domenico Scarlatti, Sonata in D Major, K. 118, tremolo and trill in a compound ornament, mm. 1–6. Heugel Urtext edition, edited by Kenneth Gilbert.

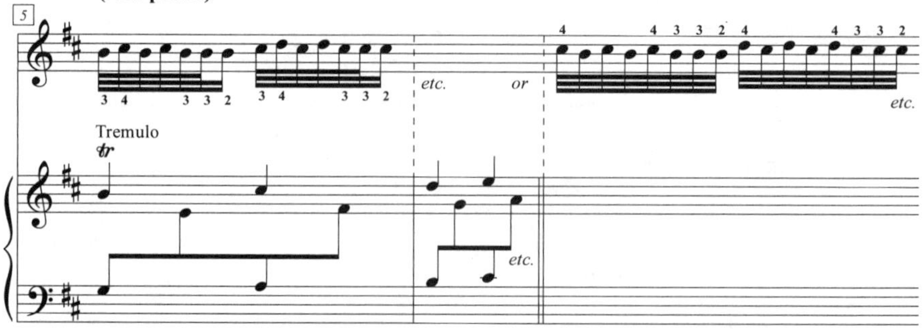

Example 8.8. Domenico Scarlatti, Sonata in D Major, K. 118, tremolo and trill in a compound ornament, two realizations (main note or upper note beginning), mm. 5–6.

Example 8.9. Domenico Scarlatti, Sonata in D Major, K. 118, compound ornament realized as only a main note trill, mm. 1–6.

Example 8.10. Domenico Scarlatti, Sonata in D Major, K. 118, compound ornament realized as only a main note tremolo, mm. 1–6.

sage, the interruption of the trill by the tremolo is a relief for the ear as well as for the hand.[18]

In K. 118 (ex. 8.7), the indication of tremolo is written over the trill sign (m. 5) in a compound ornament. The continuation of this figure is implied due to the similar passage that follows (m. 6). One possible realization is found in example 8.8 (mm. 5–6). Two choices are given: to begin with the main note trill and end with a tremolo, or to clash with the left hand by starting on the upper note of the trill and end with the tremolo. The fingering suggested for either pattern will repeat with the sequence. For reasons of aesthetic preference and tempo choice, the performer may prefer to ignore the compound ornament and opt for just one realization. In example 8.9, a short main note trill is suggested, while in example 8.10, a main note tremolo with various possible fingerings is given.

In the art of rhetoric, the repetition of a word or phrase in immediate succession causes an emotional effect (called an epizeuxis). Scarlatti's tremolo figure as a rapid repeated single note or "breath vibrato" is one example of his use of this technique. On the early fortepiano, this type of figure would not only be easier to perform but would have a more intimate and emotional appeal. Scarlatti the singer would have been aware of its impact. Jacqueline Ogeil makes a case for other repeated motives having a similar effect, such as in sonatas K. 490 (mm. 49–59); K. 285, mm. 27–32; and K. 502, mm. 39–45.[19] The entire concept as it applies to performers merits more investigation, because mainstream pianists have not adopted the concept.

An interesting solution to a final chord indicated with a trill in Scarlatti's Sonata in D Major, K. 96 (ex. 8.11), starts with the right-hand trill on both notes and then adds alternating left-hand notes, ending with a downward arpeggio (ex. 8.12). This solution would sound raucous on the harpsichord but can be thrilling on the piano.

Example 8.11. Domenico Scarlatti, Sonata in D Major, K. 96, final chord as written, m. 211.

Example 8.12. Domenico Scarlatti, Sonata in D Major, K. 96, final chord with possible trill realization in both hands, m. 211.

Near the beginning of the same sonata (ex. 8.13), the right-hand trills in m. 6 and m. 8 may be short, given the rapid tempo of allegrissimo. The pianist may wish to end this phrase with a longer trill in m. 10 and with a fermata at the end by using alternating fingers 1–3–2–3 or 2–3.

It may be remembered that this sonata was discussed in chapter 5, when a cross-hand alternative was provided (ex. 5.9). The reader/performer may wish to consider this in light of the discussion of ornamentation in this sonata.

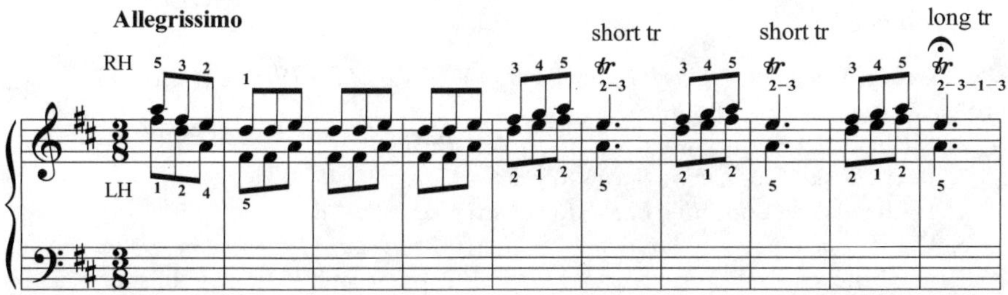

Example 8.13. Domenico Scarlatti, Sonata in D Major, K. 96, mm. 11–15, with short and long trills.

Scarlatti's Sonata in D Minor, K. 141, affords the pianist another example of a dramatic finale. Rather terminating on a single note (ex. 8.14) after breathtaking brilliance throughout the sonata, the pianist may want to make a final trill with both hands (ex. 8.15).

Example 8.14. Domenico Scarlatti, Sonata in D Minor, K. 141, mm. 157–158, ending as written.

Example 8.15. Domenico Scarlatti, Sonata in D Minor, K. 141, mm. 157–158, possible realization of ending.

While it would be impossible to give all possible solutions to ornamentation in this short chapter, it is hoped that these ideas will stimulate the performer to be creative and experiment with various possibilities. The awareness that not everything to be performed will be notated and all that is notated may not be exact is a valuable lesson in freedom and expressivity for the performer on any instrument.

Notes

1. George Kochevitsky, *Performing Bach's Keyboard Music* (White Plains, NY: ProAm Music Resources, 1996), 69.
2. Kochevitsky, *Performing Bach's Keyboard Music*, 75.
3. Kochevitsky, *Performing Bach's Keyboard Music*, 74–75.
4. Kochevitsky, *Performing Bach's Keyboard Music*, 75–76.
5. C. P. E. Bach, *Essay on the True Art of Playing Keyboard Instruments*, trans. and ed. William J. Mitchell (New York: Norton, 1949), 102, paragraph 10. First published 1753.
6. See C. P. E. Bach's chapter in *Essay* on "embellishments," especially no. 8 and no. 9.
7. C. P. E. Bach, *Essay*, 60–61, 102.
8. C. P. E. Bach, *Essay*, 103.
9. Frederick Neumann, *New Essays on Performance Practice* (Rochester, NY: University of Rochester Press, 1989), 533.
10. Frederick Neumann, *Ornamentation in Baroque and* Post-Baroque *Music* (Princeton, NJ: Princeton University Press, 1978), 515.
11. See Bruce Haynes, *The Eloquent Oboe: A History of the Hautboy 1640–1760* (Oxford: Oxford University Press, 2001), 252–254.
12. Haynes, *The Eloquent Oboe*, 254.
13. Neumann, *Ornamentation*, 519.
14. Neumann, *Ornamentation*, 515.
15. Barbara Sachs "Scarlatti's *Tremulo*," *Early Music* 19, no. 1 (February 1991): 91.
16. Sachs, "Scarlatti's *Tremulo*," 93.
17. Sachs, "Scarlatti's *Tremulo*," 93.
18. Sachs, "Scarlatti's *Tremulo*," 93.
19. See Jacqueline Ogeil, "Did Domenico Scarlatti Compose the First Great Piano Music?," in *Domenico Scarlatti Adventures: Essays to Commemorate the 250th Anniversary of His Death*, ed. Massimiliano Sala and W. Dean Sutcliffe (Bologna: Ut Orpheus Edizioni, 2008), 343–367.

9 Fingering in Chords and in Chordal Realizations

Baroque fingering in chords usually follow traditional chordal fingering used today. Earlier in chapter 5, it was seen in one of Scarlatti's most daring sonatas, Sonata in E Major, K. 264, that due to quickly moving harmonic passages the performer has several options for fingering and redistribution (ex. 5.2). In this same sonata (ex. 9.1), chordal shapes and hand size may determine the fingering for each performer.

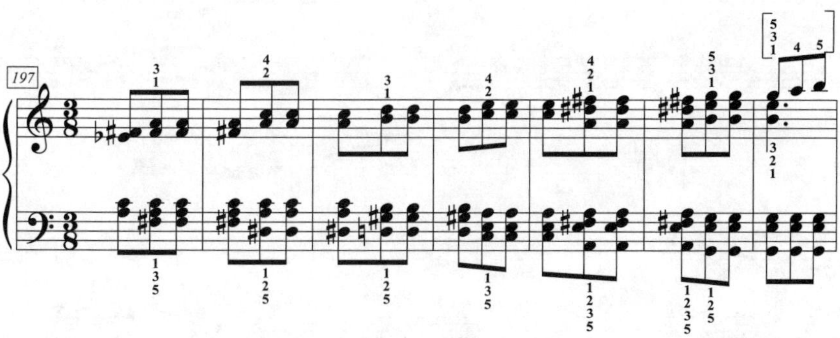

Example 9.1. Domenico Scarlatti, Sonata in E Major, K. 264, mm. 197–203.

Bach sometimes wrote out chordal realizations and sometimes only indicated the chord to be realized as in figured bass symbols over a bass line. His Prelude in C Major, WTC I, BWV 846 (ex. 9.2), features the first type of chordal realizations, which could be reduced to chordal symbols similar to figured bass or a lead sheet, if using this example pedagogically.

Example 9.2. Bach, Prelude in C Major, WTC I, BWV 846, chordal realization, mm. 1–2.

The second type, a kind of musical shorthand, or the realization and improvisation of chords, is given by Bach in a few works, such as the *Adagio* of the third Brandenburg Concerto, BWV 1048 (ex. 9.3), with only two chords and no further indications. The first violin may improvise passages to connect these two chords. Alternatively, a keyboard cadenza could be composed or improvised for these two chords, balancing the two outer movements. When I performed this work on harpsichord, the orchestral conductor had asked that I compose a cadenza. My version was rather lengthy and served as an entire second movement.

Example 9.3. Bach, Brandenburg Concerto no. 3, BWV 1048, end of first movement, followed by Adagio to be improvised, which leads to last movement, m. 1.

The question of what Bach meant, how to realize the chords in this work, and how to finger them must be addressed by the performer. In this sense, C. P. E. Bach provides important suggestions about the genre of the musical fantasy in his chapter on improvisation from his *Essay*.[1] It is important to know how to "read" the score and to consider (1) what has been done in the work by the composer himself and see if it would apply to the situation; (2) the voice leadings to determine if rolled arpeggios from top to bottom or bottom to top would apply; and (3) any other musical clues, such as character of the piece, rhythmic figures, pedal points, historical precedents, various editions, performer instructions, recordings, and treatises that would provide guidance.

J. S. Bach's *Chromatic Fantasy and Fugue*, BWV 903, gives pause for reflection in a middle section (ex. 9.4). He notates three blocked chordal passages (beginning in m. 30, m. 35, and m. 46) to play "arpeggio" and connects them with specifically written-out meandering sixteenth notes. The performer must determine how to arpeggiate these passages—rolling downward, rolling upward, or a com-

Example 9.4. Bach Fantasy, *Chromatic Fantasy and Fugue*, BWV 903 mm. 28–49.[2]

bination of the two. If performed on the harpsichord, then these arpeggios offer a good opportunity for finger pedaling or holding down the top or bottom note of the arpeggio.

In Busoni's edition of the same work, he presents an interesting solution to the arpeggiated chords, noting ample pedal for pianists.[3]

Example 9.5a. Busoni edition, 1902, realization of Bach *Chromatic Fantasy and Fugue*, mm. 28–35.

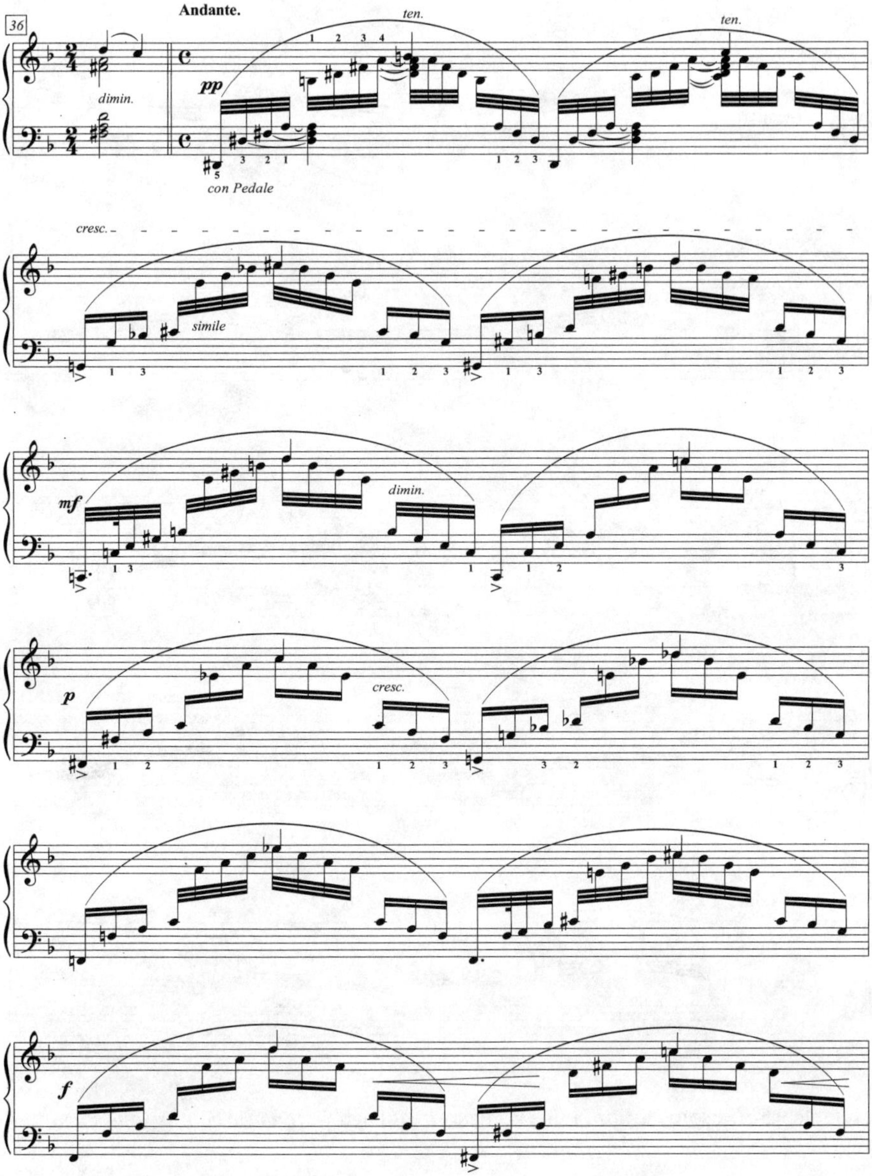

Example 9.5b. Busoni edition, 1902, realization of Bach *Chromatic Fantasy and Fugue*, mm. 36–42.

Example 9.5c. Busoni edition, 1902, realization of Bach *Chromatic Fantasy and Fugue*, mm. 43–49.

Example 9.5d. Busoni edition, 1902, realization of Bach *Chromatic Fantasy and Fugue*, mm. 50–55.

His fingering follows traditional arpeggio fingering. For the broken and sustained bass octaves, sometimes he indicates finger substitution (ex. 9.5a, andante sciolto). Sometimes he gives legato octaves with the traditional arpeggio crossing-over (ex. 9.5b, andante), making it possible to take the upper note with the left hand in order to emphasize the top note. The octave doublings that Busoni adds are particularly effective on the piano (ex. 9.5a, maestoso). Yet in a later version (1915), Busoni embellishes the A Major chord with a trill (ex. 9.6) that directly connects to the diminished chord on the bass G.[4] At the top of this arpeggio, held by the sustaining pedal, Busoni indicates to silently retake the chord before releasing the pedal. The alternating right-hand and left-hand indications in the thirty-second note descending passage reinforce Bach's manuscript indications, which are given by stemming up for the right hand and stemming down for the left hand (ex. 9.5a, allegro). The following andante (ex. 9.5b) indicates a tenuto on the top notes, which implies a light rubato and brings attention to the soprano voice. It also acts as a complement to sustained bass notes (ex. 9.5a with finger substitution; ex. 9.5c, andante).

Example 9.6. Busoni edition, 1915, realization of Bach *Chromatic Fantasy and Fugue,* m. 31.

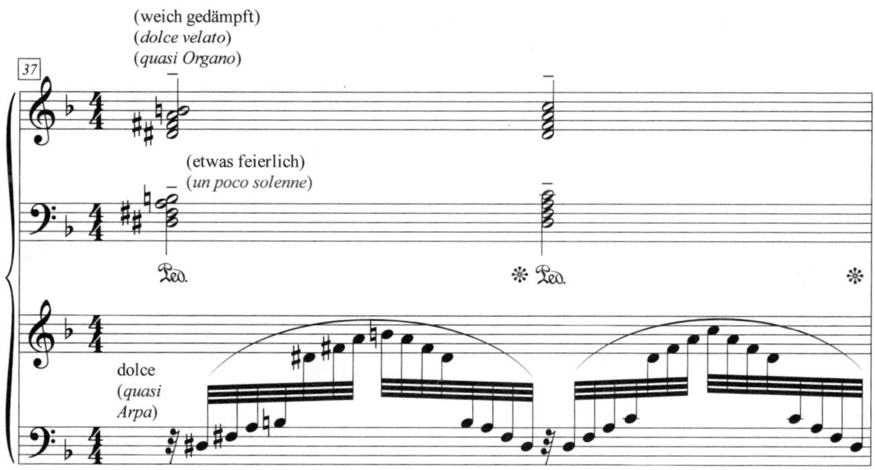

Example 9.7. Busoni edition, 1915, realization of Bach *Chromatic Fantasy and Fugue,* m. 37.

However, in this same section in the 1915 edition, Busoni indicates to play Bach's designated chord as an organ, followed by harp-like arpeggios (ex. 9.7).[5] The ensuing arpeggios are smoothly fingered without any lifts except in the pedal at certain harmonic changes (ex. 9.5b). Busoni creates tension by moving from sixteenth-note arpeggios to thirty-second note figures with the build to a dynamic climax that loses steam in its diminuendo and eventual tenuto chords (exx. 9.5c and 9.5d). It would be feasible in all arpeggiated passages to take the accented upper note with the left hand (exx. 9.5a, 9.5b, 9.5c, and 9.5d). The final andante brings the passage to the following recitative section (ex. 9.5d).[6] Pianists are well advised to compare the two editions.

Notes

1. C. P. E. Bach, *Essay on the True Art of Playing Keyboard Instruments*, trans. and ed., William J. Mitchell (New York: Norton, 1949), chapter 7, 430–445. First published 1753.

2. J. S. Bach *Chromatic Fantasy and Fugue*, BWV 903, Bach-Gesellschaft *Ausgabe*, vol. 36, ed. Ernst Naumann (Leipzig: Breitkopf & Härtel / Bach), 1890.

3. J. S. Bach, *Chromatic Fantasy and Fugue*, ed. Ferruccio Busoni (Berlin: N. Simrock, 1902).

4. J. S. Bach, *Chromatic Fantasy and Fugue*, 1915.

5. J. S. Bach, *Chromatic Fantasy and Fugue*, 1915.

6. Also see David Schulenberg, *The Keyboard Music of J. S. Bach*, 2nd ed. (New York: Routledge, 2006).

10 Bach's Poetic Meter

> Bach knows so perfectly the analogies between the working-out of a musical piece and the art of rhetoric, that people not only listen to him with satisfaction and delight when he expounds lucidly upon the resemblances and correspondences between the two, but admire the skillful application of them in his work.
>
> —Johann Birnbaum (1702–1748)[1]

Bach would have been well acquainted with musical rhetoric, because the subject was taught in the schools during the German Baroque era and referred to as "speech-in-tones."[2] Rhetoric was described as having four stages:

1. *Inventio* (the creation of appropriate thematic materials)
2. *Dispositio* (formal organization)
3. *Decoratio* (ornamentation or decoration)
4. *Pronuntiatio* (delivery or performance)[3]

Beyond speech (in which "music follows the patterns of speech, and should be articulated accordingly"), rhetoric could be applied to semantics (applied at the *Decoratio* stage for extramusical meaning) and structure (following "the principles of a good oration, as described in classical and Renaissance treatises").[4] Composition and performance were thus compared to verbal oratory in its creation and delivery. Text and music were a natural marriage; although they are easier to see in his vocal works, Bach nevertheless used these ideas in his keyboard compositions.

Rhetoric in Speech in Bach's Keyboard Works

In the context of musical discourse or musical rhetoric, musical articulation and phrasing have its basis in ancient Greek poetry. The term "feet" represented a sequence of syllables that had specific characteristics. For example, a short-long (unstressed-stressed) motive would be called an "iamb" foot; a long-short a "trochee" foot; and so on. Table 10.1 gives some examples of Bach usage of motivic poetic meter. The general Greek poetic meters are expressed here as follows:

- Short or unstressed (U)
- Long or stressed (—)
- Iambic (U—)
- Trochaic (—U)
- Spondaic (——)
- Pyrrhic (U U), consists of two syllables
- Anapestic (U U—), three syllables
- Dactylic (—U U), three syllables
- Amphibrachic (—U—), three syllables

Just a brief glance at Bach's fugues from the Well-tempered *Clavier* is enough to see how well acquainted he was with these ideas.

Table 10.1. Greek poetic meter in Bach's WTC; some examples

Meter Style (S = Short; L = Long)	**Syllabic Count**	**Bach Work**
Iambic (S–L)	Two syllables	Fugue, E-flat Minor, WTC I; Italian Concerto, BWV 971, opening
Trochaic (L–S)	Two syllables	Fugue, E-flat Major, WTC II, BWV 876, Gigues, Sicillenes
Spondaic (L–L)	Two syllables	Fugue, B-flat Minor, WTC II, BWV 891
Pyrrhic (S–S)	Two syllables	Fugue, B-flat Major, WTC I, BWV 866
Anapestic (S–S–L)	Three syllables	Fugue, F Minor, WTC II, BWV 881
Dactylic (L–S–S)	Three syllables	Fugue, E Major, WTC II, BWV 878
Amphibrachic (L–S–L)	Three syllables	Fugue, G Minor, WTC II, BWV 885

Especially relevant are the short-long-short-long (iambic) and long-short-long-short (trochaic) figures or rhythms, which abound in Baroque dances. These are closely allied to the concept of "good" and "bad" fingers with their accented and unaccented notes. According to concert pianist and scholar George Kochevitsky, most of Bach's music is constructed iambically.[5] For fingering purposes, this would imply a change of fingering on repeated-note upbeat figures. Bach's youngest son, J. C. Bach (1735–1782), suggested that in a minuet "the keyboard player must only accent the alternate measures [thereby falling into groups of two] to aid the dancer's ear."[6]

Regardless of the Greek meter used by Bach, he also incorporated these into works or motives with masculine, or downbeat, and feminine, or upbeat, beginnings. One example of a masculine beginning is the D-minor Concerto, first movement, which uses an anapestic meter of short-short-long. This meter might be considered to have a weak beginning, but in Bach's case the first short note is a strong one that leads to the long note. Another example is the Bourée of the G Major French Suite. An example of a feminine beginning is found in the theme of the E Major Prelude of WTC II. Even though this iambic motive occurs as an upbeat to the second beat, its prominent place is still heard as a feminine beginning.

Table 10.2 shows some other rhetorical concepts that Bach uses in his keyboard works.[7]

Table 10.2. Additional examples of Bach's rhetoric

Name	Description	Bach Work
Abruptio	A sudden and unexpected break in the piece	Italian Concerto, I, BWV 971, ending
Analepsis	Homophonic texture	E-flat Minor Prelude, WTC I, BWV 853, chorale preludes, many examples
Ecphonesis or Exclamatio	An outcry or a violent exclamation	D-sharp Minor Fugue, WTC I, BWV 853. Although this example is purely subjective, one interpretation of the fugue may be seen as an outcry to the pain expressed in the preceding E-flat Minor Prelude, WTC I.
Fuga	The imitation of a principal voice in other voices	WTC, toccatas, many examples
Groppo	A four-note motive in arch formation with a common first and third note	An expanded version of this idea is found in the Two-part Invention in F Major, BWV 779
Pathopoeia	Chromaticism	*Chromatic Fantasy and Fugue*, BWV 903, many other examples
Pausa	Pause in music for emphasis	Toccata in D Major, BWV 912, Adagio
Variatio, Coloratura, diminution, Passagio	An ornamentation of a melodic passage with a variety of embellishments	Italian Concerto, II, BWV 971; many other examples

Rhetoric in Semantics in Bach's Keyboard Works

The entire question of ornamentation, whether expressly written out (as in Bach's Sarabande of English Suite in A Minor or his Italian Concerto, II) or extemporaneously done by the performer at the time of performance is related to semantics. The reader is encouraged to study C. P. E. Bach's chapters from his *Essay* on ornamentation and fingering and to continue the study of rhetoric as it relates to fingering in Bach.[8] Clearly, whatever ornamentation is chosen, the melodic contour and rhythmic stability need to be considered.

Rhetoric in Structure: Some Dance Examples from Bach's Keyboard Works[9]

Musicologists Meredith Little and Natalie Jenne note that "Bach knew personally or knew the work of three eminent French dancing masters in Saxony: Johannes Pasch [1653–1710]), Pantaleon Hehenstreit [1667–1750], and Jean-Baptiste Volumier [c. 1670–1728]."[10] He had opportunities to see, know, and experience French court dance. "We may fairly conclude that French court dancing and French influences were an intrinsic, important, and graceful component of Bach's world, and that his titled dance music reflects the noble and subtle movements of early ballet."[11]

Understanding the natural flow of these dances (usually binary and AB form, or ternary and ABA form) and knowing the dance steps with their tempi will assist the pianist to find the best fingering. One of the most complex dances is the louré, described by many French writers as a "slow gigue."[12] Perhaps the best-known example is found in the G Major French Suite, BWV 816. In some editions, this louré is titled as Bourée II. Often, students perform this incorrectly, missing the large, slow pulse of the dance, and in order to get this, the music has to flow.

The choice of execution, given the variety of rhythmic figures in Bach's sarabandes (see ex. 10.1), will be of interest to the pianist when selecting a suitable fingering that aptly portrays the spirit of the Baroque dance. The sarabande rhythm usually features an elongated second beat, so careful pedaling will be important to the pianist as the sound decays. Studying the rhetorical character of the rhythm will help to understand the phrasing and thus the fingering.[13]

A. "Normal" saraband rhythm

B. English Suite in a and French Suite in d

C. English Suite in g

D. English Suite in d

E. French Suite in c

F. Partita in D

G. Partita in B-flat

Example 10.1. J. S. Bach's varying rhythms in his sarabandes.

For example, in Bach's Sarabande from the English Suite in A Minor, BWV 807, two-note slurring is implied in two-measure phrases (ex. 10.2a). The fingering given reflects this musical concept. When applying the ornaments that he prescribes, the performer will want to remain aware of the pulse (ex. 10.2b).[14]

Example 10.2a. J. S. Bach, Sarabande from English Suite in A Minor, BWV807, mm. 1–4.

Example 10.2b. J. S. Bach, Sarabande from English Suite in A Minor, BWV807, Bach's ornament realization, mm. 1–2.

Notes inégales

Music notation is an inaccurate science. During the Baroque period and even beyond, performers were supposed to have been versed in the art of understanding notational performance practice. Today, as Malcolm Bilson has pointed out, there has not been one music conservatory that teaches a course on this art.[15] As such, music conventions sometimes get ignored.

Around the eighteenth century, the organist and composer François Couperin made this observation about the problem of notating *notes inégales*:

> It seems to me that there are faults in our method of writing music which are like faults in the spelling of the French language. The fact is that we do not write as we play. What we see does not correspond to what we hear. This causes foreigners to play our music less well than we do theirs. On the contrary, Italians write their music with the true time values that they intend. For example: when there are several eighth-notes in diatonic succession, we dot them; yet we write them as equal. Our custom has enslaved us.[16]

The use of *notes inégales* became prevalent in France and in some other European countries during the Baroque and even Classical eras. It applied a rhythmic variant to passages of even notes, usually eighth or sixteenth notes. These variants were usually long-short (trochaic) groupings and sometimes were inverted to short-long (iambic) groupings. The amount of inequality of the performed notes would naturally depend on the work's character. There are basically three types of rhythmically altered conventions:

1. *Notes inégales* themselves
2. The overdot, sometimes also referred to as "double dotting" and "extra-dotting"; Leopold Mozart suggests that the "prolonging of the dot is always robbed from the quick note that follows it";[17] this practice is called *pointer* or overdotting by the French
3. Some kind of deviation from normal dotting "applied for the purposes of synchronizing dotted-note rhythms with simultaneously presented patterns of a different type."[18]

Bach was surely acquainted with works by his French colleagues, especially those of François Couperin and Jean-Philippe Rameau. In describing the French influence in Bach's works, Karl Friedrich Zelter (1758–1832) wrote to the German poet, J. W. von Goethe (1749–1832), in a letter dated June 9, 1827: "What I call the French foam in Sebastian Bach's music cannot--I must admit--be so readily lifted off that you can lay your hands on it. It is like ether: it permeates all, yet is intangible. . . . Indeed he made most successful attempts to write in this style [i.e., that of F. Couperin] himself, and in this way those curly French wigs found their way into his music."[19]

The practice of *notes inégales*, or at least writing about it, all but disappeared until the end of the nineteenth century. The French-born musician, Arnold Dolmetsch (1858–1940), in 1916, supported the practice of *notes inégales* without reservation, such as in J. S. Bach's E-flat Minor Prelude, WTC I, BWV 853, and the Sarabande from D-minor French Suite, BWV 812 (ex. 10.3b).[20]

Violinist and musicologist Frederick ("Fritz") Neumann commented on Bach's use of rhythmic inequality. He noted that Bach employed "rhythmic flexibility for the sake of a definite *Affect* . . . applied agogic accents, used *rubato* techniques of all kinds, varied the tempo, sharpened rhythm here, softened it there."[21]

Yet another scholar, the British Robert Donington (1907–1990), was unsure whether Bach used inequality in performance. However, he pointed out that his music falls "within the styles to which we can be sure from German as well as French sources that inequality might have been properly applied by good contemporary performers."[22]

American musicologist Michael Collins (d. 2001) advised that when Bach's triplets are performed, they should resolve into binary figures when the context is primarily binary, but "where the ternary rhythm dominates the dotted figures should adjust to it."[23] If the pianist opts for *notes inégales*, fingering would then be dependent on the iambic or trochaic nature of the work, as well as the binary or ternary underlying pulse.

There is a distinction between *notes inégales* and the overdot. *Notes inégales* generally takes the binary notes or duple notes, such as eighth notes or sixteenth notes, and turns them into a ternary or triplet figure. Jazz performers today are well acquainted with this concept and call them “swing” figures, such as “swing eighths” (ex. 10.3a).

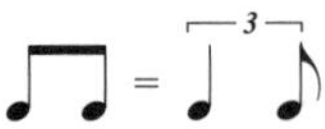

Example 10.3a. Swung eighth notes in jazz, also used in *notes inégales.*

Example 10.3b. J. S. Bach, Sarabande from French Suite in D Minor, BWV 812, mm. 1–2.

The Sarabande from Bach’s English Suite in A Minor, BWV 807, already mentioned (ex. 10.2b) could be performed with *notes inégales.* Certainly, the character of the Sarabande from Bach’s D-minor French Suite, BWV 812, (ex. 10.3b) becomes more poignant with *notes inégales.*

George A. Kochevitsky’s conclusion about the complex use of *notes inégales* in Bach’s music may or may not be accepted by pianists: “If the use of *notes inégales* was––and is––necessary in harpsichord performance to achieve accent through the prolonging of a tone, to make a small pause or to add to one’s performance some kind of expression which will compensate for the absence of dynamic shadings, such a device is not necessary in a pianoforte performance and would be perceived today as an unpleasant and strange distortion.”[24]

The Overdot

The overdot does exactly what Kochevitsky described as in the preceding paragraph as *notes inégales*: it prolongs a tone and is followed by a small breath or rest, which is then followed by a tone that is shorter than what is notated. Many such examples are found in Bach’s works.

In the example below, Bach has composed a French Overture to open his second Partita, in C Minor, BWV 826. As such, the pianist should take care to properly ensure the practice of the overdot. The fingerings and realization are given in example 10.4a and 10.4b. The acoustical properties of the piano and the

Example 10.4a. J. S. Bach, Partita in C Minor, BWV 826, opening, m. 1.

Example 10.4b. J. S. Bach, Partita in C Minor, BWV 826, rhythm of opening with overdot, m. 1.

venue will have to be taken into consideration with regard to the pedal and the amount of space between notes. Obviously, the more resonant the hall, the less pedal is needed and the more space between notes may be had.

Some other keyboard examples of works by J. S. Bach that would (already written out) or could (implied) use inequality are as follows:

- *Ouverture nach Französischer Art*, BWV 831a, Overture
- Fugue in D Major, WTC I, BWV 850
- Fugue in D Minor, WTC II, BWV 874
- Overture from the D Major Partita (sixteenth notes in the opening slow section), BWV 828
- *Kunst der Fuge*, Fugue II (or "Contrapunctus II"), BWV 1080
- Bach's ornamented version of the English Suite in A Minor (see especially mm. 5–8), BWV 807
- French Gigue, Suite in G Minor (arranged from another composer?), BWV 822
- French Gigue, Suite in F minor (fragment), BWV 823
- French Gigue, from French Suite II in C Minor, BWV 813
- French Gigue, Overture in the French Style, BWV 831
- Louré from the French Suite in G Major, BWV 816

Fingering in Metric Shifts

Metric displacement frequently occurs in the Baroque period, often in dances. Sometimes it appears as hemiola. Bach used hemiolas in many of his $\frac{3}{2}$ courantes, especially at cadence points. (His nineteen French courantes are all in $\frac{3}{2}$, except for the $\frac{6}{4}$ courante from the third French Suite in B Minor, BWV 814.)[25]

In the $\frac{6}{8}$ section of measures 71–77 of Bach's Overture in the French Style, BWV 831 (ex. 10.5), you can perceive the polymeter if you remove the bar lines and then look at the melodic entrances in each hand. This practice will help you

Example 10.5. J. S. Bach, Overture in the French Style, BWV 831, mm. 71–77.[26]

find a good fingering that will bring out the underlying metric displacements. The cadence in m. 77 is a clear case of a meter shift from a binary to a ternary pulse; the left-hand fingering and phrase groupings will especially need to emphasize this change. For example, the right-hand thumb may be used on the C-sharps in m. 71 and the left-hand fifth finger may be used on the C-sharps in mm. 72–73.

Bach's Courante from the Suite in E-flat Major, BWV 819 (ex. 10.6), although structurally regular, is actually metrically irregular. The time signature of this courante is $\frac{3}{2}$, yet the underlying pulse is felt mostly in $\frac{6}{4}$. A ternary overlay in the right hand with a binary underpinning in the left hand is found in mm. 26–27. The penultimate measure (m. 31) can be interpreted as either $\frac{3}{2}$ or $\frac{6}{4}$.[27] The left-hand octave leaps would not be connected and would be fingered with thumb and fifth finger (mm. 19–21, 23–26, 27, 30). In this same way, the G and B-flat in m. 31 would not be connected, in order to maintain the lilt of the dance.

Example 10.6. J. S. Bach, Courante from the Suite in E-flat Major, BWV 819, second half, mm. 17–32.[28]

In choosing a fingering to portray a metric shift, the performer will want to consider whether or not accents or agogics are needed. In some cases, it may be best to let the music speak for itself and to let the listener delight in the discovery of the musical joke being played.

Notes

1. Birnbaum in Albert Schweitzer, *J. S. Bach*, vol. 1, trans. Ernest Newman (New York: Macmillan, 2007), 185–186.

2. Sam Nester, "Modern Performance Trends in Bach's Sacred Music: Changing Tastes in the Performance of Bach's Weihnachtsoratorium: An Exploration of the Rhetorical Style," Bachelor of Music Honors Thesis, Western Australian Academy of Performing Arts, 2009, 13. ro.ecu.edu.au/theses_hons/1323/.

3. Nester, "Modern Performance Trends," 17. For more discussion on this topic, see Richard Troeger, *Playing Bach on the Keyboard: A Practical Guide* (Pompton Plains, NJ: Amadeus Press, 2003), chap. 12, "Musical Rhetoric."

4. Nester, "Modern Performance Trends," 17.

5. George Kochevitsky, *Performing Bach's Keyboard Music* (White Plains, NY: ProAm Music Resources, 1996), 33.

6. Margery Halford, *The Harpsichord Manual: An Introduction to the Technic, Ornamentation and Performance Practices* (Sherman Oaks, CA: Alfred, 1980), 20.

7. See Nester, "Modern Performance Trends," app. I, vii–xi.

8. Dietrich Bartel, *Musica Poetica:* Musical-rhetorical *Figures in German Baroque Music* (Lincoln: University of Nebraska Press, 1997). Sam Nester lists the rhetorical elements as follows: "1. Exordium (introduction); 2. Narratio (presenting the issue); 3. Propositio (presenting the speaker's thesis); 4. Confirmatio (presenting the main arguments supporting the thesis); 5.Confutatio (refutation of opposing arguments); 6. Peroratio/Conclusio (conclusion)," cited in "Modern Performance Trends," 19. See also Troeger, *Playing Bach*, chap. 12, "Musical Rhetoric."

9. For a comprehensive list of titled (appendix A) and untitled dances (appendix B) in Bach's works, see Meredith Little and Natalie Jenne, *Dance and the Music of J. S. Bach*, expanded ed. (Bloomington: Indiana University Press, 2009).

10. Little and Jenne, *Dance and the Music of J. S. Bach*, 13–14.

11. Little and Jenne, *Dance and the Music of J. S. Bach*, 14.

12. Little and Jenne, *Dance and the Music of J. S. Bach*, 186.

13. F. E. Kirby, *A Short History of Keyboard Music* (New York: Free Press, 1966), 136.

14. J. S. Bach, *Englische Suiten*, ed. by Rudolf Steglich and fingered by Hans-Martin Theopold, 33.

15. Malcolm Bilson is Emeritus Professor of Performance Keyboard/Fortepiano and Frederick J. Whiton Professor of Music at Cornell University in Ithaca, New York. He has made a series of DVDs on performance practice in the Classical era: *Knowing the Score,* vol. 1 (now at https://www.youtube.com/watch?v=mVGN_YAX03A) and vol. 2; and *Performing the Score* (with violinist Elizabeth Field), available at www.malcolmbilson.com. He has made a series of recordings, with some of his students, on period instruments of the complete Beethoven piano sonatas (Claves CD 9707–10). He has also recorded the complete Mozart piano concerti with John Eliot Gardiner and the English Baroque Soloists (DG Archiv E4631112) and the complete Mozart and Schubert piano

sonatas (Hungaraton 31009/14 and 31592). The asteroid 7387 Maibil, discovered in 1982, is named for him.

16. Couperin, *L'art de toucher le clavecin* (1717); cited in Kochevitsky, *Performing Bach's Keyboard Music*, 52.

17. Halford, *Harpsichord Manual*, 24.

18. Kochevitsky, *Performing Bach's Keyboard Music*, 53.

19. Zelter-Goethe correspondence cited in Hans-Joachim Schulze, "The French Influence in Bach's Instrumental Music," *Early Music* 13, no. 2 (May 1985): 180–184.

20. Kochevitsky, *Performing Bach's Keyboard Music*, 53–54.

21. Frederick Neumann in Kochevitsky, *Performing Bach's Keyboard Music*, 54.

22. Robert Donington in Kochevitsky, *Performing Bach's Keyboard Music*, 58, 63n25.

23. Michael Collins in Kochevitsky, *Performing Bach's Keyboard Music*, 57.

24. Kochevitsky, *Performing Bach's Keyboard Music*, 59.

25. Even though notated as $\frac{3}{2}$, the "proper rhythm" is $\frac{6}{4}$. According to Marpurg, Bach left "genuine models of the proper Courante time." Marpurg in Little and Jenne, *Dance and the Music of J. S. Bach*, 123.

26. Troeger, *Playing Bach*, 129.

27. Little and Jenne, *Dance and the Music of J. S. Bach*, 127.

28. J. S. Bach, *French Suite in* E-flat, Bach-Gesellschaft-*Ausgabe*, vol. 36, ed. Ernst Naumann (Leipzig: Breitkopf and Härtel / Bach Gesellschaft), 1890.v

11 Singing with the Fingers

Crossing over and turning under of the fingers are helpful techniques for ease of execution of multiple voices, whether in one hand or both. Frequent dialogue, between the hands or between different voices in one hand, occurs often in Bach's works. An unforced clarity occurs naturally on the harpsichord, due to the nature of its acoustic properties, its construction, and its evenly plucked strings. On the contrary, the pianist is forced to sculpt the polyphonic voices due to the piano's hammer action and loud-soft capabilities. Good fingering can go a long way to help produce the different articulations on either instrument and dynamic intensities on the piano.

Some solutions are explored in the following examples: (1) Bach's Allemande from the C-minor French Suite; and (2) two enharmonic versions of a Bach fugue, von Irmer's edition in D-sharp minor and Carl Czerny's later edition in E-flat minor. Notice how the fugue takes on a different character in von Irmer's edition, which was the key of the original manuscript at the *Staatsbibliothek*, Berlin, and the earlier *Bach Gesellschaft* edition, as compared to Carl Czerny's edition.[1] Both Czerny and von Irmer take the lower alto voice with the left hand (mm. 5–7), as indicated by the downward stems and by the fingering. Although it could be feasible to play the alto voice with the soprano in only the right hand, both Czerny and Irmer facilitate the execution of this passage by giving left-hand fingering.

The opening of the C-minor Allemande could be fingered as shown in example 11.1.[2] An alternate fingering of the same passage would be to start with the right-hand 2–1. This fingering would oblige a cross over from finger 5 on the D to finger 4 on the E-flat. This would then be followed by 5 on the D and then continue on as given. The fingering chosen will want to facilitate the execution of the dialogue between the upper and lower voices. The performer has to determine

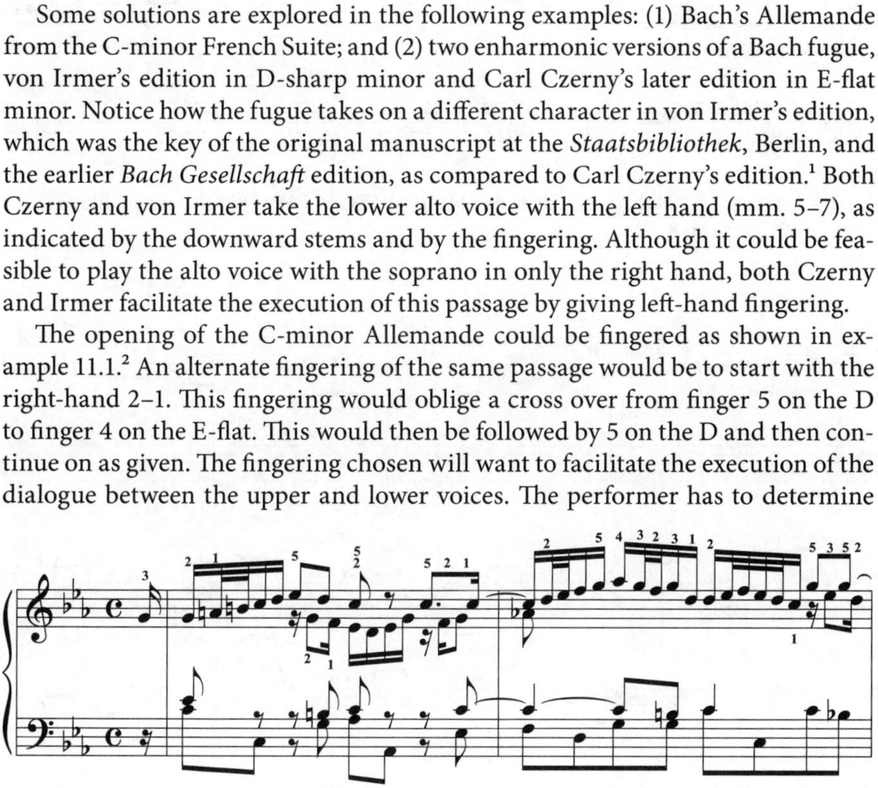

Example 11.1. J. S. Bach, French Suite in C Minor, BWV 813, Allemande, mm. 1–2.

whether all voices will be played legato or whether some non-legato will highlight a voice or motive better. This decision will be governed somewhat by the instrument.

In Bach's fugue, usually performed today as notated in E-flat minor (ex. 11.2a) but originally written as D-sharp minor fugue (ex. 11.2b), the pianist would need to determine the kind of character to be conveyed and to consider the articulation. If the goal is to play long legato lines, a careful fingering will be indispens-

Example 11.2a. J. S. Bach, Fugue in E-flat Minor, WTC, I, BWV 853, Czerny edition, mm. 5–12, see mm. 8–9.[3]

Example 11.2b. J. S. Bach, Fugue in D-sharp Minor, WTC, I, BWV 853, von Irmer *Urtext* edition, mm. 5–12, see mm. 8–9.[4]

able. It would not be within good Baroque practice, even on the piano, to make a lift after the fifth eighth note in the right hand in m. 8, which would sound then like an upbeat to the following measure and would break the line. This is because of the left-hand motivic figure in which the dotted note must connect to the following eighth note. If the performer hears the long line of the motive, there is less likely to be a break in the line when a good fingering is chosen. The main difference between the two fingering examples is found in m. 9. The Czerny edition (ex. 11.2a)[3] requires a thumb slide going from mm. 10–11, while the von Irmer edition (ex. 11.2b)[4] offers a smoother solution by virtue of the hand redistribution.

Finger Substitution

Organists and harpsichord players frequently use the art of finger substitution, pianists less so. This technique ensures a true legato and may be used in singing passages as well. Finger substitution may be done slowly or quickly as the music requires. Grace and skill are needed in fast passages so as not to have unwanted extraneous sounds or motions. For some performers, the most difficult finger substitution may be 1–5 or 5–1. When using these extremes of the hand, some performers will feel uncomfortable with the forced contraction of the hand. Keeping a supple wrist will be paramount to ensure comfort with any finger substitution.

C. P. E. advises on this practice that "when two numerals appear in succession over a single note, the first of the assigned fingers is not released until the second has arrived."[5] He continues, "Because it is not easy to employ this device skillfully it is correctly restricted to relatively long notes and cases of necessity."[6] He also noted that the thumb is especially good for this kind of device but that pupils should not use it except as a "last resort" or to avoid an even greater difficulty.[7]

Finger substitution is particularly valuable in slow movements, when a cantabile and/or legato quality is desired, even on the piano when using the pedal. In Bach's Toccata in G Major, BWV 916, Adagio (ex. 11.3),[8] the soprano voice is sustained through finger substitution.

Example 11.3. J. S. Bach, Toccata in G Major, BWV 916, Adagio, mm. 65–68.

Finger Slides

According to C. P. E. Bach, black key slides were permitted.[9] This practical technique is used to maintain rhythmic pulse and continuation of the melodic line. He points out that the "repeated finger is more natural, even on successive tied notes . . . than the replaced finger."[10] Pianists today will find this technique to be useful in many situations.

Two examples of finger slides are given. The first (ex. 11.4a), Scarlatti's Sonata in B Minor, K. 87, is probably in a moderately slow tempo, although the slide is not immediate. Most pianists will not have to use a finger slide in the opening of Scarlatti's Sonata in D Major, K. 490 (ex. 11.4b). However, those with small hands may be more comfortable playing the grace note to its resolution with right hand finger 5 in a quick slide.

Example 11.4a. Domenico Scarlatti, Sonata in B Minor, K. 87, mm. 8–11.

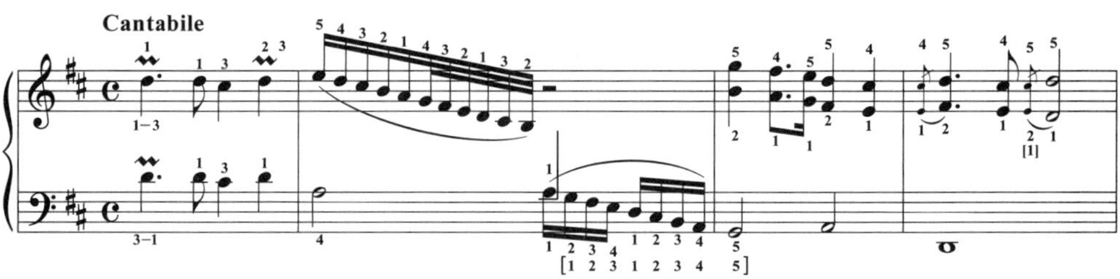

Example 11.4b. Domenico Scarlatti, Sonata in D Major, K. 490, mm. 1–4.

Finger Pedaling

In an earlier chapter, it was mentioned that the pianist and scholar Malcolm Bilson (b. 1935) noted in his film *Knowing the Score* that, to his knowledge, no music school offers a course on how to read the musical score.[11] He is referring to understanding the performance practice inherent in a musical score, not the literal notes. Two examples from Bach's works offer examples of how pianists have to understand the performance practice of this era. Both employ finger pedaling, a concept of holding down notes that are not indicated to be held in order to give a rich and more sustained sound.

In Bach's F-minor Prelude, WTC, I, BWV 857 (ex. 11.5), the quarter notes are not meant to be accented melodically, as they might be in nineteenth-century music, but rather serve as harmonic enrichment. A closer look at the score reveals that the melody is in the upper voice.[12] Therefore, a fingering should be carefully chosen and executed so that the melody is distinguished from the harmony.

Example 11.5. J. S. Bach, F-minor Prelude, WTC, I, BWV 857, mm. 1–2.

Bach often uses figures that contain two voices but are written out as one. Pianists will need to employ finger pedaling in order to convey the duality of the texture. This type of tenuto touch is immensely important in the performance of early keyboard music. It provides tonal and textural contrast, adds warmth of sound, and virtually takes the place of the sustaining pedal of a modern piano. It must be used with discretion, however, and never with notes that are extraneous to the harmony.[13] Possible fingering choices are shown in Bach's French Suite in E-Flat, BWV 815 (ex. 11.6): right hand 1–5–4–1–2–5–3–2, etc. Putting either the thumb or second finger on the lower notes will make finger pedaling possible.

Example 11.6. J. S. Bach, French Suite in E-flat, BWV 815, Allemande, mm. 3–5, as written, as played.

Finger pedaling can be an enriching technique no matter on what keyboard it is employed. The well-informed interpreter will use it effectively.

Notes

1. J. S. Bach, *Das wohltemperierte Klavier, Teil 1,* urtext edition, ed. Otto von Irmer and Hans-Martin Theopold (Munich: G. Henle Verlag, 1974); J. S. Bach, Well-Tempered *Clavichord, Book 1,* ed. Carl Czerny (New York: Schirmer, 1893).
2. J. S. Bach, "C Minor Allemande," in *Keyboard Music* (from the Bach-Gesellschaft-*Ausgabe* edition; Reprint, New York: Dover, 1970), 94.
3. J. S. Bach, Well-Tempered *Clavichord, Book 1,* ed. Carl Czerny (New York: Schirmer, 1893), 40.

4. J. S. Bach, *Das Wohltemperierte Klavier, Teil 1*, urtext edition, ed. Otto von Irmer and fingered by Walther Lampe, 40.

5. C. P. E. Bach, *Essay on the True Art of Playing Keyboard Instruments*, trans. and ed. William J. Mitchell. (New York: Norton, 1949), 72, paragraph 88. First published 1753.

6. C. P. E. Bach, *Essay*, 72, paragraph 88.

7. C. P. E. Bach, *Essay*, 72, paragraph 88.

8. J. S. Bach, *Toccaten*, urtext edition, ed. Rudolf Steglich and fingered by Hans-Martin Theopold (Munich: Henle, 1962), 83.

9. C. P. E. Bach, *Essay*, 73.

10. C. P. E. Bach, *Essay*, 73, paragraph 89.

11. Malcolm Bilson's three DVDs are essential for understanding early music performance practice: *Knowing the Score*, vol. 1 (now at https://www.youtube.com/watch?v=mVGN_YAX03A) and vol. 2; and *Performing the Score* (with violinist Elizabeth Field), available at www.malcolmbilson.com.

12. Howard Ferguson, *Keyboard Interpretation from the 14th to the 19th Century* (Oxford: Oxford University Press, 1998), 60.

13. Ferguson, *Keyboard Interpretation*, 61.

12 Dancing with the Fingers: A Guide to Understanding Scarlatti's Iberian Sonatas When Choosing Fingering

This chapter does not aim to give specific fingerings for all the Scarlatti sonatas, although some are suggested. Instead, it provides the pianist with a guide to the Iberian characteristics of these sonatas so as to make intelligent fingering choices.

It is known that Scarlatti's patron, Queen Maria Bárbara, had a passion for the dance.[1] As in Bach's dances, it is important for the pianist to understand what kind of dance is being portrayed and where the strong beats lie in Scarlatti's sonatas when choosing a fingering. Sometimes Scarlatti literally depicts an event (K. 491) or mixes Italian (tarantellas, siciliennes, Neapolitan characteristics, etc.) with Iberian elements in one sonata.

In Scarlatti's Portuguese manuscript collections (table 12.1), one sonata slipped through the catalogers' fingers. The Sonata in A Major (Fundo do Conde de Redondo [FCR] 194.1 Lx25) appears only in the collection, *Libro di Tocate per Cembalo e Tutti del Sig.nr Cavaliero D. Domenico Scarlatti*. I made the first recording on modern piano, following that by Cremilde Rosado Fernandes on the sweet-sounding Antunes harpsichord (1758) published with the *Libro*. In the Lx25 Sonata in A major, fingering follows a traditional route, while the successive left-hand thirds in m. 1 (ex. 12.1) establish a lively character.[2]

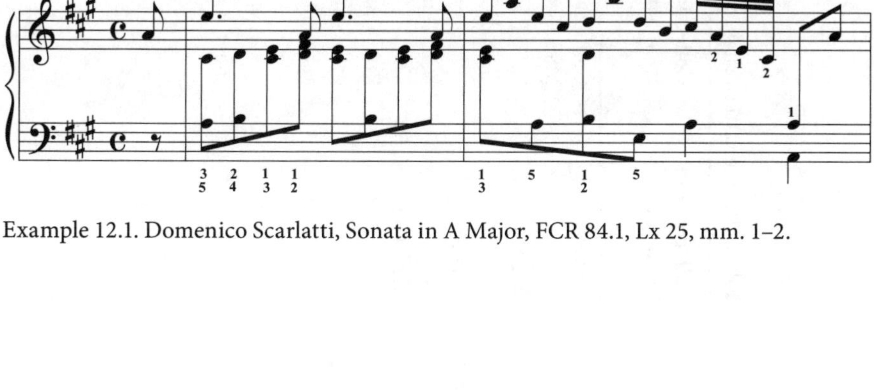

Example 12.1. Domenico Scarlatti, Sonata in A Major, FCR 84.1, Lx 25, mm. 1–2.

Table 12.1. Scarlatti sonatas in Portuguese collections

Collection and Its Sonatas	Collection and Its Sonatas	Collection and Its Sonatas	Instrument Range and Relevant Sonatas	Instrument Range and Relevant Sonatas	Other Portuguese Sonatas
Essercizi	Coimbra Manuscript, MSS 58	*Libro di Tocate per Cembalo*, FCR 94.1	Portuguese harpsicord, C–D'''	Portuguese harpsicord, C–E'''	Various Ranges
Sonatas	K. 78 (two movements: Gigha/Minuet)	FCR 194.1 Lx25	24 of the *Essercizi*	K. 44	K. 58 (Fugue). Range: C–C'''
		K. 43, 44, 53–55, 96,		K. 98	
K. 1–29		98, 101, 103, 104, 112,		K. 101	
	K. 82 (Fugue)	116, 118, 124, 125, 130,		K. 103	Fado, K. 426
"Cat" Fugue, K. 30		131, 134, 135, 145, 155,		K. 124	Range: GG–G'''
	K. 85 (maybe sketch for orchestral work for strings and continuo)	158, 159, 161, 175, 179, 182, 198, 203, 215, 216, 378, 396, 397, 410, 411,		K. 131 K. 145 K. 155	Portuguese folk music, K. 238 ("O meu menino está dormindo");
		424–427, 430, 435, 437,		K 158	
	K. 94 (Minuet). All of the sonatas are in F Major.	438, 441, 442, 445, 446, 448, 462, 463, 465–467, 474, 475, 480.		K. 159 K. 161 K. 179 K. 437 K. 448	K. 239 (corridinho). Range for both: C–D'''

Ralph Kirkpatrick, Scarlatti biographer and cataloger, pairs K. 238 (ex. 12.2) with K. 239 (ex. 12.4). The former, according to harpsichordist Cremilde Rosado Fernandes, is based on the Portuguese song from the ribatejo, “O meu menino esta dormindo” (My baby boy is sleeping).[3] If the pianist considers this piece to be a “lullaby,” then the initial motive could be played as written or as triplets (ex. 12.2), which occur later (ex. 12.3). An argument could be made that the opening motive is a form of *notes inégales*, to be played in a more gentler rhythm similar to the triplet pattern of “swing eighths.” This decision will also determine the fingering and articulations. Either way would seem viable.

Example 12.2. Domenico Scarlatti, Sonata in F Minor, K. 238, mm. 1–2.

Example 12.3. Domenico Scarlatti, Sonata in F Minor, K. 238, mm. 18–20.

Sonata K. 239 in F Minor is a corridinho or Portuguese circle dance (ex. 12.4). The inherent percussion accompaniment figure in the left hand fortifies the dance-like character of this sonata (ex. 12.5).

Example 12.4. Domenico Scarlatti, Sonata in F Minor, K. 239, mm. 1–2.

Example 12.5. Domenico Scarlatti, Sonata in F Minor, K. 239, mm. 41–43.

Some sources have cited that the Sonata in G Minor, K. 426 (ex. 12.6), is indicative of the Portuguese soulful fado, by virtue of its interrupted phrases. The fado is expressively sung, often in cafés and bars, and is accompanied by the Portuguese guitar.

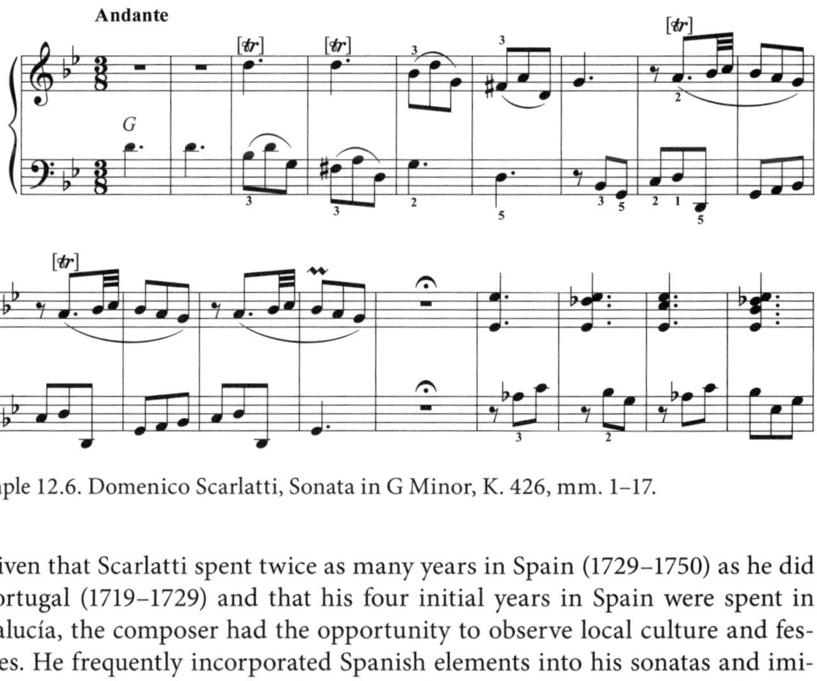

Example 12.6. Domenico Scarlatti, Sonata in G Minor, K. 426, mm. 1–17.

Given that Scarlatti spent twice as many years in Spain (1729–1750) as he did in Portugal (1719–1729) and that his four initial years in Spain were spent in Andalucía, the composer had the opportunity to observe local culture and festivities. He frequently incorporated Spanish elements into his sonatas and imitated the guitar's punteado (plucked) (ex. 12.7) and rasgueado (strummed) techniques (ex. 12.8). The rhythmic motive in example 12.8 is enhanced by beginning the left-hand 5 on each figure, with little or no pedal. Earlier in chapter 7 (exx. 7.1 and 7.2), examples of guitar-like punteado had been mentioned in the context of repeated notes or Scarlatti's indication of "mutandi i deti" (Sonata in D Major, K. 96), as well as in Sonata in D Minor, K. 141. In example 12.7, I have suggested a fingering that portrays the punteado and greatly facilitates the rapidity of the repeated note execution by allowing the left hand to take the first note on each beat followed by the right hand. At the end, the right hand will cross over in the penultimate figure, thereby allowing the left hand to play the final note with or without an ornament. In this sonata, portions of the transposed descending Phrygian scale (B–A–G–F-sharp), closely associated with Spanish music, occur in mm. 4–7 in the left hand and again in mm. 59–61 in the right hand. This sonata belongs to Scarlatti's omnibus, *Essesrcizi,* published by the Portuguese King John V in a royal-sized edition to commemorate Scarlatti's knighthood and is dated 1738–1739. By that time, Scarlatti had been living in Spain for about a decade, coming and going to other courts possibly as a musical spy for King John.[4]

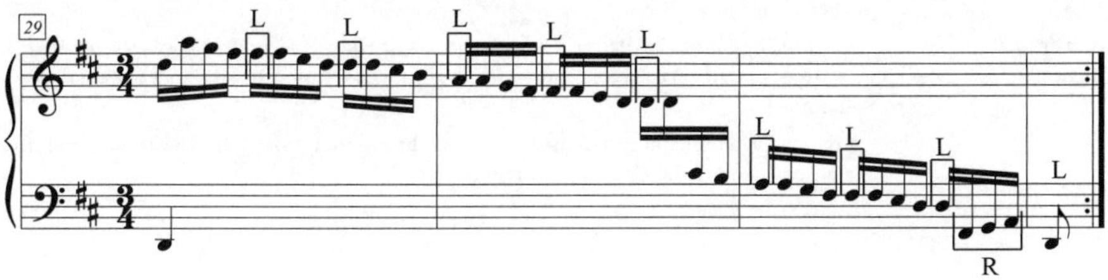

Example 12.7. Domenico Scarlatti, Sonata in B Minor, K. 27, mm. 29–32 (punteado).

Example 12.8. Domenico Scarlatti, Sonata in D Major, K. 492, mm. 26–27 (rasgueado).

Tables 12.2–12.4 give examples of the different dances that influenced Scarlatti's sonatas. They draw from several sources, predominantly the rhythmic figures suggested mostly by Linton Powell and the sonata classificiations by Powell, Dean Sutcliffe, Jane Clark, Kirkpatrick, and others.

Table 12.2. Some flamenco dances found in Scarlatti's sonatas

Spanish Flamenco element	Meaning
Cante jondo	"Deep song" or highly emotional (tragic song); *cante flamenco* (Andalusian song and dance performed by trained musicians to guitar accompaniment; some are malagueñs, peteneras, bulerías, etc.); *cante baile* (Andalusian folk dance)
Bien parado	A moment in the dance when the partners "freeze."
Bolero[3]	A dance in triple meter with a triplet on the first weak beat of the measure; the dance is more deliberate than the seguidilla.[4] The tempo of 88–96 BPM (MM) is comfortable for dancers and should be an indication for keyboard performers.[5]
Bulería	A lively flamenco song and dance in $\frac{3}{8}$ usually with the following rhythmic motive.
Fandango[9]	Old Spanish dance with strongly marked triple time; other types include the malagueña and rondeña (respectively from Malaga and Ronda) or fandangos from Granada, Múrcia, and other areas in Andalusia).
Fandanguillo or little fandango	*Tanguillo de Cádiz,* $\frac{2}{2}$ Allegro; *Tango gaditano*; Scarlatti's second wife was from Cádiz; a native from there is referred to as *gaditano.* In Roman times, street dancers were called *pullae gaditane.*[10]
Jota	A dance form that appears in many variants throughout Spain. The jota aragonesa is in fast triple time and is characterized by triplets.
Malagueña	From Málaga
Petenera	An Andalusian dance characterized by the alternation of $\frac{3}{4}$ and $\frac{3}{8}$ or between $\frac{3}{8}$ and $\frac{2}{4}$
Saeta	An Andalusian folksong sung during Lent or the Feast of the Nativity to accompany street processions and other outdoor devotional activities.
Seguidilla Seguidilla manchega ($\frac{3}{4}$)	A very popular song and dance in a quick triple meter. Several types exist, such as seguidilla sevillana from Seville.
Seguiriya andaluza "gitana"	Alternates between $\frac{6}{8}$ and $\frac{3}{4}$ Andalusian dance, possibly from seguidilla, marked by alternating meters of $\frac{3}{8}$ and $\frac{3}{4}$
Zapateado	Dance in quick time with marked heel stampings.

1. Barbara Zuber, "Wilde Blumen am Zaun der Klassik," in Dean Sutcliffe, *The Keyboard Sonatas of Domenico Scarlatti and Eighteenth-Century Musical Style* (Cambridge, UK: Cambridge University Press, 2003), 18–25.

2. Sutcliffe, *The Keyboard Sonatas of Domenico Scarlatti*, 140–41.

3. The rhythmic examples from the Spanish dances are taken from Linton E. Powell, *A History of Spanish Piano Music* (Bloomington: Indiana University Press, 1980), 184–87.

4. Powell, *A History of Spanish Piano Music*, 184.

5. Luisa Morales in Nancy Lee Harper and Luisa Morales, "European Piano Teachers' Forum: 'Dancing Scarlatti,'" *Piano Journal*, Issue 103 (2014): 29–32.

6. Morales in Harper and Morales, "Dancing Scarlatti," 31.

7. Jane Clark, "Compositor de 'Originales y afortunados Caprichos,'" in *Scherzo*, no. 116, Dosier D. Scarlatti, Año XII (July–August 1997), 112; Powell, *A History of Spanish Piano Music*, 7.

Rhythm	Scarlatti Sonata
Free	K. 193 ("ay" of vocalise or *salida*)[1]
Fermata	K. 476[2]
	Sonata-boleros: K. 380, K. 454, and K. 491, respectively, represent *Bolero de Fuente Álamo* (four sections or AABB); *Bolero de Jaén* (three sections or AAB); *Bolero de los Fernández o de Vera* (three sections or ABB or AAB).[6]
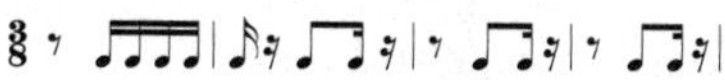	K. 492.[7] Rafael Puyana, calls this sonata a Portuguese fandango.[8] K. 492 and other sonatas in the fandanguillo category
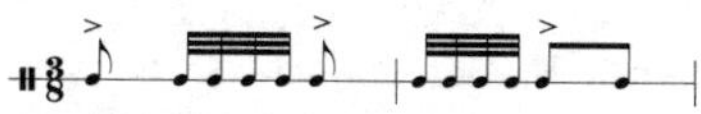 Similar to rhythm of fandango	K. 117, 230, 332, 352, 360, 364, 394, 424, 438, 441, 443, 447, 450, 452, 470, 473, 479, 509, 518, 520 (in the Coda), 526, 547, 550, 552.
	K. 112, 116, 122, 125, 130, 133, 136, 138, 155, 161, 163, 174, 178, 184, 187, 188, 193, 204a, 207, 209, 220, 221, 244, 251, 264, 278, 280, 292, 295, 297, 303, 313, 315, 327, 351, 357, 359, 369, 381, 385, 395, 399, 400, 407, 409, 421, 423, 425, 429, 436, 461, 465, 476, 484, 504, 516, 529, 538, 548. In 6/8 K. 129, 135, 137, 159, 172, 174, 218, 222, 245, 268, 278, 286, 305, 319, 323, 334, 340, 350, 372, 375, 398, 401, 403, 405, 413, 429, 433, 444, 457, 477, 494, 525, 531, 541, 543, 555.
	In 3/8 K. 21, 33, 44, 62, 79, 96, 97, 101, 102, 105, 108. K. 188[11]
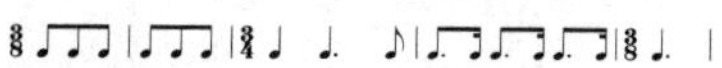	K. 502
No set rhythm; may include siguiriyas, martinets, soleares, por polos, por cañas, por fandangos. May be in 2/4 or 6/8 or may interchange between 3/4 and 6/8 Drum may accompany with this rhythm.[12] 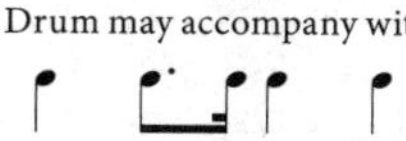	K. 490
	K. 191, 252, 530, 491. Puyana believes that this is a Majorcon bolero.[13]
	K. 203, 315 (at end), 419, 502, 521, 532, 537
	K. 119

8. Rafael Puyana, "Influencias ibéricas y aspectos por investigar en la obra para clave de Domenico Scarlatti," in *España en la música de Occidente*, vol. 2, proceedings of a conference held in Salamanca on October 29–November 5, 1985, eds. Emilio Casares Rodicio, Ismael Fernández de la Cuesta, and José Lopez-Calo (Madrid: Instituto Nacional de las Artes Escénicas y de la Música, 1987), 53, cited in Sutcliffe, *The Keyboard Sonatas of Domenico Scarlatti*, 110.
9. Powell, *A History of Spanish Piano Music*, 185.
10. Harper, "Iberian Elements in the Scarlatti Sonatas," *Piano Journal* 23, no. 67 (Spring 2002): 20.
11. Sutcliffe, *The Keyboard Sonatas of Domenico Scarlatti*, 24n, opinion of Prof. Alexandru Leahu.
12. Domenico Scarlatti, *Sonatas for the Keyboard II*, ed. Maurice Hinson (Van Nuys, CA: Alfred), 17.
13. Puyana, "Influencias ibéricas," 52, cited in Sutcliffe, *The Keyboard Sonatas of Domenico Scarlatti*, 110.

Table 12.3. Special effects in Scarlatti's sonatas[1]

Effect	**Sonata**
Acciaccatura/appoggiatura	Many sonatas
Bells	K. 482
Flutes and bagpipes	K. 513
Glissando with one finger	K. 379
Guitar	Many examples based on guitar tuning of EADGBE, either strummed (rasgueado) in chords and arpeggios, K. 119; or plucked (punteado) as found in repeated note technique, K. 96, K. 141, etc.
Trumpets and horns (fanfares)	K. 96, K. 119, many others.
Timpani and trumpets (Baroque court)	K. 380.[2]

1. Much of this material is taken from Linton E. Powell, *Spanish Piano Music* (Bloomington: Indiana University Press, 1980).

2. Ann Bond, *A Guide to the Harpsichord* (Portland, OR: Amadeus, 1997), 181, in Sutcliffe, *The Keyboard Sonatas of Domenico Scarlatti and* Eighteenth-Century *Musical Style* (Cambridge, UK: Cambridge University Press, 2003), 363n45.

Table 12.4. Scarlatti's Iberian sonatas

Identifiable Iberian sonatas	K. 21, 33, 44, 58, 62, 78, 79, 82, 85, 94, 96–98, 101–103, 105, 108, 110, 112, 116, 117, 122, 124, 125, 129, 130, 131, 133, 135–138, 145, 148, 149, 155, 158, 159, 161, 163, 172, 174, 178, 179, 184, 187, 188, 191, 193, 207, 209, 218, 220, 221, 222, 230, 238, 239, 244, 245, 252, 255, 268, 278, 286, 299, 305, 313, 315, 319, 323, 327, 332, 334, 340, 350–352, 357, 359, 360, 364, 369, 372, 375, 381, 385, 395, 398–401, 403, 405, 407, 409, 413, 421, 423–425, 429, 433, 436–438, 441, 443, 444, 447, 448, 452, 457, 461, 465, 470, 473, 476, 479, 484, 490–492, 494, 504, 509, 516, 518, 520, 525, 526, 529–531, 538, 541, 543, 547, 548, 550, 552, 555.
Sonatas with Phrygian mode (one example is the descending scale: la, sol, fá, mi).	K. 20 (mm. 82–86) juxtaposes a modal cadence with a minor scale in an original way. K. 27 has descending bass: la, sol, fá, mi. K. 116 uses the Moorish version of the Phrygian harmonic minor scale. K. 519 is modal and uses hemiola giving the effect of alternating $\frac{3}{8}$ and $\frac{3}{4}$ meters. K. 46, 60, 77, 106, 114, 115, 121, 123, 124, 140, 141, 184, 189, 203, 211, 212, 215, 223, 226, 260, 261, 278, 308, 321, 324, 337, 340, 357, 368, 394, 402, 403, 404, 411, 412, 414, 426, 429, 446, 452, 460, 461, 468, 478, 479, 491, 499, 516, 517, 521, 525, 529, 539, 547.

Brief Case Study of Scarlatti's Sonata-Bolero in D Major, K. 491

Scarlatti's Sonata in D Major, K. 491, a very danceable bolero, reveals that he was well acquainted with this flamenco art form. So literal is the depiction in this sonata that the composer has captured a moment in time for the listeners.

The origin of the bolero is that of a regional folk dance derived from the older *seguidilla.* One possible etymology of the term *bolero* is given by the Spanish writer Don Preciso (Juan Antonio Iza de Zamacola, 1756–1826) in the 1790s: "The term bolero originated in the passage of the dancer Sebastián Cerezo, one of the best dancers of his time, through the towns of La Mancha, where the lads, seeing him dance to the music's unhurried measure with a redoubling of the variations they knew of the *seguidillas,* thought that he was flying (*Volar*) . . . so people started to talk about to come to see dance the one who flew or, as they called him, the *Bolero.*"[5]

The text of the bolero is based on the type of seguidilla, in which the metrical form that consists of alternating verses of seven and five syllables lines, plus *estribillo ad libitum.* The rhyme scheme is assonant:

A la rama mas alta	To the highest branch
de tu amor subí,	Of your love I climbed
vino un ayre contrario	A gust of wind
y al suelo caí:	Blew me to the ground:
que esto sucede	Thus is the fate of whosoever
al que en alas de cera	Defies the sun
al sol se atreve.	With wings of wax.[6]

The bolero inherits from the seguidilla the latter's metrical literary form, its triple meter, and its structure, which consists of three parts known as *coplas* or *mudanzas* (table 12.5a). This format is repeated four times in the seguidillas, but three or four times in the boleros, depending upon the customs of the region and the preference of the *maestro bolero.*[7] After every section—each one with a different choreography—a break occurs known as *Bien parado* (well held or well stopped), where the dancer remains motionless while adopting a beautiful pose.[8]

The parts of the bolero after the introduction are the Salida (departure or start of the dance) y Desplante (the end of a section that marks a high point in which the dancer stops and the audience applauds—in this case, it happens at the end of the cadenza); Cadenza; Mudanza primera (first change); Paseillo (little walk); Mudanza segunda (second change); Paseíllo (little walk); Mudanza tercera (third change); Final; and Bien parado (full stop). By comparing the main characteristics of the bolero (table 12.5a) with Scarlatti's sonata (table 12.5b), one can see how closely Scarlatti follows the flamenco structure. In knowing this, the performer can approximate the correct tempo (approximately the quarter note equals 82–88 MM) and interpretation.

Table 12.5a. Main characteristics of the *Bolero*[1]

A triple-meter dance in moderate tempo (counted in six beats across two bars)
Anacrusic rhythm, starting on the last eighth note of the third beat.
Most frequent castanet rhythm patterns:

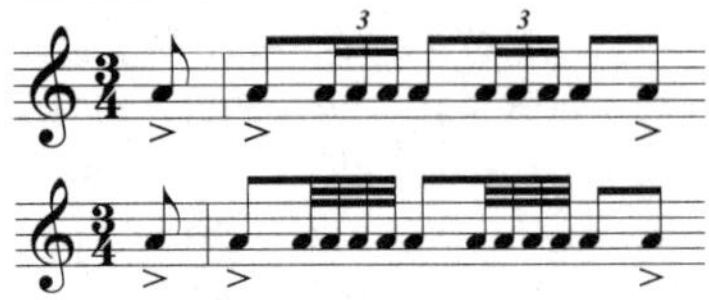

	Parts of the *Bolero*
Introducción musical	Musical introduction, mm. 1–7
Salida y Desplante	The dancer starts to evolve with bass steps, walking and bowing, mm. 8–16; cadenza follows, mm. 17–18
Mudanza primera	First part: the castanets give the starting point on the upbeat, mm. 19–25
Paseillo	Connects the parts or *Mudanzas*, mm. 26–29
Mudanza segunda	Second part, mm. 30–34
Paseillo	Connects the parts or *Mudanzas*, mm. 35–36
Mudanza tercera	Third part, mm. 37–43
Final-Bien parado	The dancer remains motionless (well held), mm. 44

This structure is repeated three or four times, depending on the region or school.

1. Luisa Morales in Nancy Lee Harper with Luisa Morales, *European Piano Teachers' Forum*: "Dancing Scarlatti," *Piano Journal*, Issue 103 (2014): 29–32.

Table 12.5b. Parts of the *Bolero* in Scarlatti's K. 491

First Half									
	Musical Introduction	*Salida y Desplante*	Cadenza	1st *Mudanza*	*Paseillo*	2nd *Mudanza*	*Paseillo*	3rd *Mudanza*	*Bien Parado*
K.491	1–7	8–17	18	18^6–26^5	26^6–30^5	30^6–35^5	35^6–37^5	37^6–44	44
Second Half									
	Musical Introduction	*Salida y Desplante*	Cadenza	1st *Mudanza*	*Paseillo*	2nd *Mudanza*	*Paseillo*	3rd *Mudanza*	*Bien Parado*
K. 491	45–49	50–60	61	61^6–69^5	69^6–73^5	73^6–77^5	77^6–80^5	80^6–87	87

The first half of this sonata is given in examples 12.9a–12.9b.[9] Scarlatti clearly depicted Spanish flamenco life in this sonata. Little pedal is required so that the rhythmic pulse is not destroyed in the repetitive left-hand quarter notes (beginning in m. 4). The right-hand thirds (mm. 40–41) will need to be overall legato, so the fingering will vary from person to person and instrument to instrument. The entire sonata needs to have a feel of lightness or a lift. If played too quickly, it loses its dance character. If play too slowly, it becomes stodgy and ungraceful. Overall fingering is not given here; rather pianists will need to let their feet determine their fingering. Observe the hemiola in bars 15–16. For those not familiar with flamenco dancing and the bolero in particular, films of these dances, like other Baroque dances, greatly aid the interpreter.[10]

K. 491

Facing Example 12.9a. Scarlatti, Sonata in D Major, K. 491, mm. 1–22.

Above Example 12.9b. Scarlatti, Sonata in D Major, K. 491, mm. 23–44.

Notes

1. W. Dean Sutcliffe, *The Keyboard Sonatas of Domenico Scarlatti and Eighteenth-Century Musical Style* (Cambridge, UK: Cambridge University Press, 2003), 112.

2. Nancy Lee Harper, *Portuguese Piano Music / Música portuguesa para piano, vol. 3*, Numérica, NUM 1228, 2012. This recording also appears with the book *Portuguese Piano Music: An Introduction and Annotated Bibliography* (Lanham, MD: Scarecrow,

2013). A modern edition of the sonata by this author will be published in *Portuguese Piano Music*, a Masterworks edition (Van Nuys, CA: Alfred, 2020).

3. Interview with Cremilde Rosado Fernandes by Nancy Lee Harper, "Iberian Elements in the Scarlatti Sonatas," *Piano Journal* 23, no. 67 (Spring 2002): 18.

4. João Pedro d'Alvarenga, "Domenico Scarlatti in the 1720s: Portugal, Traveling, and the Italianisation of the Portuguese Musical Scene," in *Domenico Scarlatti Adventures, Essays to Commemorate the 250th Anniversary of His Death*, ed. Massimiliano Sala and W. Dean Sutcliffe (Bologna: Ut Orpheus Edizioni, 2008).

5. "Este título de Bolero tuvo su origen, de que habiendo pasado á su pueblo en la Mancha Don Sebastián Zerezo, uno de los mejores baylarines de su tiempo, y viéndole baylar los mozos por alto con un compas muy pausado, al paso que redoblaba las diferencias que ellos tenian para sus *seguidillas*, creyeron que bolaba, ó á lo menos se lo figuraban asi según le veian ejecutar en el ayre; de que resultó que las gentes se citaban unas á otras para ir á ver baylar al que bolaba, ó según ellos, al *Bolero*." Juan Antonio "Don Preciso" Iza de Zamacola, *Colección de las mejores coplas de seguidillas, tiranas y polos que se han compuesto para cantar a la guitarra*, new edition (originally published in Madrid, 1797–1802; Córdoba: Ediciones Demófilo, 1982), 14. English translation by the author.

6. Iza de Zamacola, *Colección*, 13–14; Juan Jacinto Rodríguez Calderón, *La bolerología o quadro de las escuelas del bayle bolero, tales quales eran en 1794 y 1795, en la corte de España* (Philadelphia: Zacharias Poulson, 1807).

7. For instance, the *Bolero de Jaén* (Andalousia) consists of three sections; the *Bolero de Fuente Álamo* (Murcia), four sections. The traditional bolero dance is nowadays preserved mainly on the Levante coast (Castellón, Valencia, Alicante, Murcia, Almería), Jaén, the Balearic Islands, and the province of Zamora (Algodre).

8. The words "bien parado" (literally, "well held"; in other words, "full stop") were shouted by the audience at the end of each section; see Iza de Zamacola, *Colección*, 14. Nowadays, when the dance is presented on stage, as often as not, the audience spontaneously applaud at the sight of the *bien parado* pose.

9. Nancy Lee Harper and Luisa Morales, "Dancing Scarlatti," *Piano Journal* 103 (2014): 29–32.

10. Luisa Morales interpretation. For music and dance in another sonata-bolero, Scarlatti's Sonata in E Major, K. 380, see https://www.youtube.com/watch?v=K5ddBKlb1ql, with dancer Cristobal Salvador, *maestro bolero* of the Folklore School of Murcia, Spain, and harpsichordist Morales.

Conclusion

> It cannot be denied that the modern *technique*, is, after all, not superior to Bach's.
>
> —Philipp Spitta[1]

The significance of the Baroque period for the modern pianist may be somewhat underestimated. It was an exciting time of revolution, change, and experimentation. It saw the dawn of the early piano, an invention that would eventually usurp the supremacy of its first cousin, the harpsichord. With this new invention came wonderful repertoire composed for it. The appearance of Guistini di Pistoia's twelve multimovement piano sonatas in 1732 are the first known sonatas published for the early piano. On the heels of these sonatas, J. S. Bach's Italian Concerto of 1735 demarcated the possibility of it being played on the piano by virtue of its dynamic indications of "piano" and "forte." Like Bach, Domenico Scarlatti composed sonatas, such as his Sonata in G Minor, K. 88, with these same dynamic markings. Yet, he also composed in old forms, such as his Gavota, K. 64, an isolated Baroque dance. And according to one scholar, Scarlatti also gave us the first piano virtuoso etudes in his *Essercizi* of 1738–1739. Moreover, the early piano would have substituted the harpsichord in some instances of continuo playing in both instrumental and vocal music.

Having such important innovations for the early piano, Baroque fingering principles needed to be covered here not only as they apply in a theoretical way but more importantly as they apply in a practical sense—to serve the music through the performer's chosen interpretation. With these intertwined twin topics, we have discussed the pianist's dilemma of whether to play Baroque music on the piano or to opt for a purposed transcription. If the former is chosen (and that was the main objective of this work), then this question arises: In what manner is this performed? In a purist fashion? In a middle ground? Or in a historically informed performance? Most pianists would probably choose the latter. Other fingering interpretation topics addressed have included the ever-changing concepts of finger and hand positions and of "good" and "bad" fingers; crossing over and turning under of fingers; fingering in scale and chordal passages; finger substitution and finger slides; finger pedaling; fingering in various articulation choices and in ornamentation especially with regard to trills and tremolos; and fingering to portray the character of a motive or work, taking into consideration the impact of rhetoric on fingering choices and fingering in lyrical passages or in Baroque dances. In other words, the question of "what do we play?" may well determine the fingering path the performer takes. Little reference has been made to structure in the Scarlatti sonatas and its impact on the choice of fingering, although several authors, such as Nicolas Witkowski and myself, have discovered issues of symmetry, golden mean usage, and the effect of structure on performance and perception—topics that indirectly affect fingering choices.[2]

So what can a modern pianist learn from Baroque fingering and interpretation?

In a nutshell, the answer would be that fingering cannot be divorced from interpretation regardless of the instrument, but especially in the Baroque period. So important is the choice of effective fingering that without it any interpretation will suffer. With the multifaceted usage of keyboard playing in the Baroque period in solo or in continuo repertoire, the basic principle of ease of hand is of primary importance. This is true even in seemingly awkward fingerings that can sometimes be facilitated through very slight supination or pronation in hand movements. Flexible wrists, as any pianist knows, constitute an essential element of good Baroque technique, or any keyboard technique, for that matter. In general, if a fingering feels right and gives the desired articulation and expression in concert tempo, then it must be correct for that situation, that instrument, and that pianist. To rigidly adhere, merely for the sake of principle, to prescribed Baroque fingerings of a specific composer or school when performing on the modern piano could be a mistake that could lead to injury, especially if relaxation does not immediately follow any tension produced by unnatural positions. The art of fingering is a complex one and is always a matter of personal preference, even in times of change of style, taste, age, condition, and instrument.

From my harpsichord studies and through my own musical growth, I am no longer afraid to play disjointed phrases on the piano when required to allow the music to breathe in expressive musical discourse. The old, romanticized legato piano playing of Bach generally has been replaced with the ideal of a historically informed performance. Some pianists opt to use piano transcriptions of Baroque works instead, such as Bach-Busoni, Bach-Liszt, Bach-Siloti, Scarlatti-Granados, or others. Yet playing legato has its place in Baroque music performed on the piano. Ralph Kirkpatrick affirmed, "One could learn a great deal about two-part inventions, or for that matter about any two-voice pieces, by playing each voice with one finger."[3] It was Kirkpatrick's custom to finger a new piece as a completely legato expression, after which he decided on the articulations. Wanda Landowska, on the other hand, often chose fingerings that would force articulations, such as consecutive thumbs in a detached fugal statement.[4]

Contemporary Canadian harpsichordist John Sankey offers advice for pianists searching for a historically informed performance. He does not dismiss the importance of experimentation on period instruments to understand Baroque fingering concepts and why they existed:

> Must we learn early fingering techniques to properly understand the sound of early music? Knowledge of them is important to an understanding of phrasing and of tempi in many cases, particularly of French music. But, my personal judgement is that overall it will hinder more than assist a performer today, in that it forces over-specialization by today's standards. Early musicians didn't have to deal with Wm. Byrd, Louis Couperin, J. S. Bach and Domenico Scarlatti in one lifetime—we do.
>
> It took a lifetime of practise for each to do it as well as they did. Second-rate technique is an unreliable guide to first-rate music.[5]

To sum up, there is no one general Baroque concept for fingering on the piano, except perhaps to have flexibility in order to ensure comfort. By following general Baroque rules of simplicity, smooth shifts, ease of movement in whatever articulation or phrasing is chosen, and knowledge of what character is to be portrayed--what *affekt*, dance, or rhetoric--the pianist will have the required freedom of expression and technical command to be of service to the great music of the Baroque period, or any for that matter.

Reflecting an innovative spirit while anticipating the notion of finger independence, J. S. Bach's "flowing facility" may remain the goal of most pianists today. And if Julius August Philipp Spitta (1841–1894), Bach's biographer, is correct in saying that modern technique is not superior to Bach's, then it seems befitting to close with C. P. E. Bach's description of his father's technique: "How strange, how new, how beautiful were his ideas in improvising. How perfectly he realized them! All his fingers were equally skillful; all were capable of the most perfect accuracy in performance. He had devised for himself so convenient a system of fingering that it was not hard for him to conquer the greatest difficulties in the most flowing facility. Before him, the most famous clavier players in Germany and other lands had used the thumb but little."[6]

Usus est magister optimus!

Notes

1. Philipp Spitta, *Johann Sebastian Bach: His Work and Influence on the Music of Germany, 1685–1750*. 3 vols., trans. by Clara Bell and J. A. Fuller-Maitland (New York: Dover, 1951), 40.

2. N. Witkowski, "Croniques scarlatiennes," May 2016, http://delibere.fr/chroniques/chroniques-scarlattiennes/; Nancy Lee Harper, "Golden Section in the Sonatas of Domenico Scarlatti: A Re-examination of Kirkpatrick's 'Crux,'" in *Proceedings of the International Symposium for Performance Science 2007*, ed. Aaron Williamon and Daniela Coimbra, 239–244 (Utrecht: Association Européenne des Conservatoires, Académies de Musique et Musikhochschulen, 2007) http://performancescience.org/wp-content/uploads/2018/09/isps2007_proceedings.pdf; Nancy Lee Harper and Tomás Henriques, "Performing Musical Structure: Crux-phi Relationships in Domenico Scarlatti's Sonata K. 380," in *Proceedings of CIM08* Conference (Thessaloniki, Grécia, July 2–6, 2008), 80–81; Nancy Lee Harper and Tomás Henriques, "Performing Proportion: Crux Awareness in Scarlatti Interpretation," in *Proceedings of the International Symposium of Performance Science 2009*, ed. Aaron Williamon, Sharon Pretty, and Ralph Buck, 295–300

(Utrecht: Association Européenne des Conservatoires, Académies de Musique et Musikhochschulen, 2009), http://performancescience.org/wp-content/uploads/2018/08/isps2009_proceedings.pdf.

3. Ralph Kirkpatrick, *Interpreting Bach's* "Well-tempered *Clavier": A Performer's Discourse of Method* (New Haven: Yale University Press, 1984), 59.

4. Richard Troeger, *Playing Bach on the Keyboard: A Practical Guide.* (Pompton Plains, NJ: Amadeus, 2003), 216–217.

5. John Sankey, "Harpsichord Fingering," accessed May 2020, https://www.johnsankey.ca/fingers.html.

6. C. P. E. Bach in Reginald R. Gerig, *Famous Pianists and Their Technique* (Bloomington: Indiana University Press, 2007), 19.

Bibliography

Books, Articles, Dissertations

Bach, C. P. E. *Essay on the True Art of Playing Keyboard Instruments.* Translated and edited by William J. Mitchell. New York: Norton, 1949. First published 1753.

Bartel, Dietrich. *Musica Poetica:* Musical-rhetorical *Figures in German Baroque Music.* Lincoln: University of Nebraska Press, 1997.

Bodky, Erwin. *The Interpretation of Bach's Keyboard Works.* Cambridge, MA: Harvard University Press, 1960.

Bond, Ann. *A Guide to the Harpsichord.* Portland, OR: Amadeus, 1997.

Borroff, Edith. "Elisabeth-Claude Jacquet de la Guerre." In *The Norton/Grove Dictionary of Women Composers*, edited by Julie Anne Sadie and Rhian Samuel, 236–38. New York: Norton, 1995.

Calderón, Juan Jacinto Rodríguez. *La bolerología o quadro de las escuelas del bayle bolero, tales quales eran en 1794 y 1795, en la corte de España.* Philadelphia: Zacharias Poulson, 1807.

Casella, Alfredo. *Il pianoforte.* Milan: Ricordi, 1954.

Chiantore, Luca. *Historia de la técnica pianística.* Madrid: Alianza Música, 2001.

Clark, Jane. "Compositor de 'Originales y afortunados Caprichos.'" Dosier D. Scarlatti. *Scherzo* no. 116, Año XII (July–August 1997): 110–13.

Couperin, François. *L'Art de Toucher le Clavecin* (*The Art of Playing the Harpsichord*), 2nd ed. Edited and translated by Margery Halford. Van Nuys, CA: Alfred, 1974. First published 1716–17.

D'Alvarenga, João Pedro. "Domenico Scarlatti in the 1720s: Portugal, Traveling, and the Italianisation of the Portuguese Musical Scene." In *Domenico Scarlatti Adventures, Essays to Commemorate the 250th Anniversary of His Death*, edited by Massimiliano Sala and W. Dean Sutcliffe, 17–68. Bologna: Ut Orpheus Edizioni, 2008.

Dolmetsch, Arnold. *The Interpretation of the Music of the Seventeenth and Eighteenth Centuries.* Seattle: University of Washington Press, 1969.

Eigeldinger, Jean-Jacques. *Chopin: Pianist and Teacher: As Seen by His Pupils.* Cambridge, UK: Cambridge University Press, 1986.

Ferguson, Howard. *Keyboard Interpretation from the 14th to the 19th Century.* Oxford: Oxford University Press, 1998.

Fétis, François-Joseph, and Ignaz Moscheles. *Méthode des Méthodes de Piano.* Paris: Schlesinger, 1837.

Gerig, Reginald R. *Famous Pianists and Their Technique.* New ed. Bloomington: Indiana University Press, 2007.

Halford, Margery. *The Harpsichord Manual: An Introduction to the Technic, Ornamentation and Performance Practices.* Sherman Oaks, CA: Alfred, 1980.

Harper, Nancy Lee. "Iberian Elements in the Scarlatti Sonatas." *Piano Journal* 23, no. 67 (Spring 2002): 15–22.

———. "Golden Section in the Sonatas of Domenico Scarlatti: A Re-examination of Kirkpatrick's 'Crux.'" In *Proceedings of the International Symposium for Performance Science 2007*, edited by Aaron Williamon and Daniela Coimbra, 239–44. Utrecht: Association Européenne des Conservatoires, Académies de Musique et Musikhochschulen, 2007. http://performancescience.org/wp-content/uploads/2018/09/isps2007_proceedings.pdf.

———. *Portuguese Piano Music: An Introduction and Annotated Bibliography*. Lanham, MD: Scarecrow Press, 2013. Book and CD.

Harper, Nancy Lee, and Tomás Henriques. "Performing Musical Structure: Crux-phi Relationships in Domenico Scarlatti's Sonata K. 380." In *Proceedings of CIM08 Conference* (Thessaloniki, Greece, July 2–6, 2008), 80–81. http://cim08.web.auth.gr/cim08_papers/Harper-Henriques/Harper-Henriques.pdf.

———. "Performing Proportion: Crux Awareness in Scarlatti Interpretation." In *Proceedings of the International Symposium of Performance Science 2009*, edited by Aaron Williamon, Sharon Pretty, and Ralph Buck, 295–300. Utrecht: Association Européenne des Conservatoires, Académies de Musique et Musikhochschulen, 2009. http://performancescience.org/wp-content/uploads/2018/08/isps2009_proceedings.pdf.

Harper, Nancy Lee, and Luisa Morales. "Dancing Scarlatti." *Piano Journal*: "European Piano Teachers' Forum Issue" 103 (2014): 29–32.

Haynes, Bruce. *The Eloquent Oboe: A History of the Hautboy 1640–1760*. Oxford: Oxford University Press, 2001.

Hogwood, Christopher, ed. *The Keyboard in Baroque Europe*. Cambridge, UK: Cambridge University Press, 2003.

Kirby, F. E. *A Short History of Keyboard Music*. New York: Free Press, 1966.

Kirkpatrick, Ralph. *Domenico Scarlatti*. Rev. ed. Princeton, NJ: Princeton University Press, 1983.

———. *Interpreting Bach's* "Well-tempered *Clavier*": *A Performer's Discourse of Method*. New Haven: Yale University Press, 1984.

Kochevitsky, George. *Performing Bach's Keyboard Music*. White Plains, NY: ProAm Music Resources, 1996.

Le Huray, Peter. "Fingering." In *The New Grove Dictionary of Music and Musicians*, edited by Stanley Sadie, Vol. VI, 566–74. London: Macmillan, 1995.

Little, Meredith, and Natalie Jenne. *Dance and the Music of J. S. Bach*. Expanded ed. Bloomington: Indiana University Press, 2009.

Mozart, Leopold. *A Treatise on the Fundamental Principles of Violin Playing*. Early Music Series 6. Translated by Editha Knocker with a preface by Alfred Einstein. London: Oxford University Press, (1948) 1988. First published 1756.

Mozart, Wolfgang Amadeus. *The Letters of Wolfgang Amadeus Mozart (1769–1791)*. Translated from the collection of Ludwig Nohl, vol. 1. New York: Kurd and Houghton; Philadelphia: Frederick Letpoldt, 1866. https://archive.org/stream/lettersofwolfgan01moza/lettersofwolfgan01moza_djvu.txt.

Nester, Sam. "Modern Performance Trends in Bach's Sacred Music: Changing Tastes in the Performance of Bach's *Weihnachtsoratorium*: An Exploration of the Rhetorical Style." Bachelor of Music Honors Thesis, Western Australian Academy of Performing Arts, 2009. http://ro.ecu.edu.au/theses_hons/1323/. Accessed June 25, 2018.

Neuhaus, Heinrich. *The Art of Piano Playing.* 2nd ed. London: Kahn and Averill, 1993.

Neumann, Frederick. *New Essays on Performance Practice.* Rochester, NY: University of Rochester Press, 1989.

———. *Ornamentation in Baroque and* Post-Baroque *Music.* Princeton, NJ: Princeton University Press, 1978.

———. *Performance Practices of the Seventeenth and Eighteenth Centuries.* Prepared with the assistance of Jane Stevens. New York: Schirmer, 1993.

Ogeil, Jacqueline. "Did Domenico Scarlatti Compose the First Great Piano Music?" In *Domenico Scarlatti Adventures: Essays to Commemorate the 250th Anniversary of His Death,* edited by Massimiliano Sala and W. Dean Sutcliffe. Bologna: Ut Orpheus Edizioni, 2008.

———. "Domenico Scarlatti: A Contribution to our Understanding of his Sonatas through Research and Performance." PhD diss. Newcastle, Australia: University of Newcastle, 2006. Includes CDs.

Palisca, Claude. *Baroque Music.* 3rd ed. Englewood Cliffs, NJ: Prentice-Hall, 1991.

Porter, Cecilia Hopkins. *Five Lives in Music: Women Performers, Composers, and Impresarios from the Baroque to the Present.* Champaign-Urbana: University of Illinois Press, 2012.

Powell, Linton E. *A History of Spanish Piano Music.* Bloomington: Indiana University Press, 1980.

Puyana, Rafael. "Influencias ibéricas y aspectos por investigar en la obra para clave de Domenico Scarlatti." In *España en la música de Occidente: Actas del congreso internacional celebrado en Salamanca, 29 de* octubre-5 *de noviembre de 1985,* vol. 2, 51–60. Edited by Emilio Casares Rodicio, Ismael Fernández de la Cuesta, and José Lopez-Calo. Madrid: Instituto Nacional de las Artes Escénicas y de la Música, 1987.

Quantz, Johann Joachim. *On Playing the Flute.* Translated by Edward R. Reilly. New York: Schirmer, 1966. First published 1752.

Rosenblum, Sandra P. *Performance Practices in Classic Piano Music.* Foreword by Malcolm Bilson. Bloomington: Indiana University Press, 1991.

Sachs, Barbara. "Scarlatti's tremulo." *Early Music* 19, no. 1 (February 1991): 91–93.

Sankey, John. "Harpsichord Fingering." Accessed May 2020. https://www.johnsankey.ca/fingers.html.

Schulenberg, David. *The Keyboard Music of J. S. Bach.* 2nd ed. New York: Routledge, 2006.

Schulze, Hans-Joachim. "The French Influence in Bach's Instrumental Music." *Early Music* 13, no. 2 (May 1985): 180–84.

Schweitzer, Albert. *J. S. Bach.* Translated by Ernest Newman. New York: Macmillan, 2007.

Spitta, Philipp. *Johann Sebastian Bach: His Work and Influence on the Music of Germany, 1685–1750.* 3 vols. Translated by Clara Bell and J. A. Fuller-Maitland. New York: Dover, 1951. First published in 1899.

Sutcliffe, Dean. *The Keyboard Sonatas of Domenico Scarlatti and* Eighteenth-Century *Musical Style.* Cambridge, UK: Cambridge University Press, 2003.

Troeger, Richard. *Playing Bach on the Keyboard: A Practical Guide.* Cambridge, UK: Amadeus, 2003.

Watson, Derek, ed. *The Wordsworth Dictionary of Musical Quotations.* Ware, Hertfordshire, UK: Wordsworth Editions, 1994.

Witkowski, Nicolas. "Croniques scarlatiennes." *Délibérées*. May 2016. http://delibere.fr/chroniques/chroniques-scarlattiennes/.

Wolff, Christoph. "J. S. Bach." In *The New Grove Dictionary of Music and Musicians*. Edited by Stanley Sadie, vol. VI, 774–840. London: Macmillan, 1995.

Zamacola, Iza de. *Colección de las mejores coplas de seguidillas, tiranas y polos que se han compuesto para cantar a la guitarra*. Rev. ed. Córdoba: Ediciones Demófilo, 1982. Originally published in Madrid, 1797–1802.

Zuber, Barbara. "Wilde Blumen am Zaun der Klassik: Das spanische Idiom in Domenico Scarlattis Klaviermusik." Musik-Konzepte 47 (1986): 3–39.

Editions

Bach, J. S. *Brandenburg Concerto No. 3, BWV 1048*. Bach-Gesellschaft-*Ausgabe*, vol. 19. Edited by Wilhelm Rust. Leipzig: Leipzig: Breitkopf und Härtel / Bach Gesellschaft, 1871.

———. *Chromatic Fantasy and Fugue, BWV 903*. Bach-Gesellschaft-*Ausgabe*, vol. 36. Edited by Ernst Naumann. Leipzig: Breitkopf und Härtel / Bach Gesellschaft, 1890.

———. *Chromatic Fantasy and Fugue, BWV 903*. Edited by Ferruccio Busoni. Berlin: N. Simrock, 1902.

———. *Chromatic Fantasy and Fugue, BWV 903*. Edited by Ferruccio Busoni. Leipzig: Breitkopf und Härtel, 1915.

———. *Das wohltemperierte Klavier, Teil 1*. Urtext edition. Edited by Otto von Irmer and Hans-Martin Theopold. Munich: G. Henle Verlag, 1974.

———. *Das Wohltemperierte Klavier, Teil 1*. Urtext edition. Edited by Otto von Irmer and Fingered by Walther Lampe. Munich: Henle Verlag, 1995.

———. *Englische Suiten, BWV 806–811*. Urtext edition. Edited by Rudolf Steglich and fingered by Hans-Martin Theopold. Müchen: Henle Verlag, 1971.

———. *French Suite in* E-flat. Bach-Gesellschaft-*Ausgabe*, vol. 36. Edited by Ernst Naumann. Leipzig: Breitkopf und Härtel / Bach Gesellschaft, 1890.

———. "French Suite in C Minor." In *Keyboard Music* (from the Bach-Gesellschaft-*Ausgabe* edition). Reprint, New York: Dover, 1970.

———. *Partita No. 1 in* B-flat *Major*. Edited by Willard A. Palmer. Van Nuys, CA: Alfred Publishing, 1971.

———. "Sarabande." *Sechs Suiten für Clavier, gennant Französisch Suiten*, no. 1 in D Minor. Vol. 45.2, edited by Ernest Naumann. Leipzig: Breitkopf und Härtel / Bach Gesellschaft, 1895.

———. *Toccata in G Major*. Bach-Gesellschaft-*Ausgabe*, vol. 36. Edited by Ernst Naumann. Leipzig: Breitkopf und Härtel / Bach Gesellschaft, 1890.

———. *Toccaten*. Urtext edition. Edited by Rudolf Steglich and fingered by Hans-Martin Theopold. Müchen: Henle, 1962.

———. "Two Part Inventions." In *Keyboard Music* (from the Bach-Gesellschaft-*Ausgabe* edition). Ed. William Rust. Reprint, New York: Dover, 1970.

———. Well-Tempered *Clavichord, Book I*. Edited by Carl Czerny. New York: G. Schirmer, 1893.

Chopin, Frédéric. *Complete Works for the Piano, Vol. 7*. Edited by Carl Mikuli. New York: G. Schirmer, 1895.

Jacquet de la Guerre, Elisabeth-Claude. *Pieces* [*sic*] *de Clavecin*. Edited and typeset by Steve Wiberg, based on a facsimile of the first printing, 1687. Nashville, TN: Due West Editions, 2011.

Scarlatti, Alessandro. *Toccate per Cembalo*. Edited by J. S. Shedlock. London: Bach and Co., 1908.

Scarlatti, Domenico. *Essercizi per Gravicembalo, 1738–1739. Recueil des trente sonates pour clavecin*. Facsimile edition by Roy Howat. Fontenay-sous Bois, France: Stil éditions, 1977.

———. *Sonatas, Vol. 2, K. 53–103, Le pupitre. Collection de musique ancienne publiée sous la direction de François Lesure*. Edited by Kenneth Gilbert. Paris: Heugel, 1979.

———. *Sonatas, Vol. 3, K. 104–155, Le pupitre. Collection de musique ancienne publiée sous la direction de François Lesure*. Edited by Kenneth Gilbert. Paris: Heugel, 1978.

———. *Sonatas, Vol. 4, K. 156–205, Le pupitre. Collection de musique ancienne publiée sous la direction de François Lesure*. Edited by Kenneth Gilbert. Paris: Heugel, 1976.

———. *Sonatas, Vol. 5, K. 206–255, Le pupitre. Collection de musique ancienne publiée sous la direction de François Lesure*. Edited by Kenneth Gilbert. Paris: Heugel, 1974.

———. *Sonatas, Vol. 6, K. 256–305, Le pupitre. Collection de musique ancienne publiée sous la direction de François Lesure*. Edited by Kenneth Gilbert. Paris: Heugel, 1974.

———. *Sonatas, Vol. 7, K. 306–357, Le pupitre. Collection de musique ancienne publiée sous la direction de François Lesure*. Edited by Kenneth Gilbert. Paris: Heugel, 1975.

———. *Sonatas, Vol. 8, K. 358–407, Le pupitre. Collection de musique ancienne publiée sous la direction de François Lesure*. Edited by Kenneth Gilbert. Paris: Heugel, 1971.

———. *Sonatas, Vol. 9, K. 408–457, Le pupitre. Collection de musique ancienne publiée sous la direction de François Lesure*. Edited by Kenneth Gilbert. Paris: Heugel, 1972.

———. *Sonatas, Vol. 10, K. 458–406, Le pupitre. Collection de musique ancienne publiée sous la direction de François Lesure*. Edited by Kenneth Gilbert. Paris: Heugel, 1972.

———. *Sonatas for the Keyboard II*. Edited by Maurice Hinson. Van Nuys, CA: Alfred, 1996.

Collections

Guistini, Lodovico. *Sonate da Cimbalo di Piano e Forte: Lodovico Giustini di Pistoia*. Edited by Gerhard Doderer. Rio de Janeiro: Academia Brasileira de Música, 2002.

Scarlatti, Domenico. *Libro di Tocate per Cembalo e Tutti del Sigre Cavaliero D. Domenico Scarlatti*. Facsimile edition with introductory material, "Aspectos novos em torno da estadia de Domenico Scarlatti na corte de D. João V (1719–1727) / New aspects concerning the stay of Domenico Scarlatti at the court of King John V (1719–1727)," by Gerhard Doderer. CD recorded of selected Scarlatti sonatas by Cremilde Rosado Fernandes. Lisbon: Instituto Nacional de Investigação Científica, 1991.

Recordings

Fernandes, Cremilde Rosado. *Domenico Scarlatti Sonatas.* Recorded on 1758 Antunes harpsichord and includes FCR 94.1 Lx 25. Lisboa: Instituto Nacional de Investigação Científica J-CD-0102, 1991. Audio CD.

Harper, Nancy Lee. *Portuguese Piano Music/Música portuguesa para piano, vol. 3.* Numérica NUM 1228, 2012. Audio CD.

Horszowski, Mieczyslaw. *The Christofori Pianoforte 1720: Sonatas for Pianoforte (No. 1 in g minor, No. IV in e minor, No, VII in G Major, No, X in f minor) by Lodovico Giustini.* Musical Instruments from the Metropolitan Museum of Art. Recorded 1977–78. Titanic TI-78, 1980. Previously released by The Metropolitan Museum of Art as no. MMA L1803. Audio CD.

Videos

Bilson, Malcolm. *Knowing the Score, Vol. 1.* www.malcolmbilson.com. Ithaca, NY: Cornell University, 2005. DVD. https://www.youtube.com/watch?v=mVGN_YAX03A.

Bilson, Malcolm. *Knowing the Score, Vol. 2: A Supplement.* www.malcolmbilson.com. Ithaca, NY: Cornell University, 2014. DVD. https://www.youtube.com/watch?v=A7gBJtz7spE

Bilson, Malcolm (with violinist Elizabeth Field). *Performing the Score.* www.malcolmbilson.com. Ithaca, NY: Cornell University, 2010. DVD. https://www.youtube.com/watch?v=7qTN7JdiRJQ.

Index

Note: Under composers' names, musical works are listed at the end of the subentries. When a significant number of works are referenced, a separate entry for works by the composer has been created. Musical examples, figures, and tables are indicated by italicized page numbers.

agogic execution, 114, 116, 183, 187. See also *notes inégales*
d'Albert, Eugen, 62
d'Anglebert, Jean-Henri, 160
Antunes, Manuel, fortepiano by, 123, *124f*, 134n14, 195
Argerich, Martha, 155
arpeggios and arpeggiation. *See also* Moiseiwitsch, Benno, redistributions and rewritings by; rolled chords
  in Baroque music, 132, 136, *137f*, 141, 166, 171, 172, *202t*
  fingering techniques for, 18, 25, 33, 121, 175, 176
articulation. *See also* musical rhetoric
aspects of, 136
attack and decay, 136–139
  Baroque guidelines for, *137t*
  to express *affekt*, 140–141, 190, 197
  finger crossing and turning, 149–153
  importance of fingering choices to, 133, 189
  lifting, 128, 139, 142, 151, 156, 157, 191
  slurring in Baroque music, 141–143

Bach, C. P. E.
  Clavierstücke für die Rechte oder Linke Hande Allein, 129, *129f*
  Essay on the True Art of Playing Keyboard Instruments, 128, 180
  on fantasies, 170–171
  fingering technique of, 113, 125, 128–129, 149, 192
  on J. S. Bach's technique, 211
  on ornamentation, 160–161
  study of Scarlatti's *Essercizi*, 157
  "the shape of the instrument," 133
Bach, J. C., on minuets, 179
Bach, J. S.
  as father of modern piano technique, 125
  fingerings indicated by, 125–128
  flowing facility of, 211
  influences on, 117
  knowledge of French courtly dances, 181
  knowledge of Scarlatti, 157
  and musical rhetoric, 178–180, *180t*
  ornamentation of, 160, 161, 162
  Russian traditions in playing, 137
  slurring examples, 141–142, *142t*, 182
  use of thumb, 120, 149
  written chordal realizations of, 169, *169f*
Bach, J. S., works of
  "Aplicato," C Major, BWV 994, 125, *125f*, 127, *127f*, 128
  Brandenburg Concerto No. 3, BWV 1048, 170, *170f*
  Chromatic Fantasy and Fugue, BWV 903, 171–176, *171–76f*, *180t*
  Clavierbüchlein vor Wilhelm Friedemann Bach, 125, 154
  Concerto in D Minor, BWV 1052, 179–180
  English Suite in A Minor, BWV 807, *142t*, 160, 181, 182, *182f*, 184, 185
  English Suite in D Minor, BWV 811, 181
  English Suite in G Minor, BWV 809, 151, *151f*, 181
  First Sonata for Gamba and Clavier, BWV 1027, 161, *161f*
  French Suite II in C Minor, BWV 813, *142t*, 181, 185, 189–190, *189f*
  French Suite in D Minor, BWV 812, 181, 183, 184, *184f*
  French Suite in E-flat, BWV 815, 193, *193f*
  French Suite in E Major, BWV 817, 142, *142f*
  French Suite in G Major, BWV 816, 180, 181, 185
  Fugue in B-flat Major, BWV 866 (WTC), 139, *139f*, *179t*
  Fugue in B-flat Minor, BWV 891 (WTC), *179t*

Bach, J. S., works of (*continued*)
Fugue in C-sharp Major, BWV 848 (WTC), 141
Fugue in D Major, BWV 850 (WTC), 185
Fugue in D Minor, BWV 874 (WTC), 185
Fugue in D-sharp Minor, BWV 853 (WTC), *179t*, *180t*, 190–191 (*see also under* Czerny, Carl)
Fugue in E-flat Major, BWV 876 (WTC), *179t*
Fugue in E Major, BWV 878 (WTC), *179t*
Fugue in F Minor, BWV 881 (WTC), *179t*
Fugue in G Minor, BWV 885 (WTC), *179t*
Italian Concerto, BWV 971, *137f*, 141–142, *142f*, 157–158, *157–58f*, *179t*, *180t*, 209
Kungst der Fugue, BWV 1080, 185
Overture in the French Style *(Ouverture nach Französischer Art)*, BWV 831, 185–186, *185f*
Partita in B-flat Major (no. 1), BWV 825, 146, *146f*, 181
Partita in C Minor (no. 2), BWV 826, 86, *87f*, 136, *136–37f*, 184–185, *184f*
Partita in D Major, BWV 828, 181, 185
"Præambulum," G Minor, BWV 930, 125, 127, *127f*
"Praeludium and Fughetta" in C Major, BWV 870a, 125, 126–127, *126–27f*
Prelude and Fugue in E Minor, BWV 855, 152, *152f*
Prelude in C Major, BWV 846 (WTC), 169, *169f*
Prelude in C Minor, BWV 847 (WTC I), 152, *152f*
Prelude in E-flat Minor, BWV 853 (WTC), *180t*, 183, *190f*
Prelude in E Major, BWV 878 (WTC), 180
Prelude in E Minor, BWV 855 (WTC), 152, *152f*
Prelude in F Minor, BWV 857 (WTC), 192–193, *193f*
Sinfonia 15 from *Goldberg Variations*, BWV 988, 145, *145f*
Sonata in A Major for flute and cembalo, BWV 1032, 161, *161f*
Suite in E-flat Major, BWV 819, 186–187, *186f*, 188n25
Suite in F Minor, BWV 823, 185
Suite in G Minor, BWV 822, 185
Toccata in D Major, BWV 912, *180t*
Toccata in G Major, BWV 916, 147, *147f*, 191, *191f*
transcription of Marcello's Oboe Concerto, BWV 974, 162, *162f*
Two-part Invention in D Minor, BWV 775, 150–151, *150f*
Two-part Invention in F Major, BWV 779, *180t*
Badura-Skoda, Eva, 157
Baroque fingering concepts. *See also* articulation
Alessandro Scarlatti's fingering and notational system, 117, 120–123, *121–22f*, *121f*
axioms for, 133
Bach's and Scarlatti's guides to, 154
finger crossing, 128, 149
hand movement, 149, 210
heavy and light, 115–116, 151
historical changes in, 117–120
introduction of the fortepiano, 123–125
J. S. Bach's technical mastery, 125–128
use of thumb, 120, 149
Baroque fingering technique
articulation, 132
chordal fingerings, 132
finger slides, 132
on ornamented notes, 132
rolled arpeggiation, 132
Baroque performance practice. *See also* Bach, J. S.; dances; harpsichords; musical rhetoric; Scarlatti, Alessandro; Scarlatti, Domenico
Bilson and, 194n11
and historically informed piano performances, 113–115
and the modern pianist, 113–114, 209–211
and notational performance practice, 182
performer's decision making in, 132, 167, 170
and reading the musical score, 192
study of, 114
terminology and abbreviations used, 114–115
Bauer, Harold, 61, 80
bebung touch, 114, 115, 137
Beethoven, Ludwig van
controversial redistributions, 64–66
fingerings indicated by, 52, 53–56
in Moiseiwitsch's piano genealogy, 96
Beethoven, Ludwig van, works by
Piano Concerto no. 5 "Emperor," op. 73, 66, *66f*, 77, *77f*, 96
Sonata, op. 2, no. 1, 12, *13f*, 36–37, *37f*, *55f*, 96
Sonata, op. 2, no. 2, 7, *7f*, 12, *13f*, 53–55, *54f*, *55f*
Sonata, op. 2, no. 3, 8, *8f*, 38, *39f*, 50, *50f*, *56f*, 78, *78f*
Sonata, op. 7, 30, *30f*, 42, *43f*, 48, *48f*
Sonata, op. 10, no. 2, 36, *36f*, *37f*
Sonata, op. 10, no. 3, 81–82, *82f*

Sonata, op. 13, *Pathétique*, 10, *11f*
Sonata, op. 14, no. 1, 42, *44f*
Sonata, op. 14, no. 2, 74f, *74f*
Sonata, op. 31, no. 2, 34–35, *34–35f*
Sonata, op. 31, no. 3, 95–96
Sonata, op. 53 "Waldstein," 38, *39f*, 46, *47f*, 52–53, *53f*, 95
Sonata, op. 57, 23, *23f*, 32, *33f*, 38, *38f*, 39–43, *40f*, *41f*, *42f*, *46f*, 47, *47f*, 65, *65–66f*
Sonata, op. 81a, 48, *48f*
Sonata, op. 101, 19, *19f*
Sonata, op. 106, 9, *9f*, 56, *56f*, 64–65, *64–65f*
Sonata, op. 109, 7, *7f*, 14, *15f*, 70, *70f*, 81, *81f*
Sonata, op. 111, 14, *14f*, 25, *25f*, 49, *49f*, 74, *74f*, 78, *78f*, 95
Bilson, Malcolm, 116, 182, 187n15, 194n11
Knowing the Score (film), 116, 192
Birnbaum, Johann, 178
Bodky, Erwin, 137
body positions for keyboard playing, historical changes in, 117–118
boleros, *201t*, 203, *204–5t*, 206, 208nn7–8
Boni, Ana Lucia, 129
Brahms, Johannes
fingerings indicated by, 61
influence of Scarlatti on, 157
Intermezzo, op. 118, no. 1, 60, *60f*
Intermezzo, op. 118, no. 2, 90, *90f*
Intermezzo, op. 119, no. 3, 86, *86f*
Piano Concerto no. 2, *27f*
Rhapsody, op. 119, no. 4, 61, *61f*
Trio for Clarinet, Violin, and Piano, op. 114, 87, *87f*
Variations on a Theme by Schumann, op. 9, 22–23, *22f*
Brangança, Maria Teresa Bárbara de, 123, 129, 195
Bucheimer Orgelbuch (Buxheim Organ Book), 117
Bülow, Hans von, 38, 52, 64, *64f*, 78, xii
Busoni, Ferruccio
block fingerings, 25, *26f*
edition of Bach's WTC, 139, *139f*
editions of Bach's *Chromatic Fantasy and Fugue*, 172–176, *172–76f*
hand size of, 63
performers' ignorance of, xii
and using redistributions for, 63
Elegy no. 4, "Turandots Frauengemach," 25, *26f*

cadenzas, 52, 66, 106, 170. *See also* boleros
"cat hand," 117, 118, *118f*, *120f*, *138f*, 139
Cerezo, Sebastián, 203
Chopin, Frédéric
and Bach, 158
fingerings indicated by, 56–59, 76
Ballade, no. 1 in G Minor, op. 23, 4, *4f*, 8, *8f*, 17, *17f*, 21, *21f*, 29–30, *30f*, 92, *92f*
Ballade, no. 3, 82–84, *83–84f*, *83f*
Ballade, no. 4, op. 52, 16, *16f*, 26, *26f*, 44, 45, *45f*
Ballade no. 3, 9, *9f*, 68, *68f*
Étude, op. 25, no. 7, 24, *24f*
Étude, op. 25, no. 10, 42, *43f*, 44, 60
Étude in A Minor, op. 10, no. 2, 150, *150f*
Nocturne, op. 9, no. 2, 57, *57f*
Nocturne, op. 15, no. 2, 58, *58f*
Nocturne, op. 27, no. 1, 59, *59f*
Nocturne, op. 27, no. 2, 35, *35f*
Nocturne, op. 37, no. 1, 50–51, *51f*, 57–58, *58f*
Nocturne, op. 48, no. 1, 57, *57f*, 59, *59f*
Nocturne, op. 62, no. 1, 58, *58f*
Piano Concerto no. 1 in E Minor, op. 11, 33–34, *34f*, 36, *36f*, 74, *74f*, 89
Piano Concerto no. 2 in F Minor, 3, *3f*, 18–19, *19f*, 67, *67f*
Polonaise, op. 53, 92, *92f*
Polonaise-Fantasy, op. 61, 5, *5f*, 21–22, *22f*
Prelude in A Minor, op. 29, no. 2, 90–91, *91f*
Scherzo, no. 2 in B-flat Minor, 4, *4f*, 5, 6, 20, *20f*, 23, *23f*, 76, *76f*, 84, *84f*, *85f*
Scherzo, no. 4, op. 54, 15, *15f–16f*, 79, *79f*
Sonata no. 2, 80, *80f*, 89, *89f*
Sonata no. 3, 81, *81f*
chordal fingerings, 127, 132, 169–176. *See also* arpeggios and arpeggiation; rolled chords
chromatic scales, 17, 28–31, *28f*, *29f*
Clark, Jane, 199
clavichords, 113, 115, 117, 125, xii. *See also* bebung touch
Codex Faenza (Codex 117), 117
Coimbra manuscript MSS 58, 157, *196t*
Collins, Michael, 183
Cortot, Alfred, 78, 84, *84f*, xii
Couperin, François, 120, 182, 183
Couperin, Louis, 132
Craxon, Harold, *65f*
Czerny, Carl
editions of Bach's music by, 139, *139f*, 146, 189, 190–191, *190f*
in Moiseiwitsch's piano genealogy, 96
Cziffra, György, 154

dances
Baroque dances, 115, 211

dances (*continued*)
boleros, 203, *204–5t*, 206, 208nn7–8
of the French court, 181
lourés, 181, 185
sarabandes, 181–182, *181f*
and Scarlatti's Iberian sonatas, 195, 197, 199, *200–201t*
Debussy, Claude
Cloches à travers les feuilles (*Images*, Book 2), 75–76, *75f*
Estampes, no. III, *Jardins sous la pluie*, 87–88, *88f*
Étude 1 *pour les "cinq doigts" d'après Monsieur Czerny*, 76, *76f*, 80, *80f*
Descartes, René, 140
Doctrine of Affections *(affekt)*, 140–141, 162, 183, 211
Dolmetsch, Arnold, 183
Donington, Robert, 183
dynamics
accented notes, 6
in choosing fingerings, 114
and differing simultaneous touches, 47
fp techniques, 10
pp techniques, 7
redistributions for control, 79, 81
restrictions in Baroque use, 114
and testing fingering choices, 8, 30, 50, 78, 84, xiii
wrist movement and, 3, 6, 34, 56

Ecyk, Jan van
"Angel Playing the Organ" from *The Ghent Altarpiece* (painting), *118f*
embellishments. *See* ornamentation
"emergency rubato," use of, 27, 78, 86, 92
Erbach, Christian, 117

Fadini, Emilia, 115
Falla, Manuel de, influence of Scarlatti on, 157, 159n11
Ferguson, Howard, 149
Fernandes, Cremilde Rosado, 134n14, 195, 197
Fétis, François-Joseph, *Méthode des Méthodes de Piano* (with Moscheles), 133n1
figured bass, 116n3
fingering choices. *See also* legato playing; rapid passages
and the art of interpretation, 114, 133, 140, xiv
for Bach's ornaments, 160–161
and Baroque performance practice, 114
composers' indications for, 50–51, 52, 53–61, 76, 125–128, 154
factors and complexity in, xi–xii, xiii
guidelines for, xiii–xiv
for the modern pianist playing Baroque music, 209–211
provenance of, 113
reliability and expressivity, 30
and specific instruments, 133
terminology and abbreviations in Part 3 of the book, 114–115
testing of, 3, 8, xiii, xiv
fingering techniques. *See also* Baroque fingering concepts; Baroque fingering technique; dances; hand position; ornamentation; redistributions; thumb positions 5–3 for melodic projection, 24–25
"blind" octaves, 49
block fingerings, 25–28, 33, 58, 60, 61
in chords and chordal realizations, 31–34, 169–176
crossing fingers, 6–8, 61
crossing hands, 156
finger pedaling, 192–193
finger slides, 192
glissandi, 52–53, 155, 159n5
implied by musical figures, 156–158
for jumps or changes in hand position, 11–14, 19
legato octaves, 42–47
multiple notes with one finger, 20–24
pattern fingerings, 14–19
on repeated notes, 3–5, 154–155, 157
retaking notes (finger substitutions), 10–11, 175, 191
in runs, rolled chords, and arpeggios, 31–34
using same finger for clarity and portato, 49–51
Fischer, Edwin, *Beethoven's Pianoforte Sonatas*, 10
fortepiano
early example of, 123, *124f*
early works for, 123–125
invention of, xii–xiii
Fowke, Philip, xii
"To Cheat or not to Cheat" (presentation), 95
Franck, César, Prélude, Chorale, and Fugue, FWV 21, 88, *88f*
French Baroque school, 120
Friedman, Ignaz, 62, 84, *84f*

Gambarini, Elisabetta de, 129
Ganz, Rudolph, xii
Giacomini, Lorenzo, 140
Gilels, Emil, 92

Godowsky, Leopold, 90, xii
Goltzius, Hendrick, "St. Cecilia" (print), *119f*
Granados, Enrique, influence of Scarlatti on, 157, 159n12
Greek poetry, 178
Green, Gordon, 96
Guistini di Pistoia, Lodovico
Sonata in G Minor, no. 1, 124, *124f*
Sonate de Cembalo di Piano, e Forte detto volgarmente di martelletti, Op. 1, 123–124, 134n14, 209
guitar techniques
punteado, 154, 155, 198–199, *202t*
rasgueado, 198, 199, *202t*

hand position
breaking of hands, 62, 69
"cat hand," 117, 118, *118f*, *120f*, *138f*, 139
crossing hands, 156
historical changes in, 117–118, *118–20f*
preparing for changes in, 11–14, 19
rapid changes in, 80
hand splitting. *See* redistributions
Harper, Nancy Lee, 115, xiii
harpsichords. *See also* Jacquet de la Guerre, Elisabeth-Claude; Landowska, Wanda; Scarlatti, Alessandro; Scarlatti, Domenico
articulation on, 137, 138
author's experience with, 115–116
in the Baroque revival, 113
characteristics of, 124, 137, 189
and lutes, 117, 133n1
Quantz on, 116n3
Hehenstreit, Pantaleon, 181
hemiolas, 185
Hess, Myra, 65
Horowitz, Vladimir, 92
Horszowski, Mieczyslaw, 134n15

improvisation, 158, 160, 170–171
Irmer, Otto von, edition of Bach's D-sharp Minor Fugue by, 189, *190f*
Italian Baroque school, 120

Jacquet de la Guerre, Elisabeth-Claude, 129
her many firsts, 130
Pieces de la Clavessin, Suite no. 1, Prelude from Suite in D Minor, *130–32f*, 132
jazz "swing" figures, 183–184
Jenne, Natalie, 181
jeu perlé (pearly touch), 120
John V (King of Portugal), 123, 199
jumps
avoiding use of fifth finger in, 19
preparing for, 11–14, 72–75

Kirkpatrick, Ralph, 115, 140, 157, 162–163, 197, 199, 210
Kochevitsky, George A., 179, 184
Kroll, Franz, 40

Landowska, Wanda, 113, 138–139, *138f*, 210
Lebert, Sigmund, 64, *64f*
legato playing
in Baroque music, 210
changing fingerings on a repeated note, 3–5
with chords spanning an octave, 9
and finger crossing, 6, 7, 8
and harpsichord playing, 138–139
and use of thumbs on black keys, 18
using redistributions for, 70
Leschetizky, Theodor, 96
Libro di Tocate per Cembalo e Tutti del Sig.nr Cavaliero D. Domenico Scarlatti, 195, *196t*
Liszt, Franz
fingerings indicated by, 60
on Chopin's rubato technique, 158
Liszt, Franz, works by
Ballade no. 2 in B Minor, 51, *51f*, 70, *70f*
Don Juan Fantasy, 31, *32f*
Hungarian Rhapsody no. 8, 6, *6f*, 11, *11f*, 30, *31f*, 87, *88f*
Hungarian Rhapsody no. 9, 37–38, *38f*
La Leggierezza Étude, 71, *71f*
Mephisto Waltz no. 1, 73, *73f*, 84–85, *85f*
Paganini Étude no. 2, 46, *46f*, 49, *49f*
Paganini Étude no. 6 in A Minor, 20, *20f*, 32, *33f*, 49–50, *50f*, 68, *68f*, 71, *71f*
Piano Concerto no. 1, 27–28, *28f*
Réminiscences de Don Juan, S. 418, 72, *72f*
Sonetto no. 123, 67–68, *68f*
Spanish Rhapsody, 25, *25f*, 71, *72f*
Transcendental Étude no. 4, "Mazeppa," 60, *60f*
Transcendental Étude no. 8, "Wilde Jagd," *27f*, 73, *73f*
Transcendental Étude no. 9, "Ricordanza," 69–70, *70f*
Transcendental Étude no. 10 in F Minor, 69, *69f*, 85–86, *85f*
Transcendental Étude no. 11, "Ricordanza," 88–89, *89f*
Transcendental Étude no. 12, "Chasse neige," 30, *31f*
Vallée d'Obermann, 60, *60f*

Liszt, Franz, works by (*continued*)
Variations on a Basso Continuo from *"Wieinen, Klagen, Sorgen, Zagen"*, 17, *17f*, 20, *20f*, 32, *32f*
Little, Meredith, 181
Longo, Alessandro, 115
lutes, 113, *120f*, 133n1

main morte (dead hand), 120
Marpurg, Friedrich Wilhelm, 188n25
Matthay, Tobias, xii
Mattheson, Johan, *Der vollkommene Capellmeister*, 140
Merrick, Frank, 96
Michelangeli, Arturo Benedetti, 66
Moiseiwitsch, Benno, redistributions and rewritings by
Beethoven's "Emperor" Concerto, 96, 97
Rachmaninoff's Piano Concerto, no. 1, 96, 97, 98–99
Rachmaninoff's Piano Concerto, no. 2, 96, 100–105
Tchaikovsky's Piano Concerto No. 2, 96, 106–108
Moiseiwitsch Archive, 96, 108, xii
Morales, Luisa, 116
Moscheles, Ignaz
Étude in G Major, op. 70, no. 3, 150
Méthode des Méthodes de Piano (with Fétis), 133n1
Moszkowski, Moritz, 52, 64, *65f*, 78, xii
Mozart, Leopold, 183
Mozart, Wolfgang Amadeus
and Bach's Italian Concerto, 158
Nine Variations on "Lison dormait," K. 315d, 52, *52f*
Piano Concerto in A Major, K. 414, 17, *17f*
Sonata, K. 333, *18f*, 86, *87f*
Sonata in A Minor, K. 310, 21, *21f*
musical rhetoric
Bach's use of rhetoric in speech and semantics, 178–180
dance examples of, 181–182
dialog between hands or voices, 189
elements of, 187n8
and fingering choices, 210
and interpretation, 211
metric displacement in, 184–187
note inégales, 182–184
the overdot in (double dotting), 183, 184–185
stages of, 178

Nester, Sam, 187n8
Neuhaus, Heinrich, xii
Neuhaus, Heinrich, change in fingerings as older man, 152–153, *152f*
Neumann, Frederick "Fritz," 162, 183
Newman, William S., xii
notes inégales, 182–183, 197

octaves
"blind," 49
legato, 42–47
slurred, 47–48
Ogeil, Jacqueline, 124, 125, 134n10, 166
ornamentation
Bach's practice in, 160
complexity of, 160
difficulty of trills, 161–162
mordents and turns, 34–37
performer's flexibility in, 167
tremolos, 41–42, 162–163, 166
trills and tremolos in Scarlatti's works, 162–167

Pachmann, Vladimir de, redistributions on Chopin's Prelude in A Minor, op. 28, no. 2, 90–91
Paderewski, Ignaz, 62, 84, *84f*
Palisca, Claude V., 140
Pasch, Johannes, 181
Pasquali, Nicolo, 159n5
Art of Fingering the Harpsichord, 163
pedaling technique
and articulation, 136
finger pedaling, 172, 192–193
in Liszt's Ballade no. 2, 51, 70
in playing Bach, 157
performer's freedom in interpretation, 132, 167, 170
Pestelli, Giorgio, 115
piano technique, aims of, 95
pipe organs, 115
poetic meter, Bach's use of, 178–180, 183
portato touch, 51
Powell, Linton, 199
Preciso, Don, 203
Prokofiev, Sergei
Piano Concerto no. 1 in D-flat Major, 25, *26f*
Sonata no. 2 in D Minor, 8, *8f*
Sonata no. 3 in A Minor, 10, *10f*
Sonata no. 5, 23–24, *24f*
Purcell, Henry, 117
Puyana, Rafael, 143n9

Quantz, J. J., 116n3

Rachmaninoff, Sergei
  breaking of hands and rolling of chords by, 62
  and using redistributions for, 63
  Piano Concerto no. 1 in F-sharp Minor, op. 1, 96
  Piano Concerto no. 2 in C Minor, op. 18, 22, *22f*, 62, *62f*, 80–81, *81f*, 96, xii
  Prelude, op. 23, no. 6, 12–14, *13f*
Rameau, Jean-Philippe, 120, 183
rapid passages
  achieving turnabout clarity, 37–41
  block fingerings in, 27
  chromatic scales and, 28–31
  glissandos, 52–53
  redistributions for, 71
  repeated notes, 154
  turnabout clarity, 37–41
  use of pattern fingerings for, 14–19
  using redistributions for, 68
Ravel, Maurice
  Miroirs no. IV "Alborada del grazioso," 12, *12f*, 41, *41f*
redistributions
  and artistic possibility, xi–xii
  to avoid rolls, 67–72
  Baroque cross-hand techniques, 144, 147–148, 166
  in Baroque works, 144–145
  from Beethoven's fingerings, *54–55f*, 55
  by Chopin, 59
  for Chopin's Prelude in A minor, 90–91
  for clarity and clean pedal changes, 69–72
  to control voicing, 78–81
  controversies over, 63, 64–66, 78, 95–96
  decisions about, 3, 62, 63–64
  to facilitate finger pedaling, 88–90
  "inappropriate facilitation" *versus* "justifiable enablement," 95, 97
  by Moiseiwitsch, 96–108
  to prepare for jumps, large chords, and large intervals, 72–78
  to relieve stress, for speed, and for accuracy, 81–86
  for shaping phrases, 81
  stemming, 146–147, 175
  for textural and rhythmic clarity, 86–88
  videos of famous pianists using, 92
releases and decay, 137
repeated notes
  and art of rhetoric, 166
  changing fingerings on, 3–5, 9
  in chords, 9
  tremolos, 41–42, 162–167
retaking notes, 10–11
rhetoric, art of, 178. *See also* musical rhetoric
Richter, Sviatoslav, 96
Robert, Walter, xii
Robertsbridge Codex (1360), 117
rolled chords. *See also* arpeggios and arpeggiation
  pianists' techniques, 10, 12, 62
  and rapid speed, 71
  redistributions to avoid, 67–69
  top notes of, 31–34
  Rosenblum, Sandra P., 115

Sachs, Barbara, 163
Saint-Saëns, Camille, Piano Concerto no. 2, 18, *18f*, 44, *45f*
Sankey, John, 210–211
sarabandes, 181–182, *181f*
Sauer, Emil von, 51, 73, xii
scales
  chromatic scales, 17, 28–31, *28f*, *29f*
Scarlatti's interest in virtuoso technique, 153, *153f*
  various fingerings of, 128, *128f*
Scarlatti, Alessandro
  fingerings and notational system of, 117, 120–122, *121f*, 133n6
  Toccata no. 7, 122–123, *123f*, 134n10
  Toccata Primo, 121, 122f
Scarlatti, Domenico
  catalog numbers used for, 115
  and dance forms, 115
  fingerings indicated by, 154
  musical skill and contributions of, 120, 122–123, 125
  Portuguese manuscript collections of, 195, *196t*
  sonatas performed together, 157
  Spanish elements in music of, 198–207, *200–201t*
  special effects in sonatas of, *202t*
  trills and tremolos in works by, 162–167
Scarlatti, Domenico, works by
  Essercizi per gravicembalo, 125, 156–157, *196t*, 209
  Iberian sonatas of, 195–202, *202t*
  Portuguese sonatas of, *195f*, 197–198
  Sonata in A Major, FCR 194.1, Lx25, 195, *195f*
  Sonata in A Major, K. 24, 141, *141f*, 153, *153f*

Scarlatti, Domenico, works by (*continued*)
  Sonata in A Major, K. 285, 166
  Sonata in A Minor, K. 3 *(Essercizi)*, 156, *156f*
  Sonata in A Minor, K. 175, 139, *139f*, 143n9, 164, *164f*
  Sonata in B-flat Major, K. 228, 156, *156f*
  Sonata in B Minor, K. 27 *(Essercizi)*, *147f*, 198–199, *199f*
  Sonata in B Minor, K. 87, 144, *144f*, 192, *192f*
  Sonata in C Major, K. 502, 166
  Sonata in D Major, K. 96, *147f*, 148, *148f*, 154, *155f*, 163, *163f*, 166, *166–67f*, 198
  Sonata in D Major, K. 118, 163, *164–65f*, 165–166
  Sonata in D Major, K. 119, 163
  Sonata in D Major, K. 490, 166, 192, *192f*
  Sonata in D Major, K. 491, 203–207, *204–5t*, *206–7f*
  Sonata in D Major, K. 492, 198, *199f*
  Sonata in D Minor, K. 141, 155, *155f*, 163, 167, *167f*, 198
  Sonata in E Major, K. 264, 145, *145f*, 169, *169f*
  Sonata in F Major, K. 379, 155, *155f*
  Sonata in F Minor, K. 238, 197, *197f*
  Sonata in F Minor, K. 239, 197, *197–98f*
  Sonata in G Minor, K. 88, 123, *124f*, 209
  Sonata in G Minor, K. 426, 198, *198f*
Schnabel, Artur, 40
Schubert, Franz, Impromptu, op. 142, no. 4, 86, *86f*
Schumann, Robert
  "Arlequin" from *Carnival, op. 9*, 76–77, *77f*
  "Coquette," from *Carnaval*, op. 9, 11–12, *12f*
  Fantasiestücke, op. 111, no. 1, 14, *14f*
  Kinderszenen, op. 15, no. 8, "Am Kamin," 79–80, *79f*
Spitta, Julius August Philipp, 209, 211
Sutcliffe, Dean, 199

Taylor, Kendall
  Principles of Piano Technique and Interpretation, 63
Tchaikovsky, Pyotr Il'yich, Piano Concerto no. 2 in G Major, op. 44, 96
thumb positions
  and black keys, 5, 11, 14, 15, 16
  and chromatic scales, 28–31
  Couperin's and Bach's use of, 120
  multiple notes using, 20–23
Titian, "Venus with a Musician" (painting), *119f*
Tovey, Donald Francis, *65f*
tremolos, 41–42, 162–167
Türk, Daniel Gottlob, *Piano School*, 115–116

Volumier, Jean-Baptiste, 181

Well-Tempered Clavier (J. S. Bach). *See references to WTC under Bach, J. S.*
Witkowski, Nicolas, 210
women's contributions in the Baroque era, 129–132

Zelter, Karl Friedrich, 183

JOSEPH BANOWETZ, American pianist, recording artist, and pedagogue, has been heard on five continents. He is the author of *The Pianist's Guide to Pedaling* (Indiana University Press, 1985/1992), which has been published in seven languages. Banowetz's recordings have received two Grammy Award nominations.

PHILIP FOWKE is an internationally recognized British pianist, recording artist, and teacher. He is particularly known for his numerous BBC broadcasts and Promenade Concert appearances. Fowke is Fellow of the Royal Academy of Music and Professor Emeritus of the Trinity Laban Conservatoire of Music, London.

NANCY LEE HARPER is an internationally known pianist, recording artist, pedagogue, and research scholar. She has performed on four continents and is the author of a highly regarded book entitled *Portuguese Piano Music: An Introduction and Annotated Bibliography.*